GARTH OSWALD

MW01015775

VISUAL QUICKSTART GUIDE

REALBASIC

FOR MACINTOSH

Michael Swaine

Peachpit Press

Visual QuickStart Guide

REALbasic for Macintosh

Michael Swaine

Peachpit Press

1249 Eighth Street
Berkeley, CA 94710
510/524-2178
800/283-9444
510/524-2221 (fax)

Find us on the World Wide Web at: http://www.peachpit.com
To report errors, please send a note to errata@peachpit.com

Peachpit Press is a division of Pearson Education
Copyright © 2003 by Michael Swaine

Editor: Cliff Colby, Whitney Walker
Production coordinator: Gloria Marquez
Copyeditor: Kathy Simpson
Compositor: Owen Wolfson
Indexer: Emily Glossbrenner, FireCrystal Communications
Cover design: The Visual Group
Cover production: Nathalie Valette

Notice of Rights

Notice of Liability

Trademarks

ISBN 0-201-78122-0

9 8 7 6 5 4 3 2 1

Printed and bound in the United States of America

To three uncompromisers:
Tom Paine, Ted Nelson, and Richard Stallman.

Thank Yous

First, of course, the trees. Their selfless sacrifice to the cause of programmer education is profoundly appreciated. After going through the mill in writing yet another book, and once again having my pithy prose chopped, my brain rendered to pulp, and all my weekends bound up, I think I know just how the trees feel.

Thanks, too, to Brandon Dwyer for the nimble and savvy code testing, screen shooting, and reality checking. We'll have to do it again some time if we don't wise up.

Merci buckets to the pit crew at Peachpit Press, especially Cliff Colby, friend and editor, voice of reason, pillar of support, the Socratic mechanic who kept me on track. And a Platonic buss to Whitney Walker, who jumped into this moving vehicle and steered it to the finish line. My hat is also off to the rest of the team: copyeditor Kathy Simpson, production coordinator Gloria Marquez, compositor Owen Wolfson, and indexer Emily Glossbrenner.

Thanks to Andrew Barry, creator of REALbasic, and to Lorin Rivers and the gang at REAL Software for the helpful feedback and the fine product. It's been REAL.

It's finished, Nancy. Now our life can get back to normal—or to our accustomed abnormal, anyway.

TABLE OF CONTENTS

Introduction   **ix**

Chapter 1:   **Building Applications with REALbasic**   **1**

REALbasic Overview 2
The REALbasic Language. 3
What Can You Build with REALbasic? 5
Touring REALbasic. 9
Working with Projects. 10
Working with Windows 12
Working with Tools 13
Working with Object Properties 15
Working with the Code Editor. 17
Working with Menus 19
The Application Development Process 22
A REALbasic Application 23
Programming by Imitation 24

Chapter 2:   **Building an HTML Editor**   **31**

Creating the Edit Field. 32
Creating the Tags Menu 36
Creating the Symbols Menu. 46
Adding a New Menu Item. 51
Working with Files 54
Adding Save Menu Items 55
Adding an Open Menu Item 63
Creating a Save Dialog Box. 65
Building a Stand-Alone Application. 71
What's Next? 72

Chapter 3:   **Programming Object Properties**   **73**

About Objects 74
About Properties. 75
Manipulating Data and Properties in Code 76
Building a Project 80
Roughing Out the Project. 82
Managing User Input via Properties 89
Tying Up Your Project's Loose Ends. 93
Finishing the Project 98

Table of Contents

Chapter 4: **Writing REALbasic Code** **101**

Creating Behavior Without Programming 102

Using the Code Editor to Write
REALbasic Code 104

Getting Help with the REALbasic
Language 113

Mastering Dim and Assignment
Statements 116

Making Tests and Comparisons 126

Writing Code that Branches 130

Writing Code that Repeats 134

Writing Your Own Methods 137

Extending the HTML Editor 140

Creating the Indent Menu Item 141

Removing Existing Indentation 143

Inserting Indentation Before Tags 145

Handling the Indent Level 147

Extending the Project 150

Chapter 5: **Writing Object-Oriented Code** **151**

Using Inheritance 152

Creating Instances of Classes 154

Using Objects in Your Code 157

Comparing Objects 160

Creating Your Own Classes 162

Removing Classes and Objects 168

Importing and Exporting Classes 170

Deciding Where to Put the Code 172

Creating a Simple Spreadsheet 174

Creating an Instance of the Spreadsheet Class . 177

Using the Spreadsheet Class 178

Chapter 6: **Working with Files** **185**

Working with File Types 186

Working with the FolderItem Class 190

Working with Files and Folders 196

Handling File Dialogs 202

Working with Sequential Files 209

Working with Picture, Sound, and
Media Files 217

Working with Binary Files 220

TABLE OF CONTENTS

Chapter 7: **Working with Pictures** **223**

Creating Graphics with Graphical Controls.... 224

Working with Color 230

Working with Graphics File Types and
     File I/O 237

Using the Picture and Graphics Classes 240

Using Graphics-Savvy Objects. 244

Using the Canvas Control. 246

Building the Color Sliders Tool 255

Building the TurtleDraw Application. 261

Chapter 8: **Working with Animations
and Movies** **275**

Sprite Animation 276

Creating Time-Aware Applications 293

Displaying 3D Animations. 296

Working with Sound 305

Rediscovering a Classic Video Game. 307

Chapter 9: **Working with Databases** **321**

Database Basics. 322

Building a Database 325

Building a Database Viewer 333

Building a Database Front End 336

Writing Database Code 343

Chapter 10: **REALbasic and Communications** **351**

Communicating over the Internet 352

Building a Bookmarks Database. 356

Using the Bookmarks Database 364

Using Sockets 367

Printing 372

Chapter 11: **Extending REALbasic with Scripting** **375**

Making Programs RBScript Programmable 376

Extending REALbasic with AppleScript 390

Extending REALbasic with Shell Scripting 395

Chapter 12: **Being a Programmer** **401**

The Processes of Programming 402
Designing Your Applications 404
Debugging Your Applications 412
Documenting Your Applications 420
Deploying Your Applications 425

Index **429**

INTRODUCTION

For years, Macintosh users had no really satisfactory entry-level programming environment. There were authoring environments for creating educational CDs or Web sites, and there was the legendary but now-unsupported HyperCard. But there was no programming environment that mere mortals could master.

REALbasic changed that. It hits the sweet spot on ease of use versus power curve: not too challenging that it can't be learned in a few weekends by someone who has no aspiration to be a professional programmer, but powerful enough to be useful to experienced software developers.

With REALbasic, people who don't have degrees in software engineering can write useful applications such as database front ends, word processors, and Web browsers. REALbasic makes all that possible, even if it doesn't make it entirely easy.

This book will show you how to use REALbasic to create your own applications. What you need to bring to the table are a Macintosh and the desire to learn.

The REALbasic Phenomenon

REALbasic is an integrated development environment for writing application software. With it, you can write stand-alone programs that you can use or sell. Like HyperCard in another era and Visual Basic on the Windows platform, REALbasic has spawned a new market of programs. But don't be misled by the Made with REALbasic label that some products sport. A REALbasic application is a real application, every bit as much as AppleWorks or Adobe Photoshop.

Is REALbasic for you?

Multimedia authors and Web-site developers who are familiar with tools such as JavaScript, HyperCard, SuperCard, and Flash will find REALbasic a logical next step. The learning curve is slightly steeper, but the rewards are greater.

Professional programmers will find REALbasic a handy prototyping tool, and in fact Microsoft reportedly uses REALbasic to prototype some of its Macintosh applications. They will also use it to knock out an application for themselves in an afternoon.

Novice programmers will find REALbasic a good starting point. You don't have to learn everything about REALbasic or about programming to start creating your own applications; you can turn out your first one in a weekend.

Shareware authors are embracing REALbasic in droves. System administrators will find it a useful tool for rapidly developing custom applications, small or large. And art directors and other creative professionals can use it to create their own custom tools.

System requirements

To develop software with the Macintosh version of REALbasic, you need a Macintosh with at least a 68030 processor or any PowerPC processor, Mac OS System 7.6.1 or later, at least 4.5 MB of available memory, a CD-ROM drive, and a hard disk with 6.5 MB of free space (but you really need 70 MB for all the online documentation and examples).

REAL Software has also developed a Windows version of REALbasic. That version hadn't been released when this book was published, so I can't tell you its exact system requirements, but it will let you develop software in REALbasic on a Windows PC.

Regardless of which platform you use for REALbasic development, you can create software to run on Macintosh or Windows machines and in either Mac OS X or Classic Mac OS. You can even create one application and automatically generate versions for Mac and Windows—true cross-platform development. Visual Basic can't do that.

Using This Book

Like all of Peachpit's *Visual QuickStart Guides*, this book uses ample illustrations and succinct captions to walk you through REALbasic's major functions and options step by step. If you're new to REALbasic, you'll probably want to work your way through the book chapter by chapter. But if you've got an immediate REALbasic problem or question, simply scan the page tabs, illustrations, and captions to find what you need; then delve into the text for details and tips.

Here are some of the things you'll encounter in this book:

◆ When a word appears in `code font`, it indicates the literal text you need to type in your application. For example:

```
dim d as Date
d = new Date
```

In general, casing isn't important in code. I've mostly shown it the way you'll see it in the user manual and in the software, but you don't have to do it that way when you're writing your applications.

◆ Because book pages are narrower than computer screens, some of the lines of code are too long to fit on the page. So I've broken the line of code into one or more segments and inserted a gray arrow to indicate that it's a continued line and indented the rest of the line. For example:

```
Dim FullName, FirstName, LastName as
→ string
```

◆ The illustrations in this book were produced in two versions of the Macintosh operating system (OS 9 and OS X) and five versions of REALbasic, so your screens may not look just like the screens in the illustrations.

◆ Tips, signified by a ✔ in the margin, highlight shortcuts for performing common alternatives to the steps in the text.

The companion Web site

"In learning any other language, the first thing we do is learn to *read* it," writes Robert L. Glass in *Facts and Fallacies of Software Engineering* (Addison Wesley, 2003). "So how did we in the software field get stuck on this wrong track, the track of teaching writing before reading?"

Personally, I've always thought that teaching beginners to write code forces them to focus on getting all the commas and periods in place at the expense of understanding the ideas, and rewards accurate typing rather than clear comprehension. To learn REALbasic programming, you must write REALbasic programs. But it is at least as important that you *read* REALbasic code, especially early on. Fortunately, that code is easy to find. You can find REALbasic programs at the REAL Software site (www.realsoftware.com) and at the companion site for this book (www.swaine.com/realbasic.html). You'll also find examples from this book, errata, updates, and Made with REALbasic software applications on the companion site.

BUILDING APPLICATIONS WITH REALbasic

REALbasic is a powerful tool for writing application software, and the goal of this book is to get you started writing applications with REALbasic as quickly as possible. This first chapter introduces the tools that REALbasic provides you and then examines a commercial application written with REALbasic. I take it apart to show you the components from which it was built and then show you how to assemble those same components to achieve similar results.

The emphasis in this chapter is on what you can accomplish with REALbasic without doing any programming at all. By the time you finish the chapter, you will have developed a crude application. Although this application won't do anything really useful, it will show you how to use the rich set of tools in REALbasic's integrated development environment to build serious application software.

So take a look at REALbasic itself and then at an application that developers built with REALbasic to see how they did it.

REALbasic Overview

REALbasic, from REAL Software, is both a programming language and an integrated development environment.

The REALbasic IDE

Traditionally, programmers wrote their programs—the code—in a text editor and then tried them out to see whether they worked. A modern integrated development environment, or *IDE*, saves you from the necessity of writing most of the code that would otherwise make up an application. The saving can be considerable. What would take 20,000 lines of code in a language such as C or C++ might take only 200 lines of code in REALbasic.

In REALbasic's IDE (**Figure 1.1**), you build applications by dragging objects such as buttons and text fields into a window and then editing the properties and behavior of these objects to make them look and act just the way you want. You can do a great deal without doing any programming. Still, every application will require some coding, so most of this book deals with REALbasic's programming language.

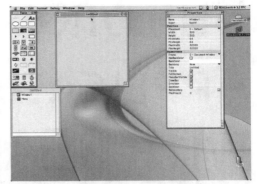

Figure 1.1 REALbasic's integrated development environment (IDE) is where you create your applications. It brings together tools for drag-and-drop user-interface building, debugging, and coding.

Where REALbasic Came From

Australian software developer Andrew Barry created REALbasic as the Mac equivalent of Visual Basic, a tool that millions of people use to develop applications quickly and easily.

REALbasic is now the product of REAL Software, based in Austin, Texas, and Andrew is no longer involved with its development. The REAL Software people have evolved Andrew's original language through several major revisions and continue to add features frequently.

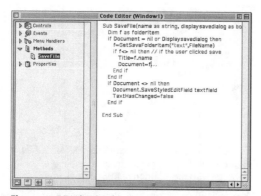

Figure 1.2 REALbasic's language is an object-oriented version of the venerable Basic language.

Figure 1.3 REALbasic's IDE provides tools that create common user interface elements such as buttons and text boxes.

The REALbasic Language

The REALbasic programming language is an object-oriented, event-driven, compiled implementation of the Basic language.

The Basic language

Basic, which is an acronym for Beginner's All-Purpose Symbolic Instruction Code, was created by John Kemeney and Thomas Kurtz back in the 1960s.

Basic programs are lists of instructions (**Figure 1.2**). The sense you have when you are writing a traditional Basic program is that you are giving detailed instructions to an extremely literal-minded being with a peculiar vocabulary.

Object-oriented programming

The approach to programming known as *object-oriented* programming, as fleshed out at Xerox Palo Alto Research Center and elsewhere in the 1970s, is a higher-level approach to software development.

In an object-oriented language, you create and manipulate objects and classes of objects. Object-oriented programming was developed in tandem with the elements of the modern computer graphical user interface—such as windows, icons, menus, and buttons—and these are in fact examples of objects that you can create and manipulate in REALbasic (**Figure 1.3**). But objects can also be more abstract. A QuickTime effect or video track, a user in a multiple-user application, and the application itself are all examples of objects.

Objects consist of properties and behavior or, to put it another way, data and code.

Event-driven programming

In *event-driven* programming, an application does nothing except respond to events.

An *event* is anything that occurs that the program can be made aware of. A keystroke is a good example of an event. When the user types something, you probably will want your application to respond in some way to the keystroke.

In event-driven programming, all the actions of an application are responses to events, whether those events are caused by the user, by some external phenomenon, or by the application itself.

Modern programming languages put these two concepts together. In an object-oriented, event-driven program, the objects respond to the events.

Compiled code

REALbasic is a *compiled* language.

Basic as originally conceived was a compiled language, but many familiar versions of Basic throughout the history of the personal computer have been *interpreted*.

Compiled code generally uses less RAM and less disk space, and compiled applications run faster than their interpreted counterparts.

REALbasic scripting

Starting with version 3.5, REALbasic includes a scripting system called RBScript. What this system means is that the applications you create with REALbasic can be scripted: This programmability in the final application, not just in its development, makes for more flexible, capable applications (**Figure 1.4**).

When you put together REALbasic's object-oriented and event-driven style with the traditional ease of use of Basic and the greater ease of use afforded by REALbasic's rich IDE, you have a powerful and friendly tool for developing application software.

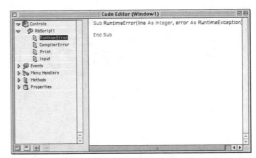

Figure 1.4 REALbasic got both easier and more powerful with the addition of RBScript, its scripting system.

Figure 1.5 Real Software's Made with REALbasic program is both a source of tools for REALbasic developers and a place to promote their wares.

What Can You Build with REALbasic?

What kinds of things can you build with REALbasic? Some limitations exist, although REAL Software comes out with new versions of REALbasic frequently and the list of limitations shrinks as the power of REALbasic grows.

Building commercial applications

Just as Visual Basic created a marketplace for Windows software developers and HyperCard launched a stackware phenomenon among Mac users back in the 1980s, a marketplace of shareware and other software has developed around REALbasic.

REALbasic is a full software development environment with debugging aids and the works. You can build anything with it that you can build with any other development environment, and REALbasic developers are proving that fact, as REAL Software's Made with REALbasic program demonstrates (**Figure 1.5**).

Prototyping applications

On the other hand, really high-performance commercial applications from companies with lots of highly trained programmers probably are not candidates for REALbasic programming. REALbasic lacks some of the tools typically used by teams of programmers working on large projects. But it is worth noting that Microsoft uses REALbasic as a prototyping language for its Macintosh applications, even though it doesn't write the final applications in REALbasic.

Programming Microsoft Office

As of version 3.5, REALbasic includes Microsoft Office Automation. With this capability, you can program every aspect of Microsoft Office 2000/2001 and Office X to manipulate Word, Excel, and PowerPoint documents and components and to create custom applications, either for your own use or to share or sell (**Figure 1.6**). Examples of this type of programming appear throughout this book.

Building Macintosh applications

If you are developing strictly for the Macintosh, your REALbasic applications can take advantage of a lot of Macintosh-only technology. You can build applications specifically for Macintosh OS X or for Mac OS 9 and earlier and for PowerPC or 680x0 Macs. You can make calls to something like 8,000 Mac OS Toolbox functions, interact with AppleScript scripts or incorporate them right into your applications, let your application communicate with other applications via Apple events, use XCMDs and XFCNs written for HyperCard stacks, and call PowerPC shared libraries. You can even harness the power of Unix under Mac OS X's hood. Although using REALbasic won't guarantee that your applications are attractive or easy to use, REALbasic will build your Mac applications in accordance with Apple user-interface guidelines, so they'll look like Mac applications (**Figure 1.7**).

Figure 1.6 With version 3.5, REALbasic added the capability to program Microsoft Office applications.

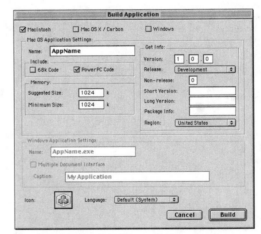

Figure 1.7 REALbasic builds applications for the Macintosh that look like Macintosh applications and applications for Windows that look like Windows applications.

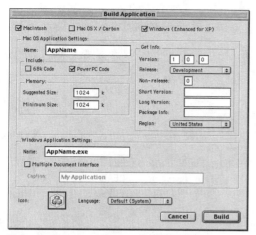

Figure 1.8 REALbasic projects can be compiled as traditional Mac OS 9 and earlier applications, Carbonized Mac OS X applications, and Windows applications.

Building Windows applications

The Pro version of REALbasic will also let you build applications for Windows (as of version 3.5, including Windows XP) while working on a Mac. Or you can write one application and painlessly build both Mac and Windows versions (**Figure 1.8**).

If you build Windows-only applications, you can include calls to the Windows Toolbox in your code. You don't even need to have a Windows machine to test your code. If you have VirtualPC from Connectix on your Mac, any REALbasic application that you build for Windows will open automatically in VirtualPC on your Mac.

A caveat: Early versions of REALbasic were spotty in their support of Windows. True, you could develop Mac applications quickly; true, you could develop applications that could be deployed on either platform; but if you wanted to develop applications quickly *and* deploy them on both platforms or even just on Windows you were out of luck. This situation has improved with each release of REALbasic.

Building applications on a Windows machine (not yet)

This task is something you *can't* do yet. Currently, REALbasic lets you create applications only on a Macintosh for use on either Windows or Macintosh machines. REAL Software has a version of REALbasic in the works for those who want to do their development on a Windows machine; that version (5.0) should be out by the time you read this book.

For Visual Basic Programmers

Andrew Barry's development of REALbasic diverged from Microsoft's Visual Basic in several ways early on and has followed its own path ever since, so don't expect to be able to port your Visual Basic projects to REALbasic without some effort. It can be done, however, and tools are available to help iron out the inconsistencies. The differences are not fundamental, so if you know Visual Basic, learning REALbasic should be a snap.

Porting Visual Basic applications

Windows already has a BASIC language tool, of course: Visual Basic from Microsoft. Thousands of applications have been written in Visual Basic just for Windows systems. Wouldn't it be nice if you could convert those applications to REALbasic and run them on a Mac?

You can, with some effort, if you can get your hands on the Visual Basic source code. If you have developed applications for Windows by using Visual Basic, REALbasic gives you the means to expand your reach to the Mac platform.

Naturally, you can run these converted applications on a Windows machine, too.

Building database applications

REALbasic comes with a built-in database, but there are also interfaces to many other database products, at least for the Mac. Developers have used REALbasic to create custom front ends for databases and to incorporate database capabilities into their applications. This book shows you how to do both things.

Building Internet applications

REALbasic simplifies the development of Internet-savvy applications. At least one Web browser is written in REALbasic, and this book contains several examples of Internet applications (**Figure 1.9**).

And you can do a lot without actually doing any programming, thanks to REALbasic's rich IDE.

Figure 1.9 Some of REALbasic's tools support Internet and serial communications. You drag this socket tool to your application's window to give the application Internet capabilities.

For HyperCard Authors

REALbasic has no relation to HyperCard and its scripting language, HyperTalk, except that it is easy to use, and REALbasic applications can incorporate external commands and functions written for HyperCard in the XCMD and XFCN formats. REALbasic won't read your existing stacks, however. Also, learning to develop applications with REALbasic is somewhat harder than learning to script stacks with HyperTalk—and significantly harder than authoring HyperCard stacks without scripting. On the other hand, the vibrant community of REALbasic developers will share ideas and code with you, REAL software actively supports and extends its product, and REALbasic is very powerful and easy to use after you get over the initial bump in the learning curve.

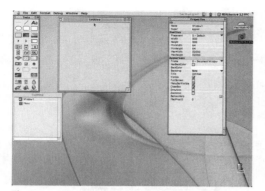

Figure 1.10 The REALbasic Integrated Development Environment, or IDE, consists of several windows for editing the appearance and behavior of your application.

Touring REALbasic

If you haven't already done so, you should get your hands on REALbasic now and install and launch it so that you can follow along with this introduction to the development environment.

REAL Software sells two versions of REALbasic: Standard and Professional. The Professional version is required if you want to build Windows applications or do serious database programming.

To install REALbasic:

◆ Open the installation CD, and drag the REALbasic folder from the CD to your hard disk.

In Mac OS X, you should place the folder inside your Applications folder.

To launch REALbasic:

◆ Double-click the REALbasic icon to launch the program.

Clicking any REALbasic document's icon in the Finder also launches REALbasic.

When it finishes launching, you should see the REALbasic IDE (**Figure 1.10**).

REALbasic's Integrated Development Environment, or IDE, is what you see when you launch REALbasic. The IDE is where you do all your application development; it consists of several windows, including the project window.

TOURING REALBASIC

Working with Projects

While you are developing your application, it is called a project. The project window contains the top-level definition of your project and helps you keep track of the different files that make up your project.

It makes sense to keep parts of the project in different files when they are different kinds of data—graphics, sounds, movies, and icons, for example.

To view the Project Window:

◆ If the Project Window is not already open, from the Window menu, choose Project.

A new Project Window appears (**Figure 1.11**).

To open an existing project:

1. From the File menu, choose Open.

2. In the Open dialog box that appears, select a REALbasic project file (other files are visible but not selectable), and click Open.

To start a new project:

◆ From the File menu, choose New.

To add a window to a project:

◆ From the File menu, choose New Window (**Figure 1.12**).

Figure 1.11 The Project Window is the control center of a REALbasic project, containing all the windows and associated files and other elements that make up the project.

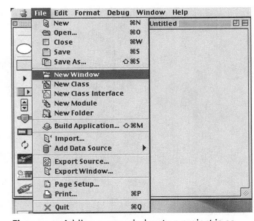

Figure 1.12 Adding a new window to a project is as simple as choosing New Window from the File menu.

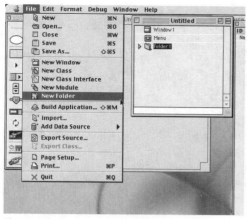

Figure 1.13 You add pictures, sound files, and QuickTime movies to your project by dragging them to the project window.

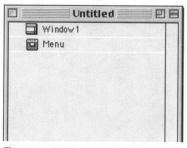

Figure 1.14 You can organize the contents of the project window by adding folders to it.

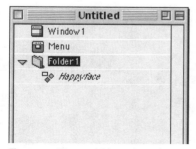

Figure 1.15 You can hide or show the contents of project window folders for clarity.

To add a movie, picture, sound, or other file to a project:

1. Locate the file in the Finder.

2. Drag the file's icon to the project window (**Figure 1.13**).

To remove items from a project:

1. Click the icon of the item to select it.

2. From the Edit menu, choose Clear.

To organize the project window:

1. From the File menu, choose New Folder. A folder appears in the project window (**Figure 1.14**).

2. Drag other items to the folder.

3. Click the disclosure triangle to the left of the folder to view or hide its contents (**Figure 1.15**).

To save a project:

◆ From the File menu, choose Save.

WORKING WITH PROJECTS

Working with Windows

The window editor contains a picture of your application as it currently exists. You drag objects to it from the Tools palette as you build your application.

To view the window editor:

◆ Double-click any window icon in the project window (**Figure 1.16**).

The window editor appears. Note that the name of the window whose icon you clicked appears in the window editor's title bar.

✔ Tip

■ The window editor is a window for editing windows. This definition can be confusing, but usually in this book, any generic reference to a window means the window that you are creating for your application.

To create a new window:

◆ From the File menu, choose New Window.

To add items to a window:

1. If the Tools palette is not visible, from the Window menu, choose Show Tools.

2. Drag any item in the Tools palette to the window editor.

To remove items from a window:

1. Click the item to select it.

2. From the Edit menu, choose Clear.

To resize a window:

◆ Drag the bottom-right corner of the window.

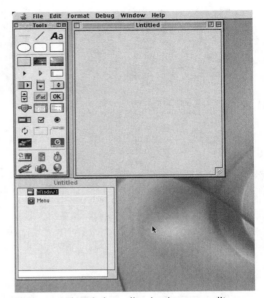

Figure 1.16 The window editor is where you edit your project's windows. It presents a more or less WYSIWYG (what you see is what you get) representation of what your application will look like.

Figure 1.17 The Tools palette is what you use to construct your application's user interface. You drag its icons to the window editor to add buttons, fields, and other user-interface elements.

Working with Tools

REALbasic applications are made up of objects. Many common objects that you need for creating the user interface of an application—collectively called *tools* or *controls*—are ready-made and stored in REALbasic's Tools palette.

REALbasic's Tools palette contains controls for displaying static text, user-editable text boxes, pop-up and contextual menus, scroll bars, sliders, progress bars, radio buttons, check boxes, bevel buttons, list boxes, tab panels, animations, movies, 3D graphics, and sounds, as well as serial and Internet socket connection tools.

✔ Tip

■ The Tools palette contains *tools,* which are also referred to as *controls* and occasionally as *interface objects*. Whatever term is used, these objects are simply the gizmos that you use to create your application's user interface.

To view the Tools palette:

◆ From the Window menu, choose Show Tools (**Figure 1.17**).

To add a tool to your project:

1. If the Tools palette is not visible, from the Window menu, choose Show Tools.

2. Drag any item in the Tools palette to the window editor.

To resize a tool:

◆ Drag any corner of the tool to resize it (**Figure 1.18**).

   To resize the tool in one direction only, Shift-drag in that direction.

   Some tools, such as the Timer, are not visible in the running application and cannot be resized.

To remove a tool from your project:

1. Click the item to select it.

2. From the Edit menu, choose Clear.

✔ Tip

■ To see the name of a tool in the Tools palette, let the cursor linger over it for a second.

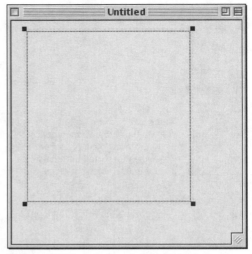

Figure 1.18 Objects in the window editor can be resized by dragging.

Working with Object Properties

REALbasic objects consist of properties and behavior. For many objects, a properties window displays the names and values of the properties of the object and allows you to edit the values.

✔ Tip

■ Object-oriented purists take note: The treatment of object-oriented programming (or *OOP*) in this chapter is intuitive rather than rigorous. I give OOP more formal treatment in later chapters, particularly in Chapter 5, "Writing Object-Oriented Code."

To view the properties window:

◆ Click any control/tool in the window editor.

or

Click the icon for any window in the project window.

or

From the Window menu, choose Show Properties.

The names of an object's properties appear on the left side of the properties window and the corresponding values on the right. REALbasic lets you edit an object's properties.

WORKING WITH OBJECT PROPERTIES

To change an object's properties:

Do any of the following:

◆ To change its value, click a property's check box (**Figure 1.19**).

To edit the text of a text property, click the text of a text property (**Figure 1.20**).

For more editing, click a button with an ellipsis to do more extensive text entry or editing of a text property in a separate edit window (**Figure 1.21**).

◆ For other kinds of properties (such as color and associated database), use Color Pickers and other editing tools (**Figure 1.22**).

◆ Press Return to see the effect of text editing in the window editor.

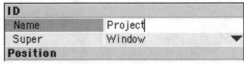

Figure 1.19 You can set some properties of objects by clicking check boxes.

Figure 1.20 Some properties, such as an object's name, are text.

Figure 1.21 Some text properties can be quite long; for them, REALbasic provides a separate window.

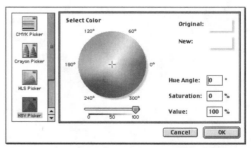

Figure 1.22 Some properties, such as the background-color property of a window, are colors, and REALbasic provides a Color Picker for setting these properties.

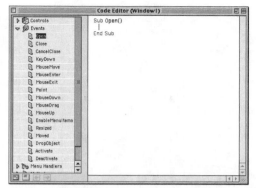

Figure 1.23 The Code Editor is where you write all your application's code.

Working with the Code Editor

REALbasic's objects consist of properties and behavior, and their behavior is embodied in their code. For every object, a Code Editor window displays and lets you edit the code associated with the object.

To view the Code Editor:

◆ In the window editor, click any control/tool, or in the project window, click the icon for any window and then press Option-Tab (**Figure 1.23**).

 or

 In the window editor, double-click any control/tool.

✔ Tip

■ The Code Editor's contents depend on the object you select. To be sure you're examining the right object's code, look for its name in the Code Editor's title bar.

About Handlers

In event-driven programming, objects respond to events. The browser pane of the Code Editor lists all the events to which a particular object responds. The code associated with each event is packaged in a *handler* and is that response.

To edit the code of an object:

1. On the left side of the Code Editor, select any code handler (**Figure 1.24**).

2. In the right panel, enter the desired code.

✔ Tip

- REALbasic code is not case-sensitive. `mywindow` is the same as `MyWindow`.

To resize the Code Editor panels:

- ◆ Drag the vertical separator between the panels (**Figure 1.25**).

✔ Tip

- The left pane of the Code Editor is a code browser; it gives access to code handlers associated with the object. Any handler selected in the left pane is displayed in the right pane for editing.

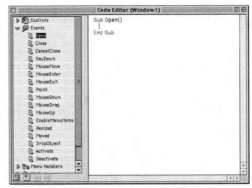

Figure 1.24 Code resides in handlers. Selecting a handler in the left panel of the Code Editor displays its code in the right.

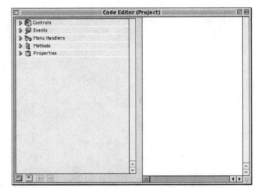

Figure 1.25 You can reallocate the space that the Code Editor gives its two panels by dragging the separator between them. This technique can be useful for viewing more of a large block of code.

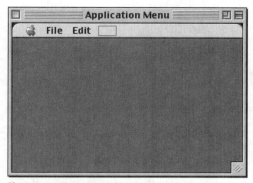

Figure 1.26 The menu editor is where you create your own menus and menu items for your application.

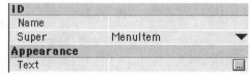

Figure 1.27 You add a new menu by clicking the blank menu that the menu editor provides at the right end of its menu bar.

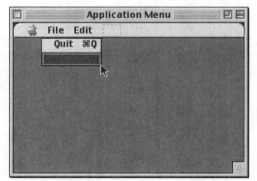

Figure 1.28 You add an item to a menu by clicking the blank item that the menu editor provides at the bottom of any menu.

Working with Menus

With exceptions that you can ignore for now, every modern computer application has a menu bar. REALbasic gives each new project a default menu bar, which you can modify with the menu editor. REALbasic supplies the Menu icon automatically in the project window when you create a new project; this icon represents the menu bar for the application. The menu editor lets you add menus to the menu bar and menu items to any menu.

To view the menu editor:

◆ In the project window, double-click the Menu icon.

The menu editor appears. (**Figure 1.26**).

To add a menu:

1. In the menu editor, click the empty menu that always appears at the right end of the menu bar.

The properties window shows the properties for this new menu (**Figure 1.27**).

2. In the properties window, enter a name and text for the menu.

To add a menu item:

1. In the menu editor, click the empty menu item that always appears at the bottom of any menu (**Figure 1.28**).

2. In the properties window, enter a name and text for the menu item.

✔ Tip

■ If a menu in your application is longer than a dozen items, consider using sub-menus to organize it.

WORKING WITH MENUS

To add a submenu to a menu:

1. In the menu editor, click the empty item that always appears at the bottom of any menu.

2. In the properties window, enter a name and text for the menu item.

3. In the properties window, click the Submenu check box.

To rearrange menus:

♦ Drag menus to the desired positions in the menu bar.

To rearrange items within a menu:

♦ Click the menu item (**Figure 1.29**) and drag it to the desired position (**Figure 1.30**).

   The item moves to its new position (**Figure 1.31**).

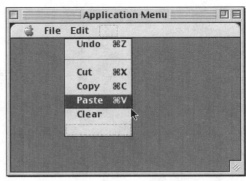

Figure 1.29 To rearrange items within a menu, click one menu item,...

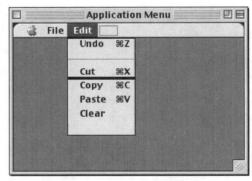

Figure 1.30 ...drag it to the desired position,...

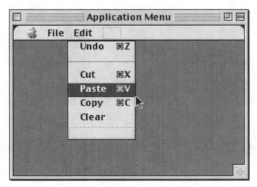

Figure 1.31 ...and drop it.

To turn a menu item into a menu:

1. Select the target menu.

2. Drag the desired item in that menu to the desired position in the target menu.

To turn a menu into a menu item:

1. Select the menu to which you want to move the desired menu.

2. In the menu bar, click the desired menu.

3. In the destination menu, drag the menu to the desired position.

4. Click this new menu item to select it.

5. In the properties window, deselect the Submenu check box unless you want this menu item to be a submenu.

To move an item from one menu to another:

1. Select the menu item.

2. Turn it into a menu (see the preceding procedure).

3. Turn it into a menu item in the destination menu (see the preceding procedure).

To remove a menu or menu item:

1. Select the menu or menu item.

2. From the Edit menu, choose Clear.

WORKING WITH MENUS

The Application Development Process

Building applications with REALbasic is a cyclical process. You create a project, add objects, edit their properties and code, test the project, and repeat this process until you are satisfied. Then you build the application and use or sell it.

A larger cycle is building and deploying applications, finding things that still need fixing, doing more editing, and building and deploying again. The process is never really finished.

Living with imperfection

The cruel truth is that your applications will crash. Often. REALbasic will crash. You can't react to these crashes in the way that you react when your word processor crashes (you know what I'm talking about). Crashes are part of the application-development process, and you have to learn to be philosophical about them. Some practices make crashes less likely, but they will happen.

Even when your application doesn't crash, it will spend the largest part of its development life in a state of brokenness. Applications don't work right until they are done, and then you stop working on them. So if you're doing things right, you typically spend most of your programming time trying to figure out why your program isn't working. This situation is normal. The process is called *debugging*, and tools that help make it less frustrating are available.

The agony of debugging is one reason why a graphical IDE such as REALbasic's is so empowering. Less of your application depends on treacherous code and more on prebuilt objects (**Figure 1.32**).

When you get it all right, you can produce applications as useful and attractive as those produced by the big boys.

Figure 1.32 REALbasic's debugging tools help track down errors.

Figure 1.33 Deus Web Wizard is one of hundreds of shareware, freeware, shrink-wrapped, custom in-house, and other applications written in REALbasic.

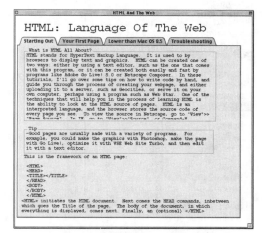

Figure 1.34 Deus Web Wizard uses the built-in user-interface features of REALbasic to display a modal dialog box with tabs.

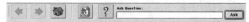

Figure 1.35 Here's another of Deus Web Wizard's windows, this one presenting buttons with custom icons.

A REALbasic Application

One of the best ways to learn application development is to take apart existing applications to see how they were built and to try to replicate interesting parts of them. You'll do that in this section and can make analyzing REALbasic applications part of your ongoing education in REALbasic application development. You'll find many REALbasic projects and applications to study at the REAL Software site.

Andrew Potter and Taylor Bond used REALbasic to create a shareware application called Deus Web Wizard, which provides help with creating Web sites and learning HTML. This application is for Mac OS 9 and earlier, at least in the version I present here, but it could just as easily have been deployed for Windows or Mac OS X (**Figure 1.33**).

Deus Web Wizard displays several windows of different kinds. The Advanced HTML window (**Figure 1.34**) is a simple movable modal dialog box, but it also has tabs that allow the user to see different content.

The window at the top of the screen is a plain box with several buttons containing custom icons and a text box for user input (**Figure 1.35**).

This application is a commercial product, and its authors expect to make some money from it. At ten dollars a pop, they may not make money very fast, but shareware is one category of commercial software, and some shareware authors make a very nice living for themselves. Aside from such crass commercial considerations, Deus Web Wizard is a handy little tool that the company tech folks might provide to less technical employees who want to put up Web sites by themselves.

Programming by Imitation

You have seen some of the main components of this application. Now you'll locate those components in the REALbasic IDE and see how you can build an application that has similar components: multiple windows of different kinds, iconized buttons, and specialized text boxes.

To start, you'll create the Deus Web Wizard toolbar—that short, wide window that Deus Web Wizard displays at the top of the screen.

To replicate the DWW toolbar:

1. To start a new project, press Command-N, choose File > New, or launch REALbasic.

2. In the project window, double-click the window icon to open the project's default window.

3. In the properties window for this window, enter Toolbar as both the title and the name of this window (**Figure 1.36**).

4. Resize the window to almost the width of your screen and approximately 64 pixels in height by dragging its bottom-right corner (**Figure 1.37**).

5. In the properties window, set the window's width and height to exactly what you want them to be.

6. Set the Frame property to Plain Box.

7. Click the HasBackColor property; then click the BackColor property, and select a light gray from the color palette that appears (**Figure 1.38**).

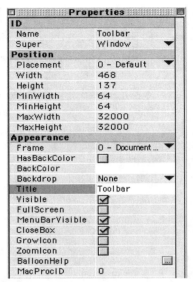

Figure 1.36 Enter Toolbar as the title of this window.

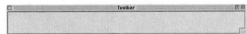

Figure 1.37 Drag the corner of the window to resize it.

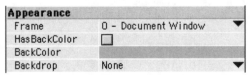

Figure 1.38 Windows have a BackColor property that controls the background color. Set this property by using the color palette.

Figure 1.39 Drag a BevelButton to the window.

Figure 1.40 Drag a PushButton to the window.

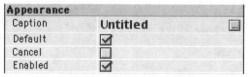

Figure 1.41 This button will be a default button, so set its Default property by checking that checkbox in the properties window.

Figure 1.42 Drop a separator to the window. This control can serve as either a vertical or a horizontal separator, depending on how you size it.

To put buttons on the toolbar:

1. Drag the BevelButton tool to the toolbar window (that is, the window editor) to place a button on the toolbar (**Figure 1.39**).

2. In the properties window for the button, select the LockLeft and LockTop properties.

3. Set the Left and Top properties to 13 and 4.

4. Set the Width and Height properties to 48.

5. In the toolbar window, Option-drag the button to make copies of it.

6. Position each copy by selecting it and then setting its Left and Top properties.

To create the toolbar's default button:

1. Drag the PushButton tool to the toolbar window to place a button near the right end of the toolbar (**Figure 1.40**).

2. Resize and position this button by dragging it or by setting its Left, Top, Width, and Height properties.

3. Select the button's Default property (**Figure 1.41**).

To create the toolbar's separator:

1. Drag the Separator tool to the toolbar window to place a separator near the left end of the toolbar.

2. Drag the separator to size and position it. Make the dragging rectangle taller than it is wide to produce a vertical separator (**Figure 1.42**).

To create the toolbar's text box:

1. Drag the EditField tool to the toolbar window to place a text box near the right end of the toolbar.

2. Drag the text box to size and position it as in the Deus Web Wizard toolbar (**Figure 1.43**).

3. Click the text box to select it.

4. If necessary, from the Windows menu, choose Show Properties to reveal the properties window.

5. In the properties window, set the properties of the field as shown in **Table 1.1**.

6. Drag the StaticText tool to just above the text box to create a static text block for labeling the text box.

7. Click the static text and set its Text property to Ask A Question (**Figure 1.44**).

Figure 1.43 Drop a TextField to the window and resize it by dragging.

Figure 1.44 Set the Text property of the StaticText control by typing the desired text in the properties window.

Table 1.1

EditField Settings

PROPERTY	VALUE	PROPERTY	VALUE
Name	EditField1	UseFocusRing	Unchecked
Index		Enabled	Checked
Super	EditField	Visible	Checked
Left	305	HelpTag	
Top	26	BalloonHelp	
Width	337	DisabledBalloonHelp	
Height	24	AutoDeactivate	Checked
LockLeft	Unchecked	TextFont	System
LockTop	Unchecked	TextSize	12
LockRight	Unchecked	Bold	Unchecked
LockBottom	Unchecked	Italic	Unchecked
Border	Checked	Underline	Unchecked
MultiLine	Unchecked	Text	
ScrollBar	Checked	ReadOnly	Unchecked
Styled	Unchecked	LimitText	0
Password	Unchecked	AcceptTabs	Unchecked
TextColor			
BackColor			

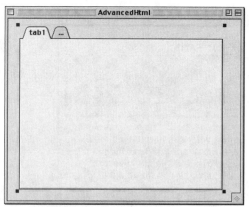

Figure 1.45 This window will be a Movable Modal window. You control this by setting its Frame property.

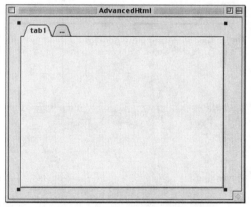

Figure 1.46 Drag a TabPanel to the window.

Position	
Left	20
Top	14
Width	353
Height	292
LockLeft	☑
LockTop	☑
LockRight	☑
LockBottom	☑

Figure 1.47 Although you can size and position objects in the window editor directly by dragging them, you can be more precise if you set the appropriate properties in the properties window.

To create more DWW windows:

1. From the File menu, choose New Window to create a new window.

   Leave the window untitled.

2. Create a third window, and title it Preview.

3. Set the Frame property of the Preview window to Movable Modal.

4. Create a fourth window, and give it the name Advanced HTML.

5. Set the Frame property of the Advanced HTML window to Movable Modal (**Figure 1.45**).

6. Size each of these windows as in Deus Web Wizard by dragging.

To create the DWW tabs:

1. Click the Advanced HTML window or choose it from the Windows menu to bring it forward.

2. Drag the TabPanel tool to the Advanced HTML window to place a tab panel in the window (**Figure 1.46**).

3. Size and position the tab panel as in Deus Web Wizard by dragging.

4. In the properties window for the tab panel, set the LockLeft, LockTop, LockRight, and LockBottom properties to ensure that the tab panel fills most of the window as it is resized (**Figure 1.47**).

5. Click the tab with the ellipsis (...) to invoke the Tab Panel Editor.

6. Select Tab 1 in the left panel of the Editor.

7. Click the Edit button in the Editor.

continues on next page

PROGRAMMING BY IMITATION

8. In the Edit Tab window that appears, enter More with Text (**Figure 1.48**).

9. Click OK.

10. Click the Add button in the Editor.

11. In the New Tab window that appears, type META Tags.

12. Click OK.

13. In the same way, add tabs labeled Tables and Java/JavaScript.

To attach text boxes to the tabs:

1. Click the Tables tab.

2. Drag the EditField control from the Tools palette to the Advanced HTML window (**Figure 1.49**).

3. Drag the corners of the EditField to size it as you want.

4. In the properties window, enter some distinctive text for this default text property.

5. Click each of the other tabs, repeating the process (**Figure 1.50**).

Each tab now has its own associated text box. As you click the tabs, you can see the default text you entered for each tab's EditField.

Although it doesn't do much, you've created an application. In the following exercise, you test it.

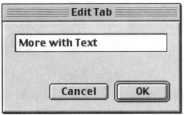

Figure 1.48 REALbasic presents custom editors whenever necessary. The Tab Panel Editor and Edit Tab window make it easy to put tab panels in your application.

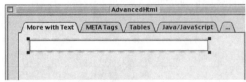

Figure 1.49 When you place a TextField in a tab panel, it is visible in the application only when that tab is selected.

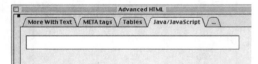

Figure 1.50 Tab panels are a good way to present a lot of information or a lot of choices in one window while avoiding a cluttered look.

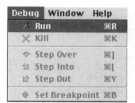

Figure 1.51 To test your project, choose Run from the Debug menu. This command puts you in testing mode, where you can try out what you've created.

Figure 1.52 To return to development mode after testing, choose File > Quit. This command quits test mode but leaves you in REALbasic.

To test the application:

1. From the Debug menu, choose Run, or press Command-R (**Figure 1.51**).

   You have now entered test mode. But where is the Advanced HTML window that you created? The answer is that an application displays only one window by default. To see more windows, you must enable them. Clearly, you have more to learn about REALbasic, but for now, there is a way to see that other window.

2. From the REALbasic menu, choose Quit.

   You haven't quit REALbasic; you were in test mode, and that's what you quit. Alternatively, you quit your application. You're now back in REALbasic's IDE.

3. From the Edit menu, choose Project Settings.

4. From the Default Window pop-up menu in the dialog box that appears, choose Advanced HTML.

5. Click OK to dismiss the dialog box.

6. From the Debug menu, choose Run again.

7. In the Advanced HTML window (which should now be visible), click the tabs in turn.

   You should see the text associated with each tab, just as you did in the IDE.

8. When you've finished testing your application, from the REALbasic menu, choose Quit, or press Command-Q (**Figure 1.52**).

In Chapter 2, "Building an HTML Editor," you'll develop a REALbasic application.

BUILDING AN HTML EDITOR

In this chapter, you will build a working application: an HTML editor. In the process, you will create working menus, create new objects, set their properties, and begin writing REALbasic code. You will learn how to enable your application to create new files, open existing files, and save files.

By the end of the chapter, you will have a rudimentary HTML editor that you can use in building Web pages, and you will know how to add features to enhance it. Because you're jumping right into building a complete application that performs useful work, occasionally you will be asked to take something on faith, not to worry about a detail, or to type code by rote. In subsequent chapters, all these skimmed-over matters will be explained in full.

Creating the Edit Field

You're going to build an HTML editor.

If you've ever created a Web page, you probably used an HTML editor such as Dreamweaver, GoLive, FrontPage, or BBEdit to generate the HTML (Hypertext Markup Language) that Web browsers read. Or you may have just entered the HTML code directly in a text editor, because HTML files are nothing but (hard-to-read) text files (**Figure 2.1**).

In fact, the HTML editor that you're going to build is really just a text editor, except that instead of having menus for choosing fonts and styles, your HTML Editor application will have menus for placing HTML tags and special symbols. In this rudimentary version, you won't worry about providing for printing, with the excuse that HTML is more naturally viewed in a Web browser than printed.

When you've finished the chapter, you'll have a working application, but while you're developing the application, it's referred to as a *project*.

```
<html>
<head>
<title>Prose Design</title>
</head>
<body bgcolor="#ffffff" text="#000000" >
<table width="700px" background=0 cellpadding=0 cellspacing=0 border=0>
   <tr>
      <td align=left valign=top><img src="pix/logo2.gif" alt="Prose Design"><img src="pix/menu2.gif" alt="Home, Servi
   </tr>
   <tr>
      <td>
         <table width="700px"   cellpadding=0 cellspacing=0 border=0>
            <tr>
               <td width="150px" align=left valign=top>
                  <table width="150px" cellpadding=0 cellspacing=0 border=0 align=left valign=top>
                     <tr>
                        <td width="146" cellpadding="0" cellspacing="0" border="0" bgcolor="#6699cc" align=left valign=top>
                           <a href="http://www.summerjo.com"><img src="pix/summerjomenu.gif" alt="www.summerjo.com" border="
                           </a> </td>
                     </tr>
                  </table>
               </td>
               <td>
                  <table width="500px" background=0 cellpadding=0 cellspacing=0 border=0>
                     <tr>
                        <td> <img src="pix/headline.gif" alt="Todays Headlines in the Tech Industry and beyond">
```

Figure 2.1 HTML, the primary language in which Web pages are written, works its magic through the use of angle-bracketed *tags*. The HTML editor you'll build will free you of the minor drudgery of entering those tags manually.

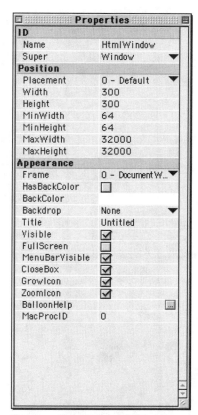

Figure 2.2 The GrowIcon and ZoomIcon properties of a window make it user-resizable. Exactly how these properties reveal themselves to the user depends on the platform (Classic Mac, OS X, or Windows).

To start the project:

1. In the Finder, double-click the REALbasic file's icon to launch REALbasic.

2. In the project window, click the name of the default window that REALbasic provides.

   The properties window for this window appears.

3. Enter `HtmlWindow` as the Name property, and press Return.

   The name of this window changes in the project window.

   Note: Leave the Title property Untitled. The Title property is what your application will display at the top of the window, and in most applications, a new document displays Untitled until the user gives it a title. The Name property names the window object so that you can refer to it in your code.

4. Still in the properties window, click the GrowIcon and ZoomIcon properties (put a check in each of their check boxes).

   These two properties let the user resize the window.

   Your properties window should look like **Figure 2.2**.

To create the HTML editing field:

1. Double-click HtmlWindow in the project window to open the window editor for it.

2. Locate the EditField control in the Tools palette, and drag it into the window editor for HtmlWindow.

   This EditField control is the workhorse control for displaying, accepting, and editing text. Most applications will have at least one EditField for accepting user input.

continues on next page

3. In the properties window, enter `HtmlField` for the Name property of this field.

4. Enter `Courier` for the Font property.

5. Select the MultiLine property.

The MultiLine property of an EditField controls whether it can accommodate multiple lines of text.

Now you'll size the field.

6. Still in the properties window, enter -1 for the Left property.

7. Enter -1 for the Top property.

8. In the window editor, drag the bottom-right corner of the field to cause it to fill the window (**Figure 2.3**).

In the properties window, note that the Width and Height properties changed to reflect what you just did (**Figure 2.4**).

In REALbasic, you often have more than one way to do a thing. You could also have just typed the numbers in the properties window, and the field would have resized accordingly in the window editor.

9. To lock in these (relative) boundaries for the field, select the LockLeft, LockTop, LockRight, and LockBottom properties.

Setting these properties specifies what should happen to the object if the user resizes the window. LockLeft locks the position of the left edge of the object with respect to the left edge of the window, and so forth. Somewhat paradoxically, if all four properties are set and the user resizes the window, the size of the window changes; if they are not set, the size stays the same.

Figure 2.3 During development, you can resize almost any user-interface object simply by dragging its corner while you're working in the window editor.

Position	
Left	- 1
Top	- 1
Width	301
Height	301

Figure 2.4 You have different ways of setting the properties of objects (dragging a corner of a user-interface control is one), but no matter how you set them, the properties window reflects the current state of an object's properties.

Figure 2.5 When you choose Run from the Debug menu, it puts you in test mode, where you can try out your application.

Figure 2.6 In test mode, your project works essentially as it will when you turn it into a stand-alone application, but you still are working inside REALbasic's IDE.

Figure 2.7 You exit test mode via the Quit command.

As an experienced computer user, you know that you should save your work regularly. You should do that now, after which you should test your application to see what you've accomplished so far.

To test your work:

1. From the File menu, choose Save (or press Command-S), and save the file with the name Html Editor.

   Note that this name now appears as the title of the project window.

2. From the Debug menu, choose Run (or press Command-R) (**Figure 2.5**).

   You are now in test mode.

3. Test your application.

   Enter some text in the field, and use the Edit menu items or their Command-key equivalents to cut, copy, and paste chunks of text (**Figure 2.6**).

   You will note that you didn't have to do anything to get these editing features. REALbasic essentially gives you the core features of a text editor for free.

   Also note that you can resize the window and the field resizes with it (thanks to your having set the LockLeft and other properties). And that font you're looking at is Courier, *n'est ce pas?*

4. If anything didn't work, make note of it before you return to the editing environment.

5. Now choose Quit from the File menu to return to the IDE, the editing environment (**Figure 2.7**).

CREATING THE EDIT FIELD

Creating the Tags Menu

So far, this application is a rudimentary text editor. Next, you'll create a Tags menu that will allow the user to enter HTML tags without typing. To be of any real use in creating Web pages, this menu needs to be a longish, hierarchical menu, because HTML has many tags. In this section, you'll just create a few menu items; you can add others by following the same steps.

To create the Tags menu:

1. In the project window, click the Menu icon.

    The menu editor appears. You use it to create menus and menu items.

2. In the menu editor, click the blank menu at the right side of the menu bar.

    This blank menu is the trick REALbasic uses to let you create new menus (**Figure 2.8**).

    The properties window shows the properties for the menu.

3. In the properties window, enter Tags for the Text property.

    The Text property of a menu is the text that the application puts in the menu.

4. Press Return.

    Note that REALbasic supplies a default value for the Name property. It's fine; leave it (**Figure 2.9**).

    As is the case with all objects, the Name property names the object, and you'll use it to refer to the object in the code that you'll be writing a lot of soon.

This new menu needs some menu items.

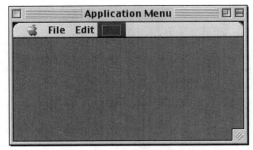

Figure 2.8 The menu editor provides a dummy menu that you use to create new menus.

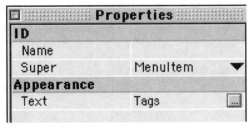

Figure 2.9 REALbasic suggests a logical name for a new menu when you create it.

Figure 2.10 The menu editor also provides a dummy menu item for creating new menu items.

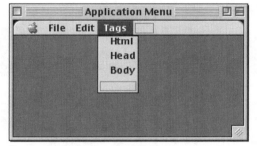

Figure 2.11 The Tags menu with its three menu items: HTML, Head, and Body.

To add an item to the Tags menu:

1. In the menu editor, select your new Tags menu.

2. Click the blank menu item at the bottom of the Tags menu.

   Like the blank-menu trick, this blank menu item is REALbasic's way of letting you create new menu items (**Figure 2.10**).

3. In the properties window for this menu item, enter HTML for the Text property.

   The Text property of a menu item is the text that the application puts in the menu item.

4. Press Return.

   Note that REALbasic supplies a default value for the Name property. It's fine; leave it.

Now you should do the same with a few more menu items.

To add more items to the Tags menu:

1. In the menu editor, select the Tags menu.

2. Click the blank menu item at the bottom of the Tags menu.

3. In the properties window for this menu item, enter HEAD for the Text property to create a Head menu item.

4. Press Return.

5. Now create a Body tag the same way.

6. In the menu editor, confirm that your Tags menu has three menu items: HTML, Head, and Body (**Figure 2.11**).

CREATING THE TAGS MENU

To test the Tags menu items:

1. From the File menu, choose Save (or press Command-S), and save the file with the name Html Editor.

2. From the Debug menu, choose Run (or press Command-R).

   You'll note that your new Tags menu is present but doesn't do any more than it did when you were looking at it in the menu editor. The menu is not enabled (**Figure 2.12**). You'll fix that problem next.

3. Now quit to return to the IDE.

To enable the Tags menu items:

1. Click the window icon in the project window to select it.

2. Press Option-Tab to open the Code Editor for the window.

3. In the left panel of the Code Editor window, click the disclosure triangle next to Events to expand it (**Figure 2.13**).

   Recall that REALbasic is an *event-driven* and *object-oriented* language. What you see in the left panel of the Code Editor are the events to which this object can respond.

4. Click EnableMenuItems to select it.

   EnableMenuItems is the event that REALbasic causes to occur just before displaying the menu items in a menu. This event is REALbasic's way of giving you, the programmer, the opportunity to enable the menu items.

Figure 2.12 The new menu items are not yet enabled.

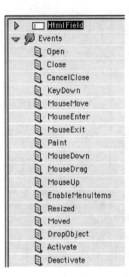

Figure 2.13 Clicking the disclosure triangle next to the Events item in the Code Editor for an object expands the event's listing, showing the events to which this object can respond.

CREATING THE TAGS MENU

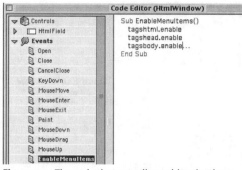

Figure 2.14 The code that actually enables the three menu items when the EnableMenuItems event occurs.

5. In the right panel of the Code Editor, type the following code at the insertion point (**Figure 2.14**):

`tagsHtml.enable`

`tagsHead.enable`

`tagsBody.enable`

You've supplied the missing piece of this event-response scenario. REALbasic will provide the EnableMenuItems event at the appropriate time, and you have written the code that is the response to that event.

✔ Tip

- REALbasic programming is all about creating objects and tweaking their properties and behavior, or code, which implies that all code belongs to some object or other. Whenever you write code, you need to ask where the code should reside—that is, to what object it logically belongs. Often, this determination is straightforward. In the preceding exercise, for example, the code to enable a Tags menu item belongs to that window. But the situation is not always that simple; you'll see examples in this chapter of how to decide where the code belongs. You'll find more detail in later chapters (particularly Chapter 5, "Writing Object-Oriented Code"), but it's good to start thinking now in object-oriented ways.

To program the HTML menu item:

1. Double-click the icon for HtmlWindow in the project window to bring up its Code Editor.

2. Choose New Menu Handler from the Edit menu.

3. In the dialog box that appears, select TagsHtml and click OK.

   You've created a handler for the Html menu item.

4. Repeat steps 2 and 3 for the Head and Body menu items, selecting TagsHead and TagsBody, respectively, in the dialog box.

5. In the left panel of the Code Editor for the HtmlWindow, click the disclosure triangle next to Menu Handlers to expand it (**Figure 2.15**).

6. Click TagsHtml to select the HTML menu item.

7. In the right panel of the Code Editor, type the following code at the insertion point (**Figure 2.16**):

   ```
   dim PreTag as string
   dim PostTag as string
   PreTag = "<html>"
   PostTag = "</html>"
   HtmlField.SelText = PreTag +
   → HtmlField.SelText + PostTag
   ```

   What this code does is insert the <html> and </html> tags in the HtmlField at the insertion point or on either side of the selected text, if any. Exactly how this code produces that effect is not important now.

Figure 2.15 Revealing the menu handlers.

```
Function Action As Boolean
   dim PreTag as string
   dim PostTag as string
   Pretag = "<html>"
   PostTag = "</html>"
   HtmlField.Seltext = Pretag + Htmlfield.Seltext + PostTag
End Function
```

Figure 2.16 The code for the Html menu item. This code is executed when the user chooses the Html menu item.

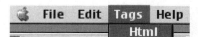

Figure 2.17 The menu items are now enabled, and if all went well, they work!

To test your programming:

1. From the File menu, choose Save (or press Command-S), and save the file.

2. From the Debug menu, choose Run (or press Command-R).

3. Test your work.

   Type some text in the field, select some of the text, and then choose the HTML menu item (**Figure 2.17**).

   If you did everything right and the gods were smiling, your Tags menu is now enabled, and its HTML item works. You'll know because your text will say html://. You have now experienced the essence of REALbasic programming: You create some objects, set their properties, and code their behavior.

   Note that the Head and Body menu items don't do anything yet, because you enabled them but didn't program them.

4. Now quit to return to the IDE.

To program the other menu items:

1. Click the window icon in the project window to select it.

2. Press Option-Tab to open the Code Editor for the window.

3. In the left panel of the Code Editor for the HtmlWindow, click the disclosure triangle next to Menu Handlers to expand it.

4. Click TagsHead to select the HEAD menu item.

continues on next page

CREATING THE TAGS MENU

5. In the right panel of the Code Editor, type this code at the insertion point (**Figure 2.18**):

dim PreTag as string

dim PostTag as string

PreTag = "<head>"

PostTag = "</head>"

HtmlField.SelText = PreTag +
→ HtmlField.SelText + PostTag

Note that this code is very similar to the code for the Html menu item.

You have programmed the Head menu item (and, earlier, the HTML menu item). Now it should be obvious how to program the Body menu item: Just repeat the preceding steps, substituting Body for Head.

There are lots of HTML tags, and if you create a menu item for each one, you'll have an awfully long menu. One way around this awkwardness would be to use hierarchical menus, grouping related tags into submenus. Now you'll see how that process works.

To add a Tables submenu:

1. In the menu editor, select the Tags menu.

2. Click the blank menu item at the bottom of the Tags menu to create a new menu item.

3. In the properties window for this menu item, enter Tables for the Text property.

4. Press Return.

Note that REALbasic supplies a default value for the Name property It's fine; leave it.

5. Choose the Submenu property (**Figure 2.19**).

```
Function Action As Boolean
  dim PreTag as string
  dim PostTag as string
  Pretag = "<head>"
  PostTag = "</head>"
  HtmlField.Seltext = Pretag + Htmlfield.Seltext + PostTag
End Function
```

Figure 2.18 The code that makes the Head menu item work.

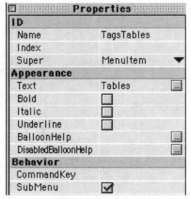

Figure 2.19 Adding a Tables submenu.

Figure 2.20 Use the dummy submenu item to create new submenu items.

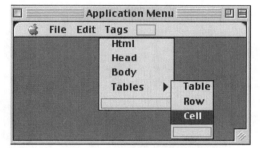

Figure 2.21 The Tables submenu, with three submenu items.

```
Sub EnableMenuItems()
  tagshtml.enable
  tagshead.enable
  tagsbody.enable
  tagstables.enable...
  tablestable.enable
  tablesrow.enable
  tablescell.enable
End Sub
```

Figure 2.22 Enabling the Tables submenu.

The Tables submenu doesn't do anything. It's just the jumping-off place for menu items below it, which you will add next.

To add items to the Tables submenu:

1. In the menu editor, select the Tables menu item.

2. Select the blank submenu item that appears next to it (**Figure 2.20**).

3. In the properties window, enter Table as the Text property.

4. Back in the menu editor, again select the blank menu item in the Tables submenu (below the Table menu item).

5. In the properties window, enter Row as the Text property.

6. Back in the menu editor, again select the blank menu item in the Tables submenu (below the Table menu item).

7. In the properties window, enter Cell as the Text property (**Figure 2.21**).

To enable these hierarchical menu items:

1. Click the window icon in the project window to select it.

2. Press Option-Tab to open the Code Editor for the window.

3. In the left panel of the Code Editor, click the disclosure triangle beside Events to expand it.

4. Click EnableMenuItems to select it.

5. In the right panel of the Code Editor, type this code at the insertion point (**Figure 2.22**):

   tagsTables.enable

   tagsTablesTable.enable

   tagsTablesRow.enable

   tagsTablesCell.enable

CREATING THE TAGS MENU

43

If you're guessing that every menu item in your application will have its own little bit of enabling code in this handler, you're *almost* right.

To program these hierarchical menu items:

1. Click the window icon in the project window to select it.

2. Press Option-Tab to open the Code Editor for the window.

3. In the left panel of the Code Editor for the HtmlWindow, click the disclosure triangle next to Menu Handlers to expand it.

4. Click TagsTablesTable to select the Table menu item of the Tables submenu of the Tags menu.

5. In the right panel of the Code Editor, type this code at the insertion point (**Figure 2.23**):

   ```
   dim PreTag as string
   dim PostTag as string
   PreTag = "<TABLE>"
   PostTag = "</TABLE>"
   HtmlField.SelText = PreTag +
   → HtmlField.SelText + PostTag
   ```

6. Repeat this procedure for the TagsTablesRow and TagsTablesCell handlers.

   You'll need to change the relevant lines of code to the following for the TagsTablesRow and TagsTablesCell handlers, respectively:

   ```
   PreTag = "<TR>"
   PostTag = "</TR>"
   ```
   and
   ```
   PreTag = "<TD>"
   PostTag = "</TD>"
   ```

Code Editor (HtmlWindow)

```
Function Action As Boolean
   dim PreTag as string
   dim PostTag as string
   Pretag = "<table>"
   PostTag = "</table>"
   HtmlField.Seltext = Pretag + Htmlfield.Seltext + PostTag
End Function
```

Figure 2.23 Programming the Table submenu item.

To test the Tags menu:

1. From the File menu, choose Save (or press Command-S), and save the file.

2. From the Debug menu, choose Run (or press Command-R).

3. Test your work.

Try out these hierarchical menu items, and convince yourself that they work like the other Tags menu items. The only difference is that putting them in a sub-menu organizes the Tags menu and lets you put more items in it without making it unwieldy.

4. Now quit to return to the IDE.

You won't do it now, but you can follow this same procedure to populate your Tags menu with all the tags in the HTML language. And you can use hierarchical menus to organize the menu further, with submenus for collections of tags such as frames, forms, fonts, and headings.

Well, you can populate the menu with *almost* all the tags. The code you've written assumes that all tags come in pairs, but some tags, such as <HR>, stand alone. Later in this chapter, you'll see how to handle them, but first, you'll look at a different HTML feature: the handling of special symbols.

Creating the Symbols Menu

HTML uses a particularly messy-looking syntax for encoding those characters that can't be entered directly in an HTML document. HTML uses the < and > characters to mark the tags, so they can't be entered directly in the text of your HTML document; the browser would try to interpret them as components of tags. These two characters are entered in an HTML document as < and > respectively. Many other such special characters exist, all encoded with this ampersand-and-semicolon syntax. You can create menu items to help you enter these characters, but they need to be handled a little differently from tags. Again, you'll create a few menu items, and you can add others by following the same steps.

To create the Symbols menu:

1. In the project window, click the Menu icon.

2. In the menu editor, click the blank menu at the right end of the menu bar (**Figure 2.24**).

3. In the properties window, enter Symbols for the Text property.

4. Press Return.

To add items to the Symbols menu:

1. In the menu editor, select your new Symbols menu.

2. Click the blank menu item at the bottom of the Symbols menu (**Figure 2.25**).

3. In the properties window for this menu item, enter LessThan for the Text property.

4. Press Return.

   Even though you are building a menu to handle these special characters, it is a little bit of a pain in the neck to have to go to the menu bar just to get quotation marks in the file. Menu items can have

Figure 2.24 The dummy menu is always available in the menu editor to let you create new menus...

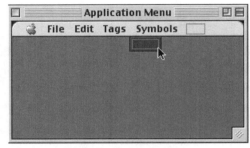

Figure 2.25 ...as is the dummy menu item.

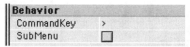

Figure 2.26 Setting the Command Key for a menu item.

```
Code Editor (HtmlWindow)
Sub EnableMenuItems()
  tagshtml.enable
  tagshead.enable
  tagsbody.enable
  tagstables.enable
  tablestable.enable
  tablesrow.enable
  tablescell.enable
  symbolsLessThan.enable|
  symbolsgreaterThan.enable
  symbolsquote.enable
End Sub
```

Figure 2.27 Every menu item needs to be enabled explicitly, and generally, you do that in this handler.

Command-key equivalents, though, and you can make good use of them in your Symbols menu.

5. Type < for the CommandKey property (**Figure 2.26**).

6. Press Return.

7. Repeat these steps to add a GreaterThan menu item with CommandKey property > and a Quote menu item with CommandKey property ".

To test the Symbols menu items:

1. From the File menu, choose Save (or press Command-S), and save the file.

2. From the Debug menu, choose Run (or press Command-R).

3. Test your work.

Again, you'll note that the new menu is there but is not enabled. But you know what to do about that.

4. Now quit to return to the IDE.

To enable the Symbols menu items:

1. Click the window icon in the project window to select it.

2. Press Option-Tab to open the Code Editor for the window.

3. In the left panel of the Code Editor, click the disclosure triangle beside Events to expand it.

4. Click EnableMenuItems to select it.

5. In the right panel of the Code Editor, type this code at the insertion point (**Figure 2.27**):

```
tagsSymbolsLessThan.enable
tagsSymbolsGreaterThan.enable
tagsSymbolsQuote.enable
```

CREATING THE SYMBOLS MENU

To program the Symbols menu items:

1. Click the window icon in the project window to select it.

2. Press Option-Tab to open the Code Editor for the window.

3. In the left panel of the Code Editor for the HtmlWindow, click the disclosure triangle next to Menu Handlers to expand it.

4. Click SymbolsLessThan to select the LessThan menu item.

5. In the right panel of the Code Editor, type this line of code at the insertion point (**Figure 2.28**):

   ```
   dim Symbol as string
   Symbol = "&lt;"
   HtmlField.SelText = Symbol
   ```

   Note that the code is simpler here than it was for the Tags menu items, because you are doing less.

6. Repeat this procedure for the GreaterThan and Quote menu items. You'll need to change the appropriate line of the code to:

   ```
   Symbol = "&gt;"
   ```

   and

   ```
   Symbol = "&quot;"
   ```

To test your programming:

1. From the File menu, choose Save (or press Command-S), and save the file.

2. From the Debug menu, choose Run (or press Command-R).

3. Test your work.

   Note that symbols are inserted into the text appropriately (**Figure 2.29**).

4. Quit to return to the IDE.

```
Code Editor (HtmlWindow)
Function Action As Boolean
   dim Symbol as string
   Symbol = "&lt;"
   Htmlfield.Seltext = Symbol
End Function
```

Figure 2.28 Programming the LessThan menu item.

Figure 2.29 These menu items insert the appropriate codes for the special characters into the HTML document.

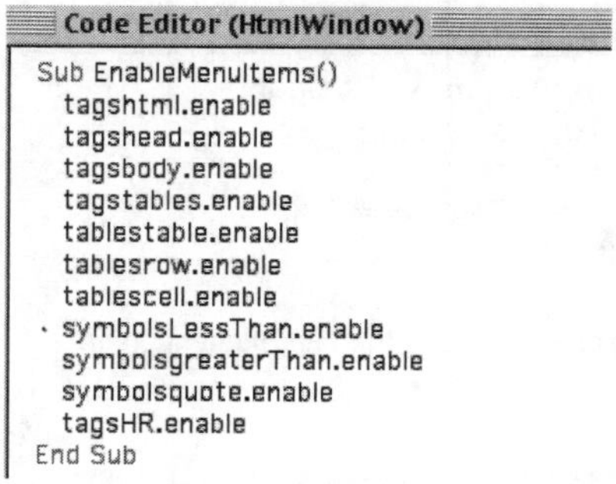

```
Code Editor (HtmlWindow)
Sub EnableMenuItems()
  tagshtml.enable
  tagshead.enable
  tagsbody.enable
  tagstables.enable
  tablestable.enable
  tablesrow.enable
  tablescell.enable
· symbolsLessThan.enable
  symbolsgreaterThan.enable
  symbolsquote.enable
  tagsHR.enable
End Sub
```

Figure 2.30 Enabling the TagsHR menu item.

Next, you'll pay off a debt that you incurred a ways back there. Some HTML tags don't bracket anything and don't come in pairs—such as the <HR/> tag for inserting a horizontal line (<HR> in some versions of HTML). You can treat such unmatched tags just like the special symbols you just dealt with. The steps and the code are almost identical.

To add an <HR> tag:

1. In the menu editor, select the Tags menu.

2. Click the blank menu item at the bottom of the Tags menu.

3. In the properties window for this menu item, enter HR for the Text property to create a HR menu item.

4. Press Return.

5. Now click the window icon in the project window to select it.

6. Press Option-Tab to open the Code Editor for the window.

7. In the left panel of the Code Editor, click the disclosure triangle beside Events to expand it.

8. Click EnableMenuItems to select it.

9. In the right panel of the Code Editor, type this code at the insertion point (**Figure 2.30**):

   `tagsHR.enable`

continues on next page

10. In the left panel of the Code Editor for the HtmlWindow, click the disclosure triangle next to Menu Handlers to expand it.

11. Click SymbolsLessThan to select the LessThan menu item.

12. In the right panel of the Code Editor, type this code at the insertion point (**Figure 2.31**):

```
dim Tag as string
Tag = "<HR>"
HtmlField.SelText = Tag
```

Compare this code with the code for any of the Symbol menu items. Although you may not know precisely what this code does (yet), it should be clear that the HR tag is being handled very much as the symbols are, and that's what you want. In the next section, you'll see how it works.

To test the <HR> menu item:

1. From the File menu, choose Save (or press Command-S), and save the file.

2. From the Debug menu, choose Run (or press Command-R).

3. Test your work.

Note that <HR> gets inserted into the text appropriately.

4. Now quit to return to the IDE.

Code Editor (HtmlWindow)

```
Function Action As Boolean
   dim Tag as string
   Tag = "<hr>"
   Htmlfield.Seltext = Tag
End Function
```

Figure 2.31 Programming the TagsHR menu item.

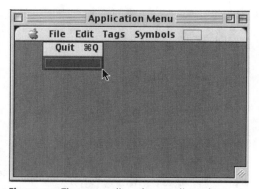

Figure 2.32 The menu editor also supplies a dummy menu item for an existing menu, such as the File menu, so that you can add menu items to it.

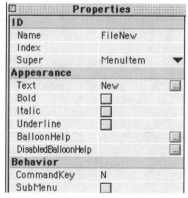

Figure 2.33 The properties of the New menu item.

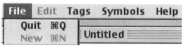

Figure 2.34 The New menu item is there but not yet enabled.

Adding a New Menu Item

Almost every application contains a New menu item, which starts a new document. You need to create such a New menu item to start building a new HTML document. You'll create the menu item, then enable it, and finally code its behavior.

To add a New item to the File menu:

1. In the menu editor, select the File menu.

2. Click the blank menu item at the bottom of the File menu (**Figure 2.32**).

3. In the properties window for this menu item, enter New for the Text property.

4. Press Return.

5. Enter N for the CommandKey property. Your properties window should look like **Figure 2.33**.

6. In the menu editor, drag the New item to the top of the File menu.

To test the New menu item:

1. From the File menu, choose Save (or press Command-S), and save the file.

2. From the Debug menu, choose Run (or press Command-R).

3. Test your New menu item.

Just verify that it's there (**Figure 2.34**). You know why the item is not enabled: You haven't written that code yet. But it's not really odd that this particular menu item is not enabled, because a window is open—and the purpose of New is to create a new window. This particular menu item needs to be enabled when no window is present, which is something you'll want to keep in mind as you write its code.

4. Quit to return to the IDE.

Here's a puzzle: You've been using the HtmlWindow's EnableMenuItems event handler to hold the menu-enabling code. But the New menu item is a little different from the other menu items you've created, in that the user is likely to choose it when no HtmlWindow is open. Because the purpose of this menu item is to open an HtmlWindow, you don't necessarily have an HtmlWindow to associate the enabling code with. How can you be sure that the New menu item is always enabled, even if no HtmlWindow is open? You'll create a new object that is always available, and you'll use that object's EnableMenuItems handler.

To enable the New menu item:

1. Click in the project window.

2. From the File menu, choose New Class (**Figure 2.35**).

   You've created a new class of object. The properties window reflects the settable properties for the class.

3. In the properties window, enter App as the name of the class.

4. Set to Super property to Application.

   The Super property will be explained later in this chapter; for now, what's important to know is that it gives your new App object all the capabilities of the Application class—in particular, the capability to enable menus.

   Your properties window should look like **Figure 2.36**.

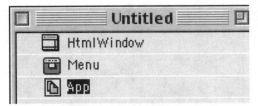

Figure 2.35 You create a new class in REALbasic via a File menu selection.

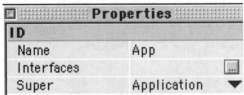

Figure 2.36 Properties of the new App class.

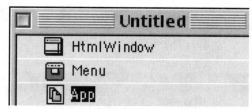

Figure 2.37 New classes are represented by icons in the project window.

```
App
Sub EnableMenuItems()
    FileNew.enable

End Sub
```

Figure 2.38 Enabling the New menu item. The code is familiar, but where the code resides is different.

```
App
Function Action As Boolean
    Dim hWin as HtmlWindow
    hWin = New HtmlWindow
End Function
```

Figure 2.39 Programming the New menu item.

To enable and program the New menu item:

1. Click the App icon in the project window (**Figure 2.37**).

2. Press Option-Tab to open the Code Editor for the App class.

3. In the Code Editor, expand the Events item.

4. Select the EnableMenuItems event.

5. In the right panel of the Code Editor, enter this code to enable the New menu item (**Figure 2.38**):

    `FileNew.Enable`

    This code enables the New menu item of the File menu just as you've been enabling the other menu items, the only difference being in where the code is stored.

6. Make sure that the Code Editor for the App class is still in front.

7. From the Edit menu, choose New Menu Handler.

8. Select the FileNew menu handler, and click OK.

9. Enter this code in the right panel of the Code Editor (**Figure 2.39**):

    `Dim hWin as HtmlWindow`

    `hWin = New HtmlWindow`

To test the menu item:

1. From the File menu, choose Save (or press Command-S), and save the file.

2. From the Debug menu, choose Run (or press Command-R).

3. Test your New menu item.

    This time, it should allow you to open a new window.

4. Quit to return to the IDE.

Working with Files

REALbasic applications can work with many file types—such as text, graphics, sound, video, and music—but you need to specify what file types you want your application to handle.

To let your application deal with text files:

1. From the Edit menu, choose File Types.

2. In the File Types dialog box, click the Add button (**Figure 2.40**).

3. In the File Types editor that appears, enter Text for the name, ???? for the Mac Creator, TEXT for the Mac Type, and .txt as the extension (**Figure 2.41**).

Now your application will know how to deal with text files, which is what HTML documents are.

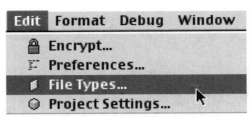

Figure 2.40 Adding a file type to your application.

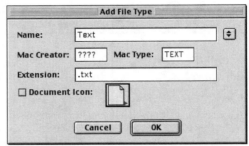

Figure 2.41 Specifying the file type.

Adding Save Menu Items

You've given your application the general capability to deal with text files, but you still need to provide the code and user-interface elements to support opening and saving files. One of these elements is a Save menu item.

As you saw when you created the New menu item, you need to consider what object the code should be associated with:

- **Is saving your work an activity that is associated with a particular window?** Yes. You do your work in one particular HtmlWindow, and it is the HTML document in that window that you want to save to a file on disk. Then it's reasonable to guess that you'll want to put the code for saving your work in either the window object or the application object. (Remember that code in the application object is available to all objects in the application.)

- **Is it necessary that the window be open to invoke Save?** Yes, because if it isn't open, no unsaved work is available to be saved. Because you can assume that the window is open when you want to save its contents, it's safe to put any content-saving code in the window object.

To create a Save menu item:

1. In the menu editor, select the File menu.

2. Click the blank menu item at the bottom of the File menu.

3. In the properties window for this menu item, enter Save for the Text property.

4. Press Return.

5. Enter S for the CommandKey property. Your properties window should look like **Figure 2.42**.

6. In the menu editor, drag the Save menu item between the New and Quit menu items in the File menu (**Figure 2.43**).

Creating your own properties

Up to now, you have been working with the properties that REALbasic has supplied. You can also create your own properties, and you need to do that now.

You need to associate a file with the current HtmlWindow so that when you choose the Save menu item, your program will know where to save it. You also need to keep track of whether text has changed since the last change. Why? Well, a Save menu item typically is enabled only if text has changed.

Two things that you need to keep track of— the file associated with the window and the changed status of the text in the window— are best seen as properties of the window. You'll create those properties in the next exercise.

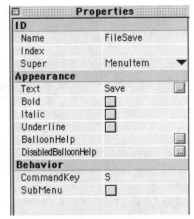

Figure 2.42 Properties of the Save menu item.

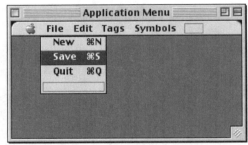

Figure 2.43 The Save menu item after it has been dragged into place in the File menu.

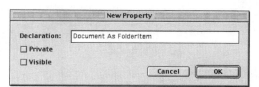

Figure 2.44 You create a new property for an object by using the New Property dialog box.

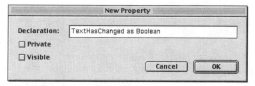

Figure 2.45 Another new property.

Figure 2.46 Your newly defined new properties don't appear in the properties window, but they do show up in the Properties list in the Code Editor. For this reason, you can edit your homemade properties only in the Code Editor.

To create new properties for the Html window:

1. In the project window, click HtmlWindow.

2. Press Option-Tab to open its Code Editor.

3. From the Edit menu, choose New Property.

4. In the New Property dialog box that appears, enter `Document As FolderItem` and click OK (**Figure 2.44**).

5. In the Edit menu, choose New Property again.

6. In the New Property dialog box that appears, enter `TextHasChanged as Boolean`, and click OK (**Figure 2.45**).

7. In the left panel of the Code Editor for HtmlWindow, click the disclosure triangle next to Properties.

   You should see the properties that you just defined (**Figure 2.46**).

You have just defined a property to keep track of the changed status. Next, you'll use that property.

You want to enable the Save menu only if the text has changed. The menu-enabling code won't be as simple as before; you will need to use an if statement and the TextHasChanged property.

To enable the Save menu item:

1. In the Code Editor for HtmlWindow, click the disclosure triangle next to Events.

2. Select EnableMenuItems.

3. Add this code in the right panel (**Figure 2.47**):

   ```
   If TextHasChanged Then
   FileSave.Enable
   End If
   ```

Next, you need to write the code that actually saves the file. To do this, you'll create a new REALbasic method.

To create the code that saves the file:

1. In the project window, select HtmlWindow.

2. Press Option-Tab to open its Code Editor.

3. From the Edit menu, choose New Method (**Figure 2.48**).

4. In the dialog box that appears, enter SaveFile as the method name.

5. In the Parameters box, enter FileName as String, DisplaySaveDialog as Boolean (**Figure 2.49**).

6. Click OK.

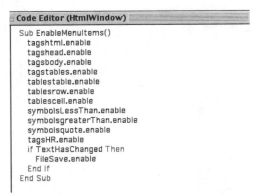

Figure 2.47 Enabling the Save menu item. This time, for a change, the enabling code is not a single line.

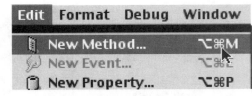

Figure 2.48 You can create your own subprograms—methods—in your REALbasic applications.

Figure 2.49 Creating a method involves real programming, but REALbasic makes part of it simple with this dialog box for specifying the method's parameters.

```
Code Editor (HtmlWindow)

Sub SaveFile(Filename as String, DisplaySaveDialog as Boolean)
  Dim Fi as FolderItem, HtmlFileName as String
  //If document has not been saved...
  If Document = Nil or DisplaySaveDialog then
     // ... then give it an html extention and save it.
     IF mid(FileName, len(FileName)- 4,5) = ".html" then
     Else
        HtmlFileName = Filename + ".html"
     End If

     fi = GetSaveFolderItem("text",HtmlFileName)
     If fi <> Nil then
        Title = fi.Name
        Document = fi
     End If
  End if
  // If the document exisits
  If Document <> Nil then
     //then just save it.
     Document.saveStyledEditField HtmlField
     textHasChanged = false
  End if

End Sub
```

Figure 2.50 Programming your new method. Note that it appears automatically in the list of methods in the Code Editor.

7. In the Code Editor for this new method, enter this code (**Figure 2.50**):

```
Dim fi as FolderItem, HtmlFileName as
string
// If the document has not been saved...
If Document = Nil or DisplaySaveDialog
→ then
// ...then give it an html extension
→ and save it
If mid(FileName,len(FileName)-4,5) =
→ ".html"then
HtmlFileName = FileName
Else
HtmlFileName = FileName + ".html"
End If
fi = GetSaveFolderItem("text",
→ HtmlFileName)
If fi <> Nil Then
Title = fi.Name
Document = fi
End if
End if
// If the document exists...
If Document <> Nil then
// then just save it
Document.saveStyledEditField HtmlField
TextHasChanged = False
End if
```

It is not at all important that you understand this code now, but merely that you recognize that this is the code that actually saves the file.

Working with event handlers

Many REALbasic objects—such as buttons, fields, and windows—come with built-in *event handlers*. These methods run whenever some particular event occurs. What actually happens when an event handler runs is up to you, though. By adding code to an event handler, you specify what your application does when the event occurs. This is the key to understanding *event-driven programming*.

Again, you need to decide where to put the code. Is TextHasChanged associated with any particular object? Yes; it's associated with the HtmlField. Then it's reasonable to put it in the HtmlField object. Part of the behavior of this field is to know what to do when its text has changed.

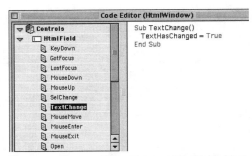

Figure 2.51 The events to which your HtmlField object can respond. You get these events automatically by virtue of the fact that the HtmlField is really a TextField object.

To manage the TextHasChanged property:

1. HtmlField is a control in HtmlWindow, so open the Code Editor for HtmlWindow.

2. Click the disclosure triangle next to Controls.

3. Click the disclosure triangle next to HtmlField to see the event handlers available for it.

   These handlers are here even though you didn't put them here, because your HtmlField is an instance of an EditField, and all EditFields come with certain pre-built properties and behavior, such as these event handlers.

4. Select the TextChange event.

5. In the right panel, enter this code (**Figure 2.51**):

   TextHasChanged = True

   Note what's going on here: TextChange is an event that REALbasic causes to occur when the text in the field has, in fact, changed. TextHasChanged, on the other hand, is a property that you defined to keep track of this fact.

Figure 2.52 Creating a new menu handler.

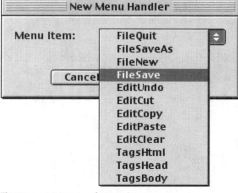

Figure 2.53 A menu of menu items.

Code Editor (HtmlWindow)

```
Function Action As Boolean
    SaveFile Title, False
End Function
```

Figure 2.54 Programming the menu item.

Figure 2.55 Properties of the Save As menu item.

To handle the Save menu item:

1. Make sure that the Code Editor for HtmlWindow is in front.

2. From the Edit menu, choose New Menu Handler to open the New Menu Handler dialog box (**Figure 2.52**).

3. Choose FileSave from the pop-up menu of menu items (**Figure 2.53**), and click OK.

4. Enter this code (**Figure 2.54**):
SaveFile Title, False

To create a Save As menu item:

1. In the menu editor, select the File menu.

2. Click the blank menu item at the bottom of the File menu.

3. In the properties window for this menu item, enter Save As... for the Text property.

4. Press Return.

Your properties window should look like **Figure 2.55**.

continues on next page

ADDING SAVE MENU ITEMS

5. In the menu editor, drag the Save As menu item below Save in the File menu (**Figure 2.56**).

6. In HtmlWindow's Code Editor, open the EnableMenuItems event.

7. Enter this code (**Figure 2.57**):
FileSaveAs.enable

8. With HtmlWindow's Code Editor front-most, from the Edit menu, choose New Menu Handler.

9. In the New Menu Handler dialog box, choose FileSaveAs from the pop-up menu, and click OK.

10. Enter this code (**Figure 2.58**):
SaveFile Title, True

To test the Save and Save As menu items:

1. From the File menu, choose Save (or press Command-S), and save the file.

2. From the Debug menu, choose Run (or press Command-R).

3. Test your new menu items.

You should be able to enter and edit text, insert HTML tags and symbols, and save your work under different file names.

4. Quit to return to the IDE.

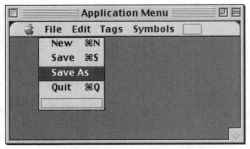

Figure 2.56 The Save As menu item dragged into place in the File menu.

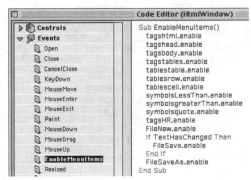

Figure 2.57 Enabling the Save As menu item.

Code Editor (HtmlWindow)

```
Function Action As Boolean
    SaveFile Title, True
End Function
```

Figure 2.58 Programming the Save As menu item.

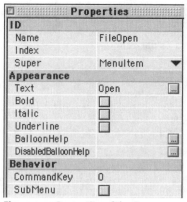

Figure 2.59 Properties of the Open menu item.

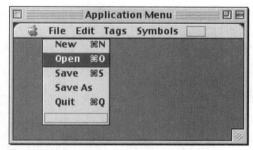

Figure 2.60 The Open menu item in its familiar position in the File menu.

```
App
Sub EnableMenuItems()
    FileNew.enable
    FileOpen.enable

End Sub
```

Figure 2.61 Enabling the Open menu item.

Adding an Open Menu Item

You also need to be able to open files; otherwise, you couldn't edit an existing file. For this purpose, you need to create an Open menu item.

To create an Open menu item:

1. In the menu editor, select the File menu.

2. Click the blank menu item at the bottom of the File menu.

3. In the properties window for this menu item, enter Open... for the Text property.

4. Press Return.

5. Enter O for the CommandKey property. Your properties window should look like **Figure 2.59**.

6. In the menu editor, drag the Open menu item below New in the File menu (**Figure 2.60**).

Again, you ask yourself where the code should go. As was the case with the New menu item, the Open menu item needs to be available even if no window is open (especially then!), so you do what you did with the New menu item: place its enabling code in an always-available object, the App object.

To enable the Open menu item:

1. Select the App object in the project window.

2. Press Option-Tab to open its Code Editor.

3. Click the disclosure triangle next to Events to expand it.

4. Select EnableMenuItems.

5. Add this code in the panel on the right (**Figure 2.61**):

    FileOpen.enable

To code the Open menu item:

1. Return to App's Code Editor.

2. From the Edit menu, choose New Menu Handler.

3. In the New Menu Handler dialog box that appears, choose FileOpen from the pop-up menu.

4. Enter this code (**Figure 2.62**):

```
Dim fi as FolderItem
Dim hwin as HtmlWindow
fi = GetOpenFolderItem("text")
If fi <> Nil then
hWin = New HtmlWindow
fi.OpenStyledEditField hwin.HtmlField
hWin.Document = fi
hWin.Title = fi.Name
End if
```

Don't worry about the details of this code now. It does quite a bit for you, though: It invokes the Open dialog box, and if the user selects a file, it opens a new window and places that file's text in the window.

To test the Open menu item:

1. From the File menu, choose Save (or press Command-S), and save the file.

2. From the Debug menu, choose Run (or press Command-R).

3. Test your Open menu item.

   Now you can open the files you've saved or other text files.

4. Quit to return to the IDE.

```
                    App
Function Action As Boolean
    Dim fi as FolderItem
    Dim hwin as HtmlWindow
    fi = GetOpenFolderItem("text")
    if fi <> Nil then
        hWin = New HtmlWindow
        fi.OpenStyledEditField hwin.HtmlField
        hWin.Document = fi
        hWin.Title = Fi.Name
    End if
End Function
```

Figure 2.62 Programming the Open menu item.

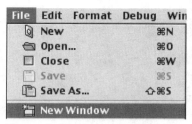

File Edit Format Debug Win

New   ⌘N
Open...   ⌘O
Close   ⌘W
Save   ⌘S
Save As...   ⇧⌘S
New Window

Figure 2.63 Creating a new window. Your REALbasic applications can have multiple windows.

Properties		
ID		
Name	SaveChanges	
Super	Window	▼
Position		
Placement	0 – Default	▼
Width	345	
Height	135	
MinWidth	64	
MinHeight	64	
MaxWidth	32000	
MaxHeight	32000	
Appearance		
Frame	1 – Movable Mod...	▼
HasBackColor	☐	
BackColor		
Backdrop	None	▼
Title	Untitled	
Visible	☑	
FullScreen	☐	
MenuBarVisible	☑	
CloseBox	☐	
GrowIcon	☐	
ZoomIcon	☐	
BalloonHelp		...
MacProcID	0	

Figure 2.64 Properties of the Save Changes dialog box.

Creating a Save Dialog Box

One chore remains: When the user closes a window or tries to quit without saving the work, a thoughtful application will display a Save Changes dialog box to allow the user to save changes. You'll create that dialog box in this section.

To create a Save Changes dialog box:

1. Click the project window.

2. From the File menu, choose New Window (**Figure 2.63**).

3. Click the New Window icon in the project window.

   Its properties window should appear.

4. In the properties window, enter SaveChanges as the Name property.

5. Select Modal Dialog for the Frame property.

6. Set the Height and Width properties to 135 and 345, respectively.

7. Deselect the CloseBox, GrowIcon, and ZoomIcon properties.

   The properties window should look like **Figure 2.64**.

To add the Save, Cancel, and Don't Save buttons:

1. Drag the PushButton control from the Tools palette to the SaveChanges window (**Figure 2.65**).

2. Repeat step 1 two more times to place three PushButton controls in the window.

3. Drag the buttons to the approximate positions of the Don't Save, Cancel, and Save buttons (**Figure 2.66**).

4. Click the leftmost button and set its properties as indicated in **Figure 2.67**.

5. Set the middle button's properties as shown in **Figure 2.68**.

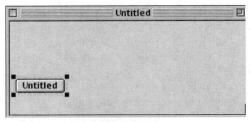

Figure 2.65 The PushButton control.

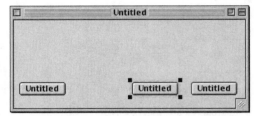

Figure 2.66 The dialog box needs three PushButtons.

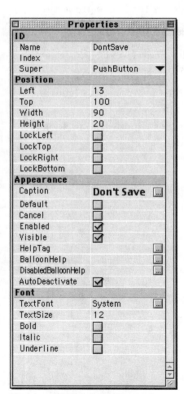

Figure 2.67 The left PushButton's properties.

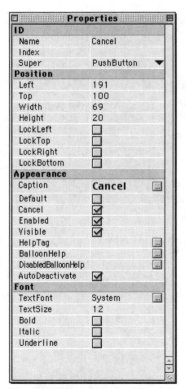

Figure 2.68 The middle PushButton's properties.

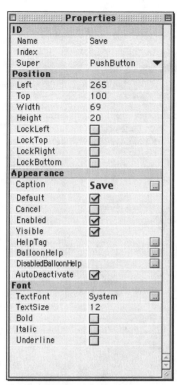

Figure 2.69 The right PushButton's properties.

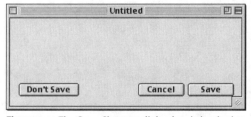

Figure 2.70 The Save Changes dialog box is beginning to look like something you'd expect to see in an application.

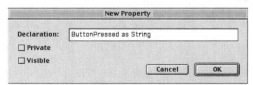

Figure 2.71 Creating the ButtonPressed property.

6. Set the right button's properties as shown in **Figure 2.69**.

The Save Changes dialog box should now look like **Figure 2.70**.

7. Select SaveChanges in the project window.

8. Press Option-Tab to open the Code Editor.

9. From the Edit menu, choose New Property to open the New Property dialog box.

10. Enter ButtonPressed as String, and click OK (**Figure 2.71**).

11. In the Code Editor for the Save Changes dialog box, click the disclosure triangle to expand Controls.

12. Expand each of the three buttons in turn, click its Action item, and enter the code as indicated in **Table 2.1.**

This code assigns a value to the ButtonPressed property that you just created. The property will reflect which button was clicked in the dialog box. For now, the code just takes note of this fact, but you'll use it later.

Table 2.1

Coding the Dialog Box's Buttons

BUTTON	CODE
Don't Save	ButtonPressed="DontSave"
	Hide
Save	ButtonPressed="Save"
	Hide
Cancel	ButtonPressed="Cancel"
	Hide

Now you'll add the Caution icon that every self-respecting dialog box ought to have.

To add the Caution icon:

1. In the project window, click SaveChanges to bring it into the window editor.

2. Drag a Canvas control from the Tools palette to the Save Changes dialog box, leaving it near the top-left corner of the window (**Figure 2.72**).

3. Click the Canvas control in the Save Changes dialog box, and in its properties window, set its properties as shown in **Figure 2.73**.

4. Click SaveChanges in the project window.

5. Press Option-Tab to open the Code Editor.

6. Expand Controls.

7. Expand Canvas1 (**Figure 2.74**).

   The Canvas control has a special event associated with it called Paint. The Paint event handler of a Canvas control runs whenever it is necessary to redraw the area of the screen occupied by the control. You will place code in the Paint event handler to draw—or redraw—that Caution icon when this situation happens.

8. Select the Paint event.

9. Enter this code in the right panel:

   `g.DrawCautionIcon 0,0`

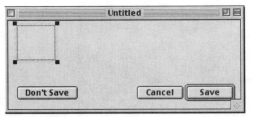

Figure 2.72 The Canvas control is useful for creating graphical elements of your application's user interface.

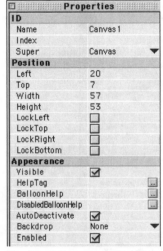

Figure 2.73 Properties of the Canvas control.

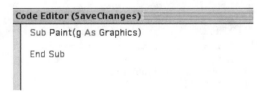

Figure 2.74 Your new Canvas control in the Code Editor.

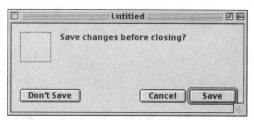

Figure 2.75 You use the StaticText control to put unchanging text in your application's user interface.

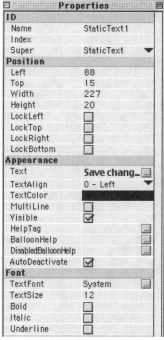

Figure 2.76 Properties of the StaticText control.

To add a caption for the Caution icon:

1. Drag the StaticText control to a position just to the right of the Caution icon in the Save Changes dialog box (**Figure 2.75**).

2. Click the StaticText control in the window, and set its properties as shown in **Figure 2.76**.

To display the Save Changes dialog box:

1. In the project window, click HtmlWindow.

2. Press Option-Tab to open the Code Editor.

3. Expand Events.

4. Select the CancelClose event.

5. Enter the code shown in **Figure 2.77**.

Again, don't worry about the details of the code for now. You might notice, though, the appearance here of the names of those three buttons you put in the dialog box and that ButtonPressed property. This property is where the information about which button got clicked is used.

```
Code Editor (HtmlWindow)
Function CancelClose() As Boolean
  If TextHasChanged then
    SaveChanges.ShowModal
    Select Case SaveChanges.ButtonPressed
    case "DontSave"
    case "Cancel"
      Return True
    case "Save"
      HtmlWindow(Window(1)).SaveFile Window(1).Title, False
    End Select
    SaveChanges.Close
  End if
End Function
```

Figure 2.77 The CancelClose event in the Code Editor.

CREATING A SAVE DIALOG BOX

Testing the whole shebang:

1. From the File menu, choose Save (or press Command-S), and save the file.

2. From the Debug menu, choose Run (or press Command-R).

3. Test to ensure that you get a proper Save Changes dialog box when you edit text in the window and then attempt to save it (**Figure 2.78**).

4. Quit to return to the IDE.

You're done. Close your project, quit REALbasic, and go reward yourself in whatever way you do that thing.

Or not. You still have one thing left to do: Turn this project into a real, stand-alone Macintosh or Windows application.

Figure 2.78 The Save Changes dialog box in action.

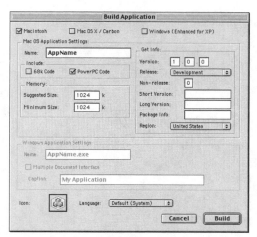

Figure 2.79 Building a stand-alone application from your project.

Building a Stand-Alone Application

You have been running your project in test mode, which works all right, but it requires the presence of REALbasic. The final step in creating your application is turning this project into a stand-alone application for Mac or Windows that doesn't require REALbasic to run.

To build a stand-alone application:

1. If you closed your project after the last section, open it in REALbasic now.

2. From the File menu, choose Build Application.

   You see the Build Application dialog box (**Figure 2.79**).

3. Click one of the check boxes at the top of the dialog box to choose the platform for which you want to create the application.

   Choose the Mac platform that you are running on so that you can see your results immediately; later, you can return to this dialog box and create a Windows version.

4. Type Html Editor in the Name text box below Mac OS Application Settings.

5. Type HtmlEditor.exe in the Name text box below Windows Application Settings.

   Leave the other settings alone for now.

6. Click Build.

   REALbasic grinds away for a while and creates your stand-alone application.

7. Quit REALbasic.

8. In the Finder, find and run your application.

   You are now a REALbasic application developer.

What's Next?

This HTML Editor application doesn't do many things, such as invoking your browser to show you what your Web page looks like; you will add some of those capabilities later in the book. But you could add several things to the project using what you know now, such as all the basic HTML tags and more special symbols in those menus. You could also create a Windows stand-alone application and test it on a Windows machine or on a Mac using VirtualPC. If you have VirtualPC installed, you can double-click the Windows application you compiled. It will start up VirtualPC and you can test it. Another possibility is: turning it into an XML editor by adding XML tags. (Mac OS X uses XML for its preferences files.)

You'll get back to this editor later in the book. In the next chapter, you'll develop a different application to explore REALbasic properties more fully.

PROGRAMMING OBJECT PROPERTIES

3

REALbasic programming is object-oriented programming. This definition means that REALbasic is all about creating objects or using built-in objects, as well as defining the properties and behavior of these objects. In this chapter, you'll learn about the properties of REALbasic's built-in objects and how to manipulate them in REALbasic code. You'll also learn how to create your own properties to extend the capabilities of REALbasic. (Manipulating objects' *behavior* is done almost exclusively by coding, which you'll learn more about in the next chapter.)

At the end of this chapter, you'll develop a simple, working REALbasic application—an electronic guestbook—that exemplifies the power of properties.

About Objects

Objects (at least, the kind of objects you find in object-oriented programming) have properties and behavior. They belong to classes, communicate via messages, and respond to events. The inventors of object-oriented programming intended their objects to model objects in the real world, and if that's how objects in the real world act, they succeeded.

At least the inventors persuaded us to think of the surface of a screen as a desktop and to pretend that we are clicking a button when we move the mouse in a particular way and see pixels change on the screen in a particular way. The objects of object-oriented programming include these buttons and windows and other user-interface objects, and so will your applications.

Files can be objects, too (as in the case of a graphic or QuickTime movie), and you can get a file into your project as an object by importing it.

Create objects in your REALbasic projects

REALbasic gives you a handful of ways to assemble your projects.

◆ Dragging files into your project window

◆ Dragging files into your window editor (**Figure 3.1**)

◆ Choosing File > Import and selecting a file to import into your project (**Figure 3.2**)

◆ Choosing the New Class menu item to create a new class of object

◆ Writing REALbasic code

✔ Tip

■ I'll flesh out the relationship between class and object in Chapter 5, "Writing Object-Oriented Code," but basically, an object is an instance of a class, or a class is the abstraction of an object.

Figure 3.1 You can create new objects in REALbasic simply by dragging files into the window editor.

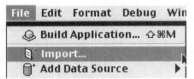

Figure 3.2 You can also create new objects by importing files into your project.

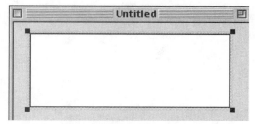

Figure 3.3 You can change an object's properties via the properties window...

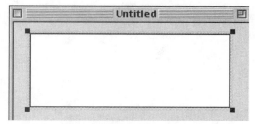

Figure 3.4 ...by manipulating the object directly in the window editor...

```
Code Editor (Hello)
Sub EnableMenuItems()
    FileQuit.enable
End Sub
```

Figure 3.5 ...or by writing REALbasic code.

About Properties

Properties are the data that make up an object; they define what it is. (An object's code defines what it does.) Objects can have many types of properties. The Height properties of a window or a text box is a number, an object's Name property is text, and a window's BackColor property is a color.

You can manipulate an object's properties in at least three ways.

- ◆ By changing the settings in its properties window (**Figure 3.3**)

- ◆ By manipulating the object directly in the window editor (**Figure 3.4**)

- ◆ By writing REALbasic code (**Figure 3.5**)

Manipulating Data and Properties in Code

You set the values of an object's properties—its data—when you create it, but the object doesn't necessarily keep those property values forever. The values can change while the application is running, under the orders of code that you have written. In Chapter 2, "Building an HTML Editor," the HtmlEditor window's Name property changes when the user saves the file.

Some built-in properties of objects can be manipulated only in the Code Editor. You can also create your own properties, and these must be coded, too.

Setting properties via the Code Editor is the simplest kind of coding, but it is still coding, and you need to know the language. Fortunately, what you need to know is pretty simple.

Variables and values

You need to know that not all data resides in the properties of objects. Your REALbasic applications can store data temporarily in *variables*.

You've seen variables in action. In Chapter 2, the line of code

```
PreTag = "<head>"
```

assigns the *value* "<head>" to the *variable* PreTag. It's important to realize that this bit of code isn't saying that PreTag equals "<head>". This code is an *assignment* statement, and it assigns the value on the right to the variable on the left. Basic was clearer about this situation at one time; the original syntax was

```
Let PreTag = "<head>"
```

Table 3.1

REALbasic Data Types

DATA TYPE	DESCRIPTION	EXAMPLES
String	Any sequence of characters	<head>
Integer	A whole number	256
Single	A decimal number	98.6
Double	A decimal number	98.6
Boolean	True or False	True

Data types

You also need to know that REALbasic recognizes several fundamental types of data, although you can add new types. The most common *data types* that REALbasic recognizes are String, Integer, Single, Double, and Boolean (**Table 3.1**).

For your REALbasic program to know what data type a variable is, you must tell it. You accomplish this task with a `Dim` statement, which must appear in your code before the first use of the variable. Here's an example of a Dim statement:

```
Dim PreTag as String
```

It tells REALbasic that PreTag is a String variable. (`Dim` is short for *dimension,* which is not a particularly helpful name.)

From Chapter 2 again:

```
Dim PreTag as String
PreTag = "<head>"
```

declares that the `PreTag` variable is of type `String` and assigns the string "<head>" to it as its value.

Referring to objects and properties

You also need to know how to refer to objects and their properties. The syntax for referring to properties is more complicated than that for referring to variables because you need to indicate the object to which the property belongs. The syntax you use for this purpose is called *dot notation.*

◆ To refer to a property of an object, place a dot between the object's name and the property's name:

```
objectname.propertyname
```

continues on next page

MANIPULATING DATA AND PROPERTIES IN CODE

77

◆ Sometimes, to be absolutely clear what object you mean, you need to supply its parent object's name also:

`parentobjectname.objectname.property`

For example,

`pushbutton1.caption`

`window1.pushbutton1.caption`

`window1.height`

Note that the last example refers to a property of the parent object.

The special term Me

In references to object and properties, the term Me means the object itself—the object to which this piece of code belongs. So if the code for a button's Action handler contains the line

`Me.Caption = "Done"`

it is setting the button's own caption to

`"Done"`.

To learn about the properties of an object:

1. From the Help menu, choose Language Reference.

2. In the left panel of the Language Reference window, select the object.

3. Read about the properties specific to objects of this class in the right panel (**Figure 3.6**).

4. Follow hypertext links in this panel to learn about other properties relevant to this object.

To set one of an object's properties in code, you use an assignment statement:

`propertyname = value`

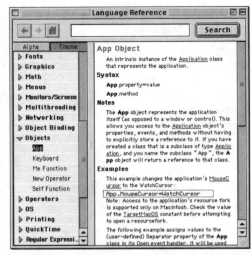

Figure 3.6 The Language Reference window is the basic reference on object properties.

Figure 3.7 You can create your own properties in REALbasic.

For example:

```
pushbutton1.caption = "Cancel"
window1.pushbutton1.caption = "Cancel"
window1.height = 320
```

And to get one of an object's properties in code, you also use an assignment statement, placing the property's value into a variable:

```
x = pushbutton1.caption
```

Later, you might use this x variable to set the value of some other property, as follows:

```
pushbutton2.caption = x
```

To create your own custom properties:

1. Press Option-Tab to open the Code Editor.

2. From the Edit menu, choose New Property (**Figure 3.7**).

3. In the dialog box that appears, enter a declaration.

    A declaration is to a property what a dimension statement is to a variable; it establishes its data type. The syntax is:

    ```
    propertyname as datatype
    ```

    For example:

    ```
    Strength as Integer
    Nickname as String
    Spayed as Boolean
    ```

4. Click OK to dismiss the dialog box.

5. In the Code Editor, click the disclosure triangle next to Properties.

    Your new property should appear here.

MANIPULATING DATA AND PROPERTIES IN CODE

Building a Project

In the remainder of this chapter, you will build a simple electronic guestbook, a project that will give you some experience in manipulating object properties.

The product concept

The situation is this: You and your partner are the owner-operators of a small bed-and-breakfast in the California wine country, and you want to replace the leatherette-bound book in which your guests write their names and addresses with an electronic equivalent. Your guests don't mind the current system, but you're getting tired of having to enter their data in your Mac for your mailing list. You want to make the guests do the work so that you can get away once in a while to sample the products for which this region is famous, but so as not to annoy the guests too much, you want to design the electronic guestbook to mirror the paper one fairly closely.

The product spec

From these desiderata you first develop the product specification, or *spec* (**Figure 3.8**). Creating a spec is good programming practice. It looks like you're going to want an application that displays a horizontal window that looks like one entry in the paper guestbook, including the following:

◆ A friendly welcoming message

◆ The friendly logo of your business

◆ A place to enter a name

◆ A place to enter an address

◆ A place to enter a city

◆ A place to enter a state

◆ A place to enter a ZIP code

Figure 3.8 Describing the features you'll want in your guestbook application.

Guestbook features:

• *friendly welcoming message*

• *business logo*

• *place for guest to enter name*

• *ditto address, city, state, zip code*

• *and ??*

Telephone numbers, email address, country, Canadian province? Maybe later, but you'll start with just this much.

A paper guestbook has many pages of names, but yours need have only one person's worth of data-entry space, because you can write each guest's data out to a file as soon as it's entered, for use in that mailing list. So you'll need to supply the user a button to click when he or she is finished. Clicking this button says, "I'm done. Accept my data, write it to the file, and clear the fields so that someone else can use this thing."

You want to keep the guestbook friendly, so maybe there should also be a little hint now and then about what to do next, to prod users gently to fill in any missing information.

For that matter, it might be good to force users (gently, of course) to fill in all the fields. An entry with a missing city isn't going to do you much good come mailing-list time. Maybe that button doesn't clear the fields and write the data until the fields are all filled in.

Well, that's a pretty casual product spec, but it's adequate for this simple project. Now you'll try to put the pieces into place.

Roughing Out the Project

Now you'll build a REALbasic project based on your product spec.

To create the application's main window:

1. Choose New from the File menu to start a new project.

2. Double-click the window icon in the project window to open the window editor.

3. In the properties window, set the window's properties as follows:

   Name: GuestbookWindow

   Title: Our Guestbook

   Width: 512

   Height: 190

   Frame: Plain Box

4. Set the following properties to true by, if necessary, clicking their check boxes:

   HasBackColor

   Visible

   CloseBox

5. Set the following properties to false by, if necessary, clicking their check boxes:

   FullScreen

   GrowIcon

   ZoomIcon

   Your properties window should look like **Figure 3.9**.

6. Click the space next to BackColor in the properties window, and in the Color Picker that appears, set the color to white.

   In an RGB Color Picker, this step means moving all the sliders to the right (**Figure 3.10**).

Figure 3.9
The properties settings for the guestbook's main window.

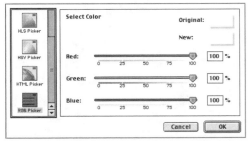

Figure 3.10 Setting the background color of the window.

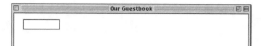

Figure 3.11 Drop six instances of the EditField control in the window editor to create the guestbook's user-input fields.

Figure 3.12
The properties window should look like this figure.

7. From the File menu, choose Save (or press Command-S), and save the file with the name Guestbook.

✔ Tip

- You can use the Tab key to jump between text properties in the properties window. This technique won't help you with the properties that are set via check boxes, but it can speed the process of setting multiple text properties.

To create the user-input fields:

1. Drag the EditField control to the window editor six times, positioning the six fields one above the other, the first at the top (**Figure 3.11**).

These fields will be your user-input fields for name, address, and so on, as well a hint field to prompt the user about what to do next.

2. Select the first field, and in the properties window, set its properties as follows:

Name: HintField

Left: 256

Top: 48

Width: 192

Height:26

TextSize: 18

Enabled, Visible, AutoDeactivate, Bold, Italic: true

Border, ScrollBar, UseFocusRing: false

3. Click the space next to TextColor in the properties window, and in the Color Picker that appears, choose a dark blue.

Your properties window should look like **Figure 3.12**.

continues on next page

ROUGHING OUT THE PROJECT

4. Select the second field, and in the properties window, set its properties as follows:

Name: NameField

Left: 4

Top: 92

Width: 504

Height:30

TextSize: 18

Enabled, Visible, AutoDeactivate,
Bold: true

Border, ScrollBar, UseFocusRing: false

5. Click the space next to TextColor in the properties window, and in the Color Picker that appears, choose a dark blue.

6. Select the third field, and in the properties window, set its properties as follows:

Name: AddressField

Left: 4

Top: 124

Width: 504

Height:30

TextSize: 18

Enabled, Visible, AutoDeactivate,
Bold: true

Border, ScrollBar, UseFocusRing: false

7. Click the space next to TextColor in the properties window, and in the Color Picker that appears, choose a dark blue.

8. Select the fourth field, and in the properties window, set its properties as follows:

Name: CityField

Left: 4

Top: 156

Width: 308

Height:30

TextSize: 18

Enabled, Visible, AutoDeactivate,
Bold: true

Border, ScrollBar, UseFocusRing: false

Figure 3.13 The user-input fields for the guestbook, neatly arranged.

9. Click the space next to TextColor in the properties window, and in the Color Picker that appears, choose a dark blue.

10. Select the fifth field, and in the properties window, set its properties as follows:

    Name: StateField

    Left: 316

    Top: 156

    Width: 32

    Height:30

    TextSize: 18

    Enabled, Visible, AutoDeactivate, Bold: true

    Border, ScrollBar, UseFocusRing: false

11. Click the space next to TextColor in the properties window, and in the Color Picker that appears, choose a dark blue.

12. Select the sixth field, and in the properties window, set its properties as follows:

    Name: ZipField

    Left: 352

    Top: 156

    Width: 72

    Height:30

    TextSize: 18

    Enabled, Visible, AutoDeactivate, Bold: true

    Border, ScrollBar, UseFocusRing: false

13. Click the space next to TextColor in the properties window, and in the Color Picker that appears, choose a dark blue.

14. From the File menu, choose Save (or press Command-S) to save your work. Your window editor should look something like **Figure 3.13**.

continues on next page

ROUGHING OUT THE PROJECT

This procedure should give you nice big, bold text for easy reading. Your HintField, which will prompt the user what to do next, shouldn't look like a data-entry field, so you've made its text italic and a different color. If you were doing this without help, you'd have tried some different sizes for the fields and text before settling on these, but these settings will do. The window is just big enough to accommodate the fields, with some room for a friendly greeting, your friendly logo, and the button the guest will click when he or she is finished entering data. To create these features, you'll use the Canvas, StaticText, and PushButton controls.

To add an image:

1. Drag the Canvas control to the window editor (**Figure 3.14**).

2. In the control's properties window, set these properties:

Name: Canvas1

Left: -2

Top: 0

Width: 144

Height: 72

Visible, AutoDeactivate, Enabled: true

3. In the Finder, locate an image that you'd like to use as your logo.

You may want to use a JPEG, GIF, PICT, or TIFF file, ideally no larger than 144 pixels wide and 72 pixels high, but any image will work.

4. Drag the image file to your project window to import it into the project (**Figure 3.15**).

The image is now available to use in your project.

5. In the window editor, click the Canvas control.

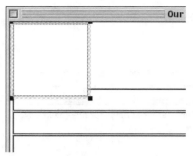

Figure 3.14 The Canvas control allows you to incorporate graphics into your application.

Figure 3.15 Importing an image file by dragging it to the project window.

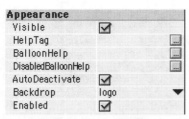

Figure 3.16 Selecting the imported image as the backdrop for the Canvas control.

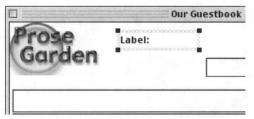

Figure 3.17 The StaticText control allows you to place fixed text in a window.

Figure 3.18
The properties window for the StaticText control.

6. In the properties window, choose the image you just imported from the Backdrop pop-up menu (**Figure 3.16**).

7. From the File menu, choose Save (or press Command-S) to save your work.

To add text :

1. Drag the StaticText control to the window editor (**Figure 3.17**).

2. In the control's properties window, set its properties as follows:

Name: Greeting

Left: 168

Top: 6

Width: 324

Height: 30

Text: Please sign our guestbook!

Visible, AutoDeactivate: true

FontSize: 24

3. Click the space next to TextColor in the properties window, and in the Color Picker that appears, choose a dark blue.

Your properties window should look like **Figure 3.18**.

4. From the File menu, choose Save (or press Command-S) to save your work.

To add a button:

1. Drag the PushButton control to the window editor (**Figure 3.19**).

2. Set the control's properties as follows:

Name: DoneButton

Left: 442

Top: 162

Width: 60

Height: 20

Caption: Done

Default, Enabled, Visible,
AutoDeactivate: true

Your properties window should look like **Figure 3.20**.

3. From the File menu, choose Save (or press Command-S) to save your work.

To test your project:

1. From the Debug menu, choose Run (or press Command-R).

2. Try out the application.

You should find that most of the pieces are in place (**Figure 3.21**). You have the window and the fields and can type your name and address data in them.

Note that the button doesn't do anything when you click it, because you haven't given it any behavior by writing code. You'll do that soon.

Note also that you can enter data in the HintField field—that space just below the Welcome message. But you don't really want this: your guests shouldn't be able to modify the hint field. You have another bug to stomp.

3. From the File menu, choose Quit to return to the development environment.

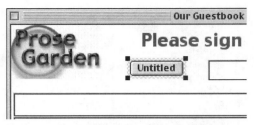

Figure 3.19 The PushButton control is a generic button that you can customize to your needs.

Figure 3.20
The properties window for the PushButton control, showing how you've customized it.

Figure 3.21 The guestbook, or part of it.

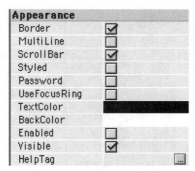

Figure 3.22 You can prevent data entry in a field via the Enabled property of the field.

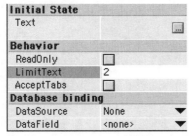

Figure 3.23 You can control how much text a user can enter in a field via the LimitText property of the field.

Managing User Input via Properties

Next month, when you're generating the mailing for your bed-and-breakfast, it'll be too late to ask an absent guest for the street address she forgot to enter. You'd like to write the guest-book program so that it helps your guests fill in all the needed data. To do so, you'll use object properties to manage user input.

For starters, since you don't want your guests entering data in the HintField, you'll disable it.

To prevent entry in a field:

1. Click the field named HintField in the window editor.

2. In the field's properties window, click the Enabled check box to turn off the Enabled property (**Figure 3.22**).

   The Enabled property for a field permits user interaction. Turning it off tells the field to ignore the user.

You'd also like to restrict your guests to entering two-letter state abbreviations and five-digit ZIP codes. Following is one way to accomplish that task.

To limit entry in a field:

1. Click the StateField field in the window editor.

2. In the field's properties window, enter 2 for the LimitText property (**Figure 3.23**).

   This setting tells the field to accept a maximum of two characters.

3. Click the ZipField field in the window editor.

4. In the field's properties window, enter **5** for its LimitText property.

   This setting tells the field to accept a maximum of five characters. You aren't restricting input to digits, which you'll do next.

To limit field entry to numbers:

1. Click the window icon in the project window to select it.

2. Press Option-Tab to open the Code Editor.

3. Click the disclosure triangle next to Controls to expand it.

4. Click the disclosure triangle next to ZipField to expand it.

5. Click the LostFocus handler in the left panel (**Figure 3.24**).

6. Enter this code in the right panel:
   ```
   If Me.Text <> "" And Val(Me.Text) <
   → 10000 Then
   Me.Text = ""
   Me.SetFocus
   End if
   ```

7. From the File menu, choose Save (or press Command-S) to save your work.

Figure 3.24 A field's LostFocus handler lets your code take some action whenever the user leaves the field.

The code does this: If the ZIP-code field is not empty, and its contents don't look like a number larger that 10000, the code clears whatever is in the field and keeps the focus. Recall that Me refers to the object itself—in this case, the ZipField field. The <> characters mean "is not equal to." And val(somestring) turns the string somestring into a number, ignoring nonnumeric characters. Because you've limited this field to five characters maximum, these machinations more or less guarantee that you get a five-digit number in this field or nothing. (This method is neither the only nor the most logical way to restrict field data to numbers, but it serves the present purpose.)

You might also like to control the order of entry for the fields. When the guest has entered a name in the Name field and pressed the Tab key, the insertion point for text entry should appear in the Address field, and so

Figure 3.25 Only one object at a time can have the focus. Your code can take advantage of knowing what object has the focus.

AddressField
- KeyDown
- GotFocus
- **LostFocus**
- MouseDown
- MouseUp
- SelChange

Figure 3.26 The LostFocus handler again.

Table 3.2

Coding the LostFocus Handlers

EDITFIELD	ENTER THIS CODE
NameField	AddressField.SetFocus
AddressField	CityField.SetFocus
CityField	StateField.SetFocus
StateField	ZipField.SetFocus
ZipField	NameField.SetFocus

forth. One way to do that is set the *focus* in your code (**Figure 3.25**).

One object at a time can have the focus; in the case of EditField objects, having the focus means that this field has the insertion point for entering text (assuming that the field is enabled). EditFields know when they get the focus and when they lose the focus, and they can take actions via their code when either of these events occurs.

To control the order of entry in fields:

1. Click the window icon in the project window to select it.

2. Press Option-Tab to open the Code Editor.

3. Click the disclosure triangle next to Controls to expand it.

4. Click the disclosure triangle next to NameField to expand it.

5. Click the LostFocus handler in the left panel (**Figure 3.26**).

6. Enter this code in the right panel:

   `AddressField.SetFocus`

7. Now do the same with each of the other four user-input fields, entering code in their LostFocus handlers as shown in **Table 3.2**.

continues on next page

8. In the properties window for each user-input field, click the UseFocusRing check box (**Figure 3.27**).

This property displays a visual cue to show the user when the field has the focus.

9. From the File menu, choose Save (or press Command-S) to save your work.

When the NameField has the focus and something happens to cause it to lose the focus, the AddressField is given the focus. In particular, when the user is typing in NameField and presses the Tab key, the insertion point will appear in the AddressField.

Does the user have no control of where text is entered? Let's find out.

To test the controls on user input:

1. From the Debug menu, choose Run (or press Command-R).

2. Type some text in the fields.

You should find that you are restricted to two characters in the state field and five in the ZIP-code field.

Although you can type arbitrary characters in the ZIP-code field, when you leave the field, it rejects the entry and holds onto the focus if it doesn't recognize the entry as a five-digit number.

3. Press Shift-Tab.

Normally, this action moves you to the preceding field. Your code should be overriding this behavior.

4. From the File menu, choose Quit to return to the development environment.

If you find the tight management of the order of user input to be too controlling, just delete the offending LostFocus handler code in those five fields. Good programming involves responding to what feels right to the user.

Figure 3.27 An object's UseFocusRing gives the user a visual cue when the object has the focus.

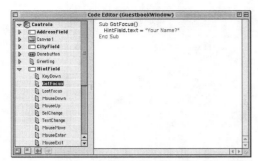

Figure 3.28 When an object gets the focus, the GotFocus handler comes into play.

Table 3.3

Coding the GotFocus Handlers	
EDITFIELD	ENTER THIS CODE
NameField	HintField.Text = "Your Name?"
AddressField	HintField.Text = "Your Address?"
CityField	HintField.Text = "Your City?"
StateField	HintField.Text = "Your State?"
ZipField	HintField.Text = "Your Zip Code?"

Tying Up Your Project's Loose Ends

Several things are yet undone. You created a HintField to prompt the guest but haven't done anything with it. Then there's the matter of saving the guest's input to a file and clearing the fields for the next guest. And you might want to thank the guest for doing your data-entry work for you. In this section, you'll take on each of these tasks in turn.

To prompt the user for input:

1. Click the window icon in the project window.

2. Press Option-Tab to open the Code Editor.

3. Click the disclosure triangle next to Controls to expand it.

4. Click the disclosure triangle next to NameField to expand it.

5. Click the GotFocus handler in the left panel (**Figure 3.28**).

6. Enter this code in the right panel:
   HintField.Text = "Your name?"

7. Now do the same with each of the other four user input fields, entering code in their GotFocus handlers as shown in **Table 3.3**.

8. From the File menu, choose Save (or press Command-S) to save your work.

When the NameField gets the focus, a message appears in the HintField, prompting the user to enter his or her name. A similar prompt appears for the other user-input fields.

To code a button:

1. Click the window icon in the project window.

2. Press Option-Tab to open the Code Editor.

3. Click the disclosure triangle next to Controls to expand it.

4. Click the disclosure triangle next to Done to expand it.

5. Click the Action handler in the left panel (**Figure 3.29**).

6. Enter this code in the right panel:

```
// Prompt user for missing data.
If NameField.Text = "" Then
  NameField.SetFocus
ElseIf AddressField.Text = "" Then
  AddressField.SetFocus
ElseIf CityField.Text = "" Then
  CityField.SetFocus
ElseIf StateField.Text = "" Then
  StateField.SetFocus
ElseIf ZipField.Text = "" Then
  ZipField.SetFocus
Else
  // All data entered, so write the
  → data to the file
  // ...and clear the data from the
  → fields.
  NameField.Text = ""
  AddressField.Text = ""
  CityField.Text = ""
  StateField.Text = ""
  ZipField.Text = ""
End if
```

Figure 3.29 A button's Action handler comes into play when the button is clicked.

Figure 3.30 The Timer control lets you add time-dependent behavior to your application.

Properties	
ID	
Name	ThanksTimer
Index	
Super	Timer ▼
Position	
Left	124
Top	6
Behavior	
Mode	0 – Off ▼
Period	3000

Figure 3.31 The properties window for the Timer control.

This code gets executed when the guest clicks the Done button. It looks like a lot of code, but it does just one or two simple things several times: First, it checks each data-entry field in turn to see whether it's empty; if so, it gives the field the focus to encourage the guest to enter the missing data. When all the fields contain data, the code does the other simple thing: clears all the fields to make room for the next guest's data. The procedure is sort of like cleaning the room.

7. From the File menu, choose Save (or press Command-S) to save your work.

At this point, when the guest has entered the data and clicked the Done button, and your program has cleared the field, it would be nice to say "Thank you for entering the data," but you don't want the thank-you message to be hanging around forever. You'd like the message to appear in the HintField for a few seconds and then be replaced by the welcoming prompt for the next guest. To incorporate time into the equation, you need to use a Timer control.

To add a time-controlled text message:

1. Drag the Timer control from the Tools palette to the window editor (**Figure 3.30**).

2. In the properties window for the timer, set its properties as follows:
   Name: ThanksTimer
   Mode: 0 – Off
   Period: 3000
   Location: (doesn't matter)
   Your properties window should look like **Figure 3.31**.

continues on next page

The timer object's Period property represents the number of milliseconds that the timer will run. A setting of 3000 means that the timer will count off 3 seconds.

The timer's Mode property is set to 0, 1, or 2. A setting of 0 means that the timer is turned off. A setting of 1 means that it will count down from the value of its Period setting to zero; then its Action handler will execute, and its Mode will change to 0. A setting of 2 means that the timer will count down to 0, its Action handler will execute, and then it will start counting down again.

You'd use a setting of 1 to create a time that starts counting down immediately and executes its Action handler once; a setting of 2 will give you a timer that starts counting down immediately, and keeps restarting itself every time it counts down to 0 and executes its Action handler. You'll use a setting of 0 to start with, because you don't want the time to start immediately. Your application's code will change the Mode setting of the timer to start the timer at certain times while the application is running.

Figure 3.32
Programming the action of the Timer control.

3. Click the window icon in the project window.

4. Press Option-Tab to open the Code Editor.

5. Click the disclosure triangle next to Controls to expand it.

6. Click the disclosure triangle next to ThanksTimer to expand it.

7. Click the Action handler in the left panel (**Figure 3.32**).

8. Enter this code in the right panel:
```
Me.Mode = 0
NameField.SetFocus
```

Figure 3.33
Programming the
Done button.

To code the button for timer action:

1. Click the Window icon in the project window.

2. Press Option-Tab to open the Code Editor.

3. Click the disclosure triangle next to Controls to expand it.

4. Click the disclosure triangle next to Done to expand it.

5. Click the Action handler in the left panel (**Figure 3.33**).

6. Add this code just before End if in the right panel:

   ```
   // Then show a 3-second thank you message.
   ZipField.SetFocus
   HintField.Text = "Thank you!"
   ThanksTimer.Mode = 1
   ```

   Here's where your code changes the timer's Mode setting, which causes it to start counting down.

7. From the File menu, choose Save (or press Command-S) to save your work.

To test the timer:

1. From the Debug menu, choose Run (or press Command-R).

2. Type some text in the fields and tab from field to field, click the Done button, and so on.

   The HintField should prompt you properly for input, and the Done button should prod you for missing data and clear the fields when all fields are filled.

3. From the File menu, choose Quit to return to the development environment.

Finishing the Project

Last of all, you need to save the data to a file.

To write field data to a file:

1. Click the window icon in the project window.

2. Press Option-Tab to open the Code Editor.

3. Click the disclosure triangle next to Controls to expand it.

4. Click the disclosure triangle next to Done to expand it.

5. Click the Action handler in the left panel (**Figure 3.34**).

6. Enter this line:

   ```
   WriteCustomerData(NameField.Text,
   → AddressField.Text,CityField.Text,
   → StateField.Text,ZipField.Text)
   ```

   before the line

   ```
   // ...and clear the data from the fields.
   ```

WriteCustomerData is a *method*: a chunk of code that can be invoked by name. This particular method reads the data from the data-entry fields and writes them to a file called Customers.txt—very handy, if the WriteCustomerData method existed. Because it doesn't, you'll create the file next.

To create a new method:

1. Click the window icon in the project window.

2. Press Option-Tab to open the Code Editor.

3. From the Edit menu, choose New Method (**Figure 3.35**).

4. In the dialog box that appears, enter WriteCustomerData for the Name.

Figure 3.34 More code for the Done button.

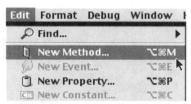

Figure 3.35 Creating a method that will write the data to the file. Creating your own methods is like adding your own verbs to REALbasic's language.

Figure 3.36 The parameters of a method are the means by which it gets and returns data values.

5. In the Parameters text box, enter F1 as String, F2 as String, F3 as String, F4 as String, F5 as String (**Figure 3.36**).

6. Click OK to dismiss the dialog box.

7. In the Code Editor, click the disclosure triangle next to Methods to expand it.

8. Click WriteCustomerData.

9. Enter this code in the right panel:

```
Dim CustomerFile as FolderItem
Dim CustomerData as TextOutputStream
CustomerFile = GetFolderItem
→ ("Customers.txt")
If Not CustomerFile.Exists then
CustomerData =
CustomerFile.CreateTextFile
End If
CustomerData = CustomerFile.
→ AppendToTextFile
CustomerData.WriteLine(F1)
CustomerData.WriteLine(F2)
CustomerData.WriteLine(F3)
CustomerData.WriteLine(F4)
CustomerData.WriteLine(F5)
CustomerData.Close
Return True
```

10. From the File menu, choose Save (or press Command-S) to save your work.

This code looks very different from what you went through to save a file in the Html Editor in Chapter 2. For the guestbook application, you don't want to engage your B&B guests in file-save dialog boxes, so you use this stripped-down technique.

To test the project:

1. From the Debug menu, choose Run (or press Command-R).

2. Enter some guest data, filling in all the fields and clicking Done (**Figure 3.37**).

3. Enter more data, clicking Done each time.

4. In the Finder and in same folder as REALbasic, locate the Customers.txt file.

5. Double-click Customers.txt to open it in your preferred text editor.

   The guest data that you typed should be there.

6. Click the guestbook to return to REALbasic.

7. From the File menu, choose Quit to return to the development environment.

To build a stand-alone application:

1. From the File menu, choose Build Application (**Figure 3.38**).

2. Click one of the check boxes at the top of the dialog box that appears, to choose the platform for which you want to create the application.

3. Type Guestbook in the Name box below Mac OS Application Settings.

4. Type Guestbook.exe in the Name box below Windows Application settings.

5. Click Build.

This application is a very simple one, but you could enhance it in ways that would make it more useful. For some purposes, saving the guests' names and addresses to a text file may be adequate, but you might want to format the data so that it's more accessible to other programs. In Chapter 9, "Working with Databases," you'll see how to make your REALbasic applications play nicely with, for example, database programs such as FileMaker Pro.

Figure 3.37 Testing the guestbook. It should now be able to accept, constrain, and save guest data just as you have programmed it to.

Figure 3.38 All that remains is to turn your project into a stand-alone application.

WRITING REALbasic CODE

4

As you saw in Chapter 3, "Programming Object Properties," object-oriented programming is all about objects and the properties and behavior of those objects. In that chapter, you learned how to manipulate the properties of objects. In this chapter, you'll learn how to control objects' behavior by writing code in REALbasic's programming language.

Unlike the original BASIC programming language, REALbasic is an object-oriented language. In this sense, it is more like C++ or Java than it is like BASIC. As you'll see in Chapter 5, "Writing Object-Oriented Code," this distinction affects how you structure your programs. But at the level of the individual command, REALbasic code looks a lot like traditional BASIC code. The *syntax* is similar.

In this chapter, you will learn that syntax. You'll also learn how to get the most out of REALbasic's Code Editor, your primary tool for writing REALbasic code. In the process, you will add code that extends the capabilities of the HTML editor that you built in Chapter 2, "Building an HTML Editor." By the end of this chapter, you will know how to write your own REALbasic code.

Creating Behavior Without Programming

In some cases, you can program the behavior of objects in REALbasic without writing any code. Certain objects, such as PushButton controls, have obvious and natural behaviors associated with them. A handy REALbasic feature called *object binding* lets you assign the obvious behavior to the appropriate object without doing any coding. In every case, the obvious behavior involves another object and binds the two objects together. Creating a binding between a PushButton control and a MoviePlayer control, for example, can cause the movie to play when the button is clicked. Note, though, that object binding works only with controls and only with certain controls.

To create an object binding between two controls:

1. Holding down the Shift and Command keys, drag from the source object (the one that will do the controlling) to the destination object (the one that is to be controlled).

2. In the New Binding dialog that appears, choose the desired behavior, and click OK (**Figure 4.1**).

A line will appear, connecting the two objects and signifying the binding (**Figure 4.2**).

To examine an object binding:

◆ Select the line connecting the objects by clicking it.

In the Properties window that appears, you see the active object binding that is represented by this line.

Note that an object can have more than one binding. A CheckBox control, for example, might have an object binding that causes a

Figure 4.1 By creating an object binding between two objects, you can cause one to control the other.

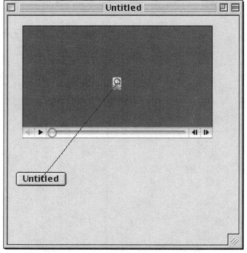

Figure 4.2 When you create an object binding between two objects, the IDE shows it as a line connecting the objects.

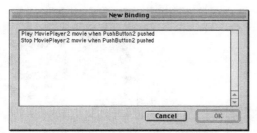

Figure 4.3 A pair of objects can have more than one object binding.

MoviePlayer control to play its movie when the CheckBox is checked and another that causes the movie to stop playing when the CheckBox is unchecked.

To modify an object binding:

1. Select the line representing the binding.

2. Press the Delete key.

3. Create a new binding as described earlier in this section.

To find out what object bindings are available for a given object:

◆ Holding down the Shift and Command keys, drag from the source object to the destination object as though you were creating a binding.

You can read the possible bindings between these objects in the dialog that appears (**Figure 4.3**).

Consult the *REALbasic Developer's Guide* for the full list of possible bindings for all objects.

Object binding is one way of controlling the behavior of objects. After it has been created, an object binding controls the objects' behavior just as though you had written the appropriate REALbasic code. But no REALbasic code is being written in the background by the object binding. The only way to modify an existing object binding is to follow the preceding procedure.

Object binding is a useful tool, and it's worth your time to build some object bindings to experience how this feature works. But although object bindings can save you time and effort, the only way to build full REALbasic applications is to write REALbasic code. And you do that in the Code Editor.

Using the Code Editor to Write REALbasic Code

Although some behavior of some objects can be controlled by object binding, most behavior is implemented in code. The lines of REALbasic code that you write as you create your application spell out what its objects can do and, consequently, what the application can do. You write that code in the Code Editor.

As mentioned earlier in this book, REALbasic code is object-oriented and event-driven. The Code Editor is your key to object-oriented, event-driven programming in REALbasic. Through it, you explicitly associate chunks of code with the relevant objects and with the events that trigger their action. You open the Code Editor for a PushButton control to edit the code for that object.

The Code Editor has two parts: the browser, which is the left pane; and the editor, which is the right pane (**Figure 4.4**). Because the Code Editor it is your primary tool for programming in REALbasic, it pays to learn how to use all its features.

To open the Code Editor for a control:

1. Open the window that contains the control.

2. Double-click the control.

The Code Editor for the control's parent window opens, with the desired control selected and the primary handler for that control opened.

Every control lives in some window. When you open the Code Editor for a control, you have access to the code for all the controls in that window.

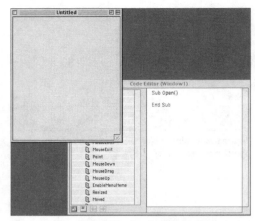

Figure 4.4 The Code Editor has two parts: the browser and the editor.

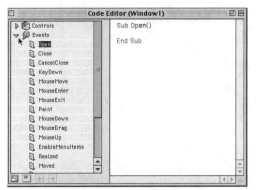

Figure 4.5 The browser pane (left) shows all the events to which a control can respond.

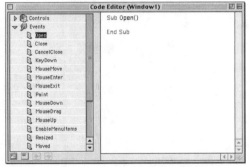

Figure 4.6 The editor pane (right) shows the code associated with the selected event.

To open the Code Editor for a window:

◆ Double-click anywhere in the window itself (not a control).

or

◆ Press Option-Tab.

or

◆ Click the desired window in the Project window, and press Option-Tab.

To see all the controls for a window:

1. Open the Code Editor for the window.

2. Click the disclosure triangle next to controls in the browser pane.

To see all the events to which a control can respond:

1. Open the Code Editor for the window.

2. Click the disclosure triangle next to Controls in the browser pane.

3. Click the disclosure triangle next to the name of the control (**Figure 4.5**).

Like a control, a window is an object and has a set of events to which it can respond.

To see the code associated with a control's event handler:

1. Open the Code Editor for the window.

2. Click the disclosure triangle next to Controls in the browser pane.

3. Click the disclosure triangle next to the name of the control.

4. Click the name of the event handler. The editor pane will display the code, if any, that is executed when this event occurs (**Figure 4.6**).

The window itself can respond to events, just as controls can.

USING THE CODE EDITOR TO WRITE REALBASIC CODE

105

To see all the events to which a window can respond:

1. Open the Code Editor for the window.

2. Click the disclosure triangle next to Events in the browser pane.

3. Click the disclosure triangle next to the name of the event.

To see the code associated with a window's event handler:

1. Open the Code Editor for the window.

2. Click the disclosure triangle next to Events in the browser pane.

3. Click the disclosure triangle next to the name of the event.

   The editor pane will display the code, if any, that is executed when this event occurs.

What are these events to which your code needs to respond? One common and important category of event that your code should be able to handle is the user's selection of an item from a menu. Menu handlers are so common that they have their own section in the Code Editor's browser pane.

To see all the menu handlers for a window:

1. Open the Code Editor for the window.

2. Click the disclosure triangle next to Menu Handlers in the browser pane (**Figure 4.7**).

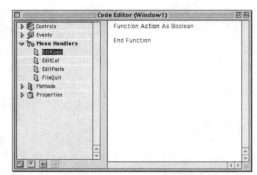

Figure 4.7 Menu handlers are listed separately in the browser pane.

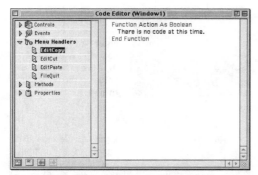

Figure 4.8 The code associated with a menu item.

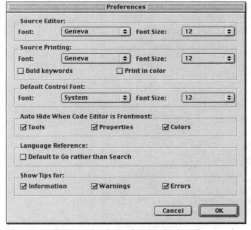

Figure 4.9 Setting the fonts for the Code Editor, code printing, and the default for controls.

To see the code associated with a menu handler:

1. Open the Code Editor for the window.

2. Click the disclosure triangle next to Menu Handlers in the browser pane.

3. Click the name of the menu handler.

The editor pane will display the code, if any, that is executed when this menu item is selected (**Figure 4.8**).

You can create your own handlers, called *methods,* and your own custom properties for objects. You'll learn about methods and custom properties later in this chapter.

You may find it useful to customize the editor to suit your preferred way of working.

To change the Code Editor's fonts:

1. Open the Preferences dialog via the Preferences menu.

In Mac OS X, the Preferences item is in the REALbasic menu; in Mac OS 9, it's in the Edit menu.

2. Set the fonts for the Code Editor, code printing, and the default for controls (**Figure 4.9**).

USING THE CODE EDITOR TO WRITE REALBASIC CODE

To get more space for writing code:

◆ Select a smaller code font in the Preferences dialog.

or

◆ Drag the resize bar between the panes to the left (**Figure 4.10**).

or

◆ Press Shift-Tab.

This last action will hide the browser. Pressing Shift-Tab a second time will make the browser visible again.

Note: This last method will work only if you have been navigating the items in the browser by using the keyboard arrow keys. If you have been using the mouse and clicking items, Shift-Tab only moves the focus between the browser and the Code Editor.

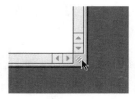

Figure 4.10 To get more space for writing code, drag the resize bar between the panes to the left.

Figure 4.11 To hide all the handlers that don't have any code associated with them, click the Show and Hide Empty Methods button at the bottom of the window.

✔ Tips

■ To get more room for editing in the Code Editor, you can drag the resize bar between the editing and browser panes to the left. If you drag it all the way, the browser pane disappears. To bring it back, Control-click anywhere in the Code Editor. Unlike the Shift-Tab method for hiding and showing the browser, this method always works.

■ Clicking the disclosure triangle next to an item in the Code Editor's browser pane is one way to eliminate some of the Code Editor's information overload. But you can hide all the handlers that don't have any code associated with them by clicking the Show and Hide Empty Methods button at the bottom of the window (**Figure 4.11**).

```
Function Action As Boolean

End Function
```

Figure 4.12 The Code Editor always supplies the first and last lines of a handler or method. You get to write the rest.

When you select a method in the browser pane of the Code Editor, its associated code appears in the editor pane. Even for an "empty" method, some code is supplied automatically: the first and last lines (**Figure 4.12**). You can't enter, delete, or change these lines directly, but you can ignore them except for the parameters listed in the first line. Parameters are explained later in this chapter in the discussion on writing your own methods.

To enter code in the code panel:

1. Type anywhere between the first and last lines.

    REALbasic tries to guess what you are going to type. As you type, it offers its guess in light-gray type.

2. If the guess REALbasic offers is what you want, press Tab to accept it.

    If REALbasic finds several plausible completions for what you are typing, it will display an ellipsis (...).

3. If REALbasic displays an ellipsis, press Tab to see a contextual menu of choices; if you are offered a menu, click one of the menu items to accept it.

    This guesswork is called *autocompletion.*

✔ Tips

■   You can use autocompletion in many places in REALbasic. Just watch what you type. If you see gray text appearing ahead of the characters you are entering, they are REALbasic's guess at what you intend to type. Press Tab to accept the guess or to see a contextual menu of guesses. If the guess is wrong, just go on typing.

■   Keep your eyes peeled for the Tips Window. It will give you good suggestions for writing code.

USING THE CODE EDITOR TO WRITE REALBASIC CODE

To edit your code:

◆ Cut, copy, paste, and clear code via the Edit-menu items, just as you would do it with text.

Command-key alternatives work as you would expect, too.

or

◆ Use the Edit-menu items Undo and Redo or their Command-key alternatives to retract unwise editing actions or reinstate wise ones.

or

◆ Highlight text to be moved, and drag it to where you want it.

This technique works within a handler, between handlers, from the Online Language Reference to the Code Editor, and between the Code Editor and any word processor or text editor that supports drag and drop. You can also drag text clippings from the Desktop to the Code Editor.

✔ Tips

■ Hold down the Shift key when you choose the Cut or Copy menu item or their Command-key equivalents to perform a "cut and append" or "copy and append" operation. The cut or copied text is appended to the text that's already in the Clipboard, rather than replacing it. This method is handy when you want to gather up several snippets of code and move them all to one new location.

■ To copy and paste a single word quickly, click the location where you want to paste, hold down the Option key, and click the word you want to paste. You can also use this technique to copy property or method names from the browser pane to your code. The real benefit of this shortcut is not speed but accuracy. Every word that you can copy rather than typing is one word that you can't mistype.

Figure 4.13 The Code Editor supports Find and Replace operations within code.

To find/replace code in the Code Editor:

1. Choose Edit > Find.

   The Find/Replace window appears.

2. Enter the text to find.

3. Enter the text to replace it with, if any.

4. Select the scope of the search:

   ▲ **Source:** search within the current handler/method.

   ▲ **Module:** search within the current module. (Modules are explained in Chapter 5.)

   ▲ **Project:** search anywhere in the current project.

5. Click one of the three buttons to find, replace and find again, or replace all occurrences (**Figure 4.13**).

✔ Tips

- You can jump immediately to the last method you were editing by clicking the Back button (the small arrow at the bottom of the Code Editor window). The Back button and the Forward button (next to it) work similarly to the Back and Forward buttons in a Web browser; they let you step backward and forward through the methods you have been editing (**Figure 4.14**).

- You will find yourself frequently jumping back and forth between the Code Editor for a window and the window itself in the IDE. A quick way to open the window from its Code Editor is to click the leftmost icon at the bottom of the Code Editor window (**Figure 4.15**).

To print your code:

1. Choose File > Print, or press Command-P. The Print dialog appears.

2. Specify how much code to print: the current method, the current module, or the whole project.

3. Click Print.

Figure 4.14 The Back button and the Forward button work similarly to the Back and Forward buttons in a Web browser; they let you step backward and forward through the methods you have been editing.

Figure 4.15 A quick way to open the window from its Code Editor is to click the leftmost icon at the bottom of the Code Editor window.

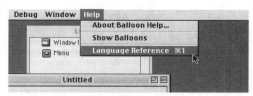

Figure 4.16 The Online Language Reference is a searchable, browsable database of documentation on REALbasic syntax.

Figure 4.17 When you're browsing the Online Language Reference, click the Alpha button to see all entries in alphabetical order.

Figure 4.18 The Online Language Reference documentation contains hyperlinks to other parts of the documentation.

Getting Help with the REALbasic Language

This chapter covers the rudiments of the syntax and vocabulary of REALbasic. But I don't address many instructions and features here. You can find documentation on nearly all of them in the Online Language Reference, but you have to know where to look.

To access the online language reference:

◆ Choose Help > Language Reference (**Figure 4.16**).

   or

◆ Press Command-1.

   or

◆ Press the Help key, if your keyboard has one.

To browse the online language reference alphabetically:

1. Click the Alpha button (**Figure 4.17**).

2. Scroll the left pane (the browser) to find the item.

3. Select the item in the left pane to view its documentation in the right pane.

To browse the online language reference by theme:

1. Click the Theme button.

2. Scroll the left pane (the browser) to find the item.

3. Select the item in the left pane to view its documentation in the right pane.

✔ Tip

■ Any text that appears in blue underlined format in the Online Language Reference is a link. Click it to view its documentation (**Figure 4.18**).

GETTING HELP WITH THE REALBASIC LANGUAGE

To view the documentation for a particular control in the Online Language Reference:

1. Select the control in a window.

2. Open the Online Language Reference. The documentation for the control will appear.

To search the online language reference for a particular term:

1. Type the term in the text box at the top of the window (**Figure 4.19**).

   You can search for only a single word. No spaces can appear in your entry.

   As you type each character, REALbasic tries to guess what you may be looking for. To accept its guess, press Tab.

2. If you see three dots, press Tab to get a list of choices.

3. Click Search, or press Return.

4. Choose the item in the browser pane.

To cancel a search:

◆ Click Home.

   This action will cancel the search and return the browser to its normal state.

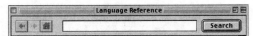

Figure 4.19 Searching the Online Language Reference.

The Online Language Reference includes code examples in its documentation. You are free to include these code snippets directly in your programs, and the Online Language Reference makes it easy to do just that.

To use code examples from the online language reference in your own programs:

◆ Drag the gray rectangle surrounding the code example to the place where you want to insert it in your code (**Figure 4.20**).

or

◆ Click the point in your code where you want to insert the code; then Option-click the code in the Online Language Reference.

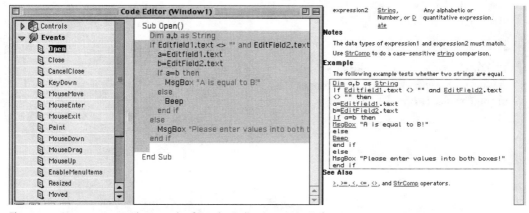

Figure 4.20 You can copy code examples from the Online Language Reference to your own programs.

Mastering Dim and Assignment Statements

The code that you write in a REALbasic handler or method is like a recipe: It's a sequence of instructions to be carried out in order. Many of these instructions manipulate data, and the assignment statement is the primary way to manipulate data in REALbasic programs. You met the assignment statement in Chapter 3; here, you'll see how to use it with specific types of data and with variables and properties.

Before a variable can be used, it must have a data type assigned to it. You do this with the Dim statement.

To create a variable:

◆ Use the Dim statement:

```
Dim myVar as string
Dim lengthMyVar as integer
Dim i,j,k as integer
```

✔ Tip

■ Any Dim statements in a handler must appear first, before any other statements in the handler (**Figure 4.21**).

```
Function Action As Boolean
  Dim Myvar as string
  Dim lengthmyvar as integer
  Dim i, j, k as integer
  //Dim statements must appear first, before
  //any other statements in the hander
End Function
```

Figure 4.21 Any Dim statements in a handler must appear before any other statements.

To create a variable that is an object:

◆ Use the Dim statement:

```
Dim c as clipboard
```

Now you can access the properties of this object:

```
me.text = c.text
```

Variables can be created as simple data types such as integer, string, and Boolean, as shown earlier in this section; or as specific object types, such as windows, list boxes, and the Clipboard. They can also be created as containers for more than one value at a time. A variable that contains several values of the same type is called an *array*.

To create an array:

◆ Use the Dim statement, specifying the *dimension* of the array:

```
Dim customer (100) as string
```

This statement sets aside space for 100 strings, each of which can be referred to by its *index:*

```
customer(0) = "Charlie Adams"
customer(99) = "D. Zanuck"
```

Arrays are zero-based: Their indexes start at 0 and go to 1 less than the dimension in the Dim statement. So the preceding two strings are the first and last in the customer array.

To create a multidimensional array:

◆ Use the Dim statement, and supply two or more dimensions:

```
Dim Chessboard (8,8) as string
```

This code creates an 8 x 8 array of values whose type is string. You could refer to a cell in this array this way:

```
Chessboard(0,0) = WhiteQueensRook
```

After you have created a variable, you can use it.

To assign a string value to a variable:

◆ Place the variable on the left side of the equals sign (=) and the value it is to get on the right side (**Figure 4.22**):

Dim Mother, Father, Child (20) as string

Mother = "Barb"

Father = "Earl"

Child(1) = "Doc"

Child(2) = "Mark"

Child(3) = "Ginny"

You can also use this form of the assignment statement, which makes clearer what is being assigned to what:

Let Mother = "Barb"

To assign a string to a property:

◆ Whatever appears on one side of the equals sign in an assignment must be the same type as what appears on the other side. So both of these statements work

window.title = "Dorothy's Dog"

window.title = someStringVariable

because the window.title property is of type string.

To assign a property's value to a string variable:

◆ Assuming that someStringVariable has been created as a string variable, someStringVariable = window.title will put the window's title in someStringVariable.

✔ Tip

■ You can never put a quoted string on the left side of an assignment statement. It's easy to see why. Unlike variables and properties, a string such as "Hello Dolly" is not a container to put a value in; it *is* a value. In general, you can't place a value to the left of an assignment statement.

Figure 4.22 Assigning a string value to a string variable.

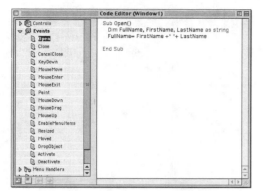

Figure 4.23 Concatenation: building up long strings from short ones.

To concatenate strings:

◆ Use the plus-sign operator (+) to combine two strings:

```
Dim FullName, FirstName, LastName as
→ string
FullName = FirstName + LastName
```

You can combine any number of strings in this way. To make the preceding example work, you probably want to put a space between the first and last names (**Figure 4.23**):

```
FullName = FirstName + " " + LastName
```

To determine the length of a string:

◆ One of the methods that REALbasic supplies for working with strings is `len`. `len` is a function, which means that it returns a value to you. When you give it a string, `len` returns an integer that is the number of characters in the string:

```
Dim s as string, ls as integer
s = window1.title
ls = len(s)
```

✔ Tip

■ Functions return values. Anywhere in your code that a value of a particular data type is appropriate, a call to a function that returns that data type is appropriate. If `i` is of integer type, you can assign an integer value to it:

```
i = 47
```

You can also assign the value of a function that returns an integer value to it:

```
i = len(s1).
```

To extract part of a string:

◆ REALbasic supplies three methods for extracting part of a string: left, right, and mid. You give left a string and n, the number of characters you want, and the method returns the first n characters of the string. Similarly, right returns the last n characters. mid takes three parameters: the string, the starting position in the string, and the number of characters to grab, counting from that position. So the following will put "The" in L, "Beagle" in R, and "Voyage" in M (**Figure 4.24**):

```
Dim S, L, R, M
S = "The Voyage of the Beagle"
L = left(S,3)
R = right(S,6)
M = mid(S,5,6)
```

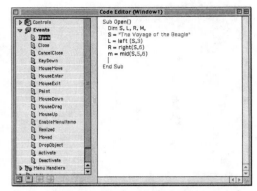

Figure 4.24 Using string functions to extract part of a string.

Another string method, instr, can be used to get the location of a substring in a string. instr takes the string and the substring as parameters and returns an integer that is the position of the beginning of the first occurrence of the substring in the string. If the substring isn't in the string, instr returns 0.

```
instr("The Voyage of the Beagle",
→ "Voyage")
```

returns a value of 5, whereas

```
instr("The Voyage of the Beagle", "Trip")
```

returns a value of 0. To test for the occurrence of a substring in a string and get a Boolean result, compare the result of instr with 0 (**Figure 4.25**):

```
instr(theString,theSubstring) > 0
```

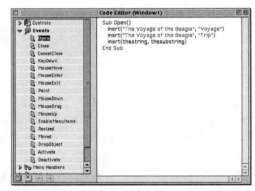

Figure 4.25 Using the instr function to search for one string inside another.

✔ Tip

- Information stored in computers is normally measured in bytes; kilobytes; megabytes; or if there is a lot of it, gigabytes. A single byte of text is equal to one character—sometimes. Sometimes, it isn't. REALbasic supplies string functions for both situations. Normally, you'll use `len`. But if you know that the string represents binary data rather than characters, use `lenb`. Other string functions (such as `left`, `mid`, and `right`) also have their binary versions (`leftb`, `midb`, and `rightb`).

To replace part of a string:

- If `s1`, `s2`, and `s3` are strings,

  `replace(s1,s2,s3)`

  returns `s1` with the first occurrence of `s2` replaced by `s3`.

  If `s3` is empty, this same code deletes the first instance of `s2` in `s1`.

  If `s1` or `s2` is empty, the code does nothing.

  To replace all instances of `s2` in `s1` with `s3`, use

  `replaceAll(s1,s2,s3)`.

  `replace` and `replaceAll` are case-insensitive; they treat uppercase and lowercase letters the same.

MASTERING DIM AND ASSIGNMENT STATEMENTS

To remove spaces from the beginning or end of a string:

Use one of the following:

◆ dim s as string

  s = " Holly Golightly "

  s = trim(s)

  leaves "Holly Golightly" in s
  (**Figure 4.26**).

◆ dim s as string

  s = " Holly Golightly "

  s = ltrim(s)

  leaves "Holly Golightly " in s.

◆ dim s as string

  s = " Holly Golightly "

  s = rtrim(s)

  leaves " Holly Golightly" in s.

To change the case of string data:

◆ This string function returns the string given to it, with all uppercase letters converted to lowercase:

  lowercase(s1)

◆ This one converts all the characters to uppercase:

  uppercase(s1)

◆ And this one converts all the characters to lowercase and then converts the first letter of each word to uppercase:

  titlecase(s1)

  The result, for example, is This Is Titlecase (**Figure 4.27**).

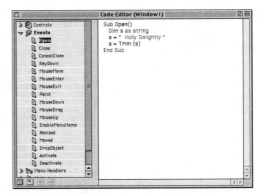

Figure 4.26 Functions for manipulating strings.

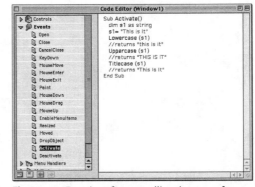

Figure 4.27 Functions for controlling the case of string data.

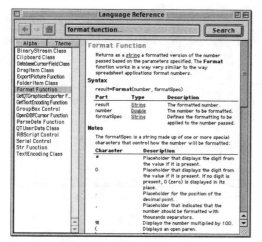

Figure 4.28 Converting a number to a string.

To determine the ASCII value of a string:

◆ Use the asc or ascb function:

i = asc("z")

newAsc = asc(c1) + 32

To convert a number to a string:

Use one of the following:

◆ dim s as string, n as integer

n = str(s)

◆ dim s as string, n as integer

n = cstr(s)

The cstr function uses the settings in your International Preferences dialog or Numbers control panel to interpret numbers. Use it if your Mac is not using a period (.) as the delimiter for decimal numbers.

◆ dim s, fmtspec as string, n as integer

s = format(n, fmtspec)

The format function gives you detailed control of the formatting of a number as a string. The fmtspec parameter specifies the formatting according to a simple code. See the Online Language Reference for details (**Figure 4.28**).

MASTERING DIM AND ASSIGNMENT STATEMENTS

To convert a string to a number:

Use one of the following:

◆ dim n as double

   n = val("27")

   puts the value 27 into n.

◆ dim n as double

   n = cdbl("27")

does the same, but uses the settings in your Mac's International Preferences dialog or Numbers control panel to determine how to interpret the number.

Both functions, val and cdbl return a double as their result. The string passed to these functions is assumed to represent a decimal number unless it is prefixed by &0, &H, or &b, which indicate an octal, hexadecimal, or binary number, respectively. The string that follows this prefix must be appropriate to that number's base. A binary number can contain only 1s and 0s, for example. Both functions ignore any characters after and including the first character that is not a proper character in the indicated base (**Figure 4.29**).

Figure 4.29 Converting a string to a number.

Table 4.1

Mathematical Operators		
OPERATOR	MEANING	USE
+	Addition	A + B
-	Subtraction	A - B
-	Negation	- B
*	Multiplication	A * B
/	Division	A / B
\	Integer division	A \ B

To assign a numeric value to a variable:

Use one of the following:

◆ `dim n as integer`

`i = 365`

An *integer* is a whole number in the range -2,147,483,648 to 2,147,483,648.

◆ `dim n as single`

`i = 3.14159`

A *single* is a real number—that is, a decimal number. It takes up 4 bytes of memory.

◆ `dim n as double`

`i = 3.14159`

A *double* is a real number—that is, a decimal number. It takes up 8 bytes of memory, double the number of bytes used by a single. Doubles give higher precision in calculations than singles do, but calculations with doubles run slower.

To do math with variables:

◆ You can combine mathematical values by using any of the basic mathematical operators in any combination (**Table 4.1**).

MASTERING DIM AND ASSIGNMENT STATEMENTS

Making Tests and Comparisons

Next to getting and setting values, the most common thing to do with values is compare them. Comparisons are highly useful in programming to control the order of execution of program statements. The result of any comparison—whether of strings, numbers, or other types of data—is always of Boolean type (true or false).

Using Boolean values

Boolean values can enter your code in many ways. A Boolean might be the value of a user-interface property that you set in the IDE, the result of a computation, or a directly assigned value. Booleans have their own kind of arithmetic by which they can be combined. There are three important operators for combining Booleans: not, and, and or. The result of any combination of Booleans is a Boolean.

To negate a Boolean value:

◆ Use the not operator.

The result is true if, and only if, the argument is false (**Figure 4.30**).

An operator's *arguments* are the values to which it is being applied.

To perform the logical and of two Boolean values:

◆ Use the and operator.

The result is true if, and only if, both the arguments are true (see Figure 4.30).

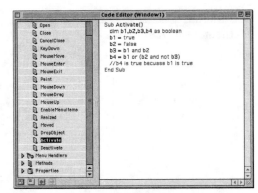

Figure 4.30 Boolean operations.

Table 4.2

Comparison Operators		
OPERATOR	MEANING	USE
=	Equality	A = B
<>	Inequality	A <> B
>	Greater than	A > B
<	Less than	A < B
>=	Greater than or equal to	A >= B
<=	Less than or equal to	A <= B

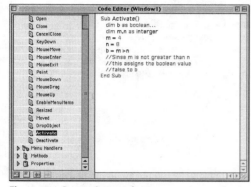

Figure 4.31 Comparing numbers.

To perform the logical or of two Boolean values:

◆ Use the or operator.

The result is true if, and only if, at least one of the arguments is true (see Figure 4.30).

✔ Tip

■ Booleans can be combined in expressions of great complexity. Use parentheses to group elements of complex expressions to help improve clarity. The expression

b1 and b2 and b3 and b4

is unambiguous, for example, but

(b1 and b2) and not (b2 or b3)

would be hard for either a human or the REALbasic compiler to understand without the parentheses.

Comparing data items

You can use Booleans to compare the sizes of numbers or compare strings for alphabetic priority. Surprisingly, the syntax is often the same.

To compare two numbers:

◆ Use any of the comparison operators in **Table 4.2.**

The result of comparing two numbers is a Boolean. Here's an example:

```
dim b as boolean
dim m,n as integer
m = 4
n = 8
b = m > n
```

Because m is not greater than n, this code assigns the Boolean value false to b (**Figure 4.31**).

✔ Tip

■ Generally, the values you are comparing must be of the same data type. REALbasic, however, is forgiving enough to allow you to compare two numbers of different numeric types, such as an integer and a single.

MAKING TESTS AND COMPARISONS

127

To compare two strings:

◆ For case-insensitive comparison, use any of the comparison operators in Table 4.2.

  When these operators are used to compare strings, they test alphabetic priority rather than size. These comparisons all return true:

  house > horse

  then > the

  ford = Ford

◆ For case-sensitive comparison, use the strComp function:

  strComp(s1,s2,mode)

  strComp returns an integer: -1, 0, or 1. It returns:

  1 if s1 > s2,

  -1 if s1 < s2

  0 if s1 = s2

  The mode parameter should be set to 0 for case-insensitive comparison. See the REALbasic documentation for details on its use.

✔ Tips

■ The strComp function differs from the other comparison operators. For one thing, it is a function, not an operator; for another, it returns an integer value rather than a Boolean.

■ The equals sign (=) performs two quite different functions: test for equality and value assignment. The REALbasic compiler always knows which meaning is correct in any context, and you, the programmer, *should* always know what you intended (**Figure 4.32**).

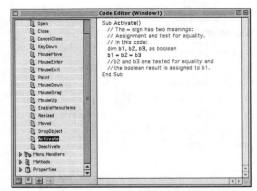

Figure 4.32 The equals sign (=) performs two functions: equality testing and value assignment. Here, the equals sign on the left side assigns the value to its right to the variable on its left, and the equals sign on the right side tests for the equality of two values.

Using tests to control the sequence of instruction execution

Although a handler or method is a sequence of instructions, sometimes you want to change the order in which those instructions are carried out. If you want to select among instructions to execute or want to execute a set of instructions repeatedly, you are manipulating the sequence of the instructions. The next sections show you how to do this.

MAKING TESTS AND COMPARISONS

Writing Code that Branches

REALbasic provides two tools to let you create *branching code*—that is, code that executes one set of statements or another, depending on some condition that is assessed at run time. These tools are the If structure and the Select Case structure.

The If structure

The If structure spans several lines of code and involves some or all of the keywords If, Then, Else, ElseIf, and End If. The keywords bracket tests and blocks of code to execute based on the tests. The If structure uses a Boolean value in its tests to decide which branch of code to execute (**Figure 4.33**).

To branch code in one of two directions:

◆ Use the If-Then-Else version of the If structure:

```
If [Boolean condition] Then
    [first block of statements]
Else
    [second block of statements]
End If
```

If the Boolean condition evaluates to true, the first block of statements will be executed; otherwise, the second block will be executed.

Figure 4.33 The If structure.

To execute one block of code conditionally:

◆ Use the If-Then version of the If structure:

```
If [Boolean condition] Then
   [block of statements]
End If
```

If the Boolean condition evaluates to true, the block of statements will be executed; otherwise, execution will continue with the next statement after End If.

To branch code in any of several directions:

◆ Use the If-Then-ElseIf version of the If structure:

```
If [Boolean condition 1] Then
   [first block of statements]
ElseIf [Boolean condition 2] Then
   [second block of statements]
ElseIf [Boolean condition 3] Then
   [third block of statements]
Else
   [last block of statements]
End If
```

If Boolean condition 1 evaluates to true, the first block of statements is executed. Otherwise, each successive Boolean condition is evaluated in the same way, and as soon as one is found that evaluates to true, the block of code following it is executed. Any number of EndIfs can be used in an If structure.

To perform complex branching of code:

◆ Place one or more If structures inside another If structure:

```
If [Boolean condition 1] Then
    If [Boolean condition 2] Then
        [first block]
    Else
        [second block]
    End If
Else
    [third block]
End If
```

If Boolean condition 1 evaluates to true, the second If structure is evaluated, resulting in the execution of the first or second block of code. If the first condition evaluates to false, the third block is executed.

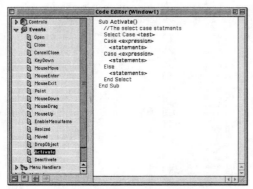

Figure 4.34 The Select Case structure.

The Select Case structure

The Select Case structure does what the If structure does but often produces clearer code. Instead of the Boolean test used by the If structure, the Select Case structure uses an integer or string value to choose among several possibilities (**Figure 4.34**).

To branch code in one of several directions with the Select Case structure:

◆ Follow this pattern:

```
Select Case [test expression]
Case [first expression]
    [first block of statements]
Case [second expression]
    [second block of code]
Else
    [last block of statements]
End Select
```

The test expression is evaluated; then each other expression is evaluated in turn until one is found that matches the test expression. The block of statements following the first matching expression is executed, and execution continues with the next statement after End Select. If no expression matches the test expression, any statements following the Else are executed.

Writing Code that Repeats

Often, you want to repeat a section of code several times. You may know exactly how many times, or the number of times that you want the code to be executed may be a function of some variable quantity that you can put a name to. Or you may want to keep executing a section of code until something happens. REALbasic provides three tools for executing a section of code repeatedly: the For...Next structure, the While structure, and the Do...Loop structure.

Figure 4.35 The For...Next structure.

The For...Next structure

You use the For...Next structure when you know, or can figure out at run time, exactly how many times you want the code section to repeat (**Figure 4.35**).

To repeat a section of code N times:

◆ Use the For...Next structure:

```
Dim N, counter as integer
For counter = 1 To N
   [statements]
Next
```

N is an integer. counter is an integer variable, which can be named anything and which gets incremented by 1 each time through the loop—that is, the block of statements repeats. After N repetitions, execution continues with the first statement after the Next.

To repeat a section of code N times with a countdown variable:

◆ Use the For...Next structure with the DownTo keyword:

```
Dim N, counter as integer
For counter = N-1 DownTo 0
   [statements]
Next
```

counter is decremented by 1 each time through the loop until it reaches 0. The integers on either side of the To or DownTo keyword can be any integer constant, variable, or expression, but the value to the right of a To or to the left of a DownTo must be the larger of the two; otherwise, no statements will get executed.

To repeat a section of code, skipping every other repetition:

◆ Use the For...Next structure with the Step keyword:

```
Dim N1,N2,counter as integer
For counter = N1 To N2 Step 2
   [statements]
Next
```

The integer value following the Step keyword can be a constant, variable, or expression. For a Step value of 2, the structure executes the statements the first time through the loop and then skips the second and every even-numbered pass through the loop. This variation of the For...Next structure is used when the starting and ending values (N1 and N2 here) are particularly meaningful variables. Otherwise, it usually is simpler to use a value for N2 that is half the size.

To break out of a For...Next loop:

◆ Use the Exit keyword:

```
Dim N1,N2,counter as integer
For counter = N1 To N2 Step 2
   [statements]
   Exit
   [statements]
Next
```

Although doing so is not good coding practice, it can be useful, especially when you are debugging your code, to put an Exit inside a loop. When the Exit is encountered, execution immediately transfers to the first statement after the Next.

WRITING CODE THAT REPEATS

135

The While and Do...Loop structures

Sometimes, you don't know how many times you need to repeat a section of code; you just know that you want to keep on doing it until something happens or while some condition holds. For these cases, REALbasic provides the `While` and `Do...Loop` structures (**Figure 4.36**).

To repeat a section of code while or until some condition holds:

◆ Use one of the following:

```
While [condition]
   [statements]
Wend
```

or

```
Do Until [condition]
   [statements]
Loop
```

or

```
Do
   [statements]
Loop Until [condition]
```

The `While` structure executes the statements while the condition holds true. The `Do...Loop` structure executes the statements until the condition becomes true. Placing the test at the end of the `Do...Loop` structure causes the condition to be evaluated after each time through the loop, so the statements will be executed at least once.

✔ Tip

■ In any `While` or `Do...Loop` structure, the statements that are executed must at some point cause the test condition to change to `false` (for a `While`) or `true` (for a `Do...Loop`). Otherwise, the loop will never terminate.

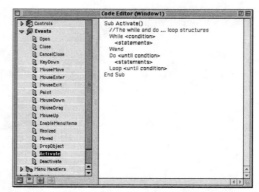

Figure 4.36 The `While` and `Do...Loop` structures.

WRITING CODE THAT REPEATS

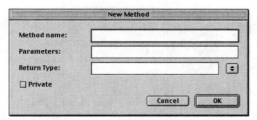

Figure 4.37 The parts of a method.

Writing Your Own Methods

The code you write for a REALbasic application resides in its *methods*. Event handlers and menu handlers are methods, and you can create your own custom methods, as you did in Chapter 3. The code is packaged in these discrete chunks because this type of programming is event-driven. The code in an event handler springs into action when the events that the handler handles occurs; a menu handler's code performs its magic when the user selects a menu item; and the code in a custom method is executed when the method is invoked by some other piece of code.

The parts of a method (**Figure 4.37**) are:

◆ **The method's name.** The name is used to refer to or call the method in your code.

◆ **The parameters** (optional). If you pass values to your method, the method needs a way to refer to those values. A method's parameters are the names by which it refers to these values.

◆ **The return value** (optional). The return value is used to return a value to the calling code.

◆ **The method body.** The method body is the code that the method executes.

To create a method:

1. With the Code Editor open, choose Edit > New Method.

2. In the New Method dialog, enter a name, parameters (optional), and a return value for the method.

3. In the Code Editor, click the disclosure triangle to show the user-defined methods.

4. Click the name of the method you just created, and enter its code in the editor pane of the Code Editor (**Figure 4.38**).

To use a method in your code:

◆ If your method has no return value, use it as you would a built-in REALbasic command:

`indent(HtmlField.text,lt)`

Note that the parameters are enclosed in parentheses.

or

◆ If your method has a return value, use it as a value, where a value of that type would be appropriate:

`HtmlField.text =`
`indent(HtmlField.text,lt)`

To pass values to a method:

◆ Put the values in parentheses after the method name.

The values you supply may be literal values or variables. They must appear in the same order as the parameters you defined for the method, matching their data types, and they must be separated by commas if you use more than one parameter.

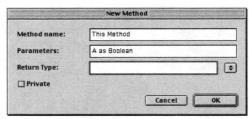

Figure 4.38 Creating a method.

To return a value from a method:

◆ If you have defined a return value for a method, use the call to the method just as you would use a value of the data type of the return value.

To delete a method:

1. Open the Code Editor for the window in which the method resides.

2. Click the disclosure triangle next to Methods in the left pane to see the method's name.

3. Click the icon next to the method's name to select it.

4. Choose Edit > Delete, or press Command-Delete.

✔ Tip

■ A method that does not return a value is sometimes called a *procedure*. You can use it in your code as though it were a built-in REALbasic command. A method that returns a value is called a *function*; you can use it in your code as though it were a variable of the appropriate data type. Think of functions as being nouns and procedures as being verbs.

WRITING YOUR OWN METHODS

Extending the HTML Editor

In Chapter 2, you created a simple HTML editor. Although that application eases the process of entering HTML tags and special characters in a document, it doesn't do much else. In particular, it doesn't produce especially attractive or readable HTML documents.

In the remainder of this chapter, you will write a REALbasic method that you can use to generate cleanly formatted HTML. The method, called Indent, will put each tag on a separate line and indent the tags to show the level of nesting of tags. Sets of tags nested inside other sets of tags will be indented farther to show this nesting.

Creating this method requires only a few of the REALbasic programming techniques covered in this chapter.

Figure 4.39 The Indent menu item.

Creating the Indent Menu Item

Before you create the Indent method, you need to think about the user interface. How will the user invoke your Indent method? The most obvious way is via an Indent menu item (**Figure 4.39**).

To create the Indent menu item:

1. In the Project window, double-click the Menu icon to open the Menu Editor.

2. Click the Edit menu.

3. Click the blank menu item.

4. In the Properties window, enter Indent for the Text property, and accept (or enter) EditIndent as the Name property.

5. Close the Menu Editor.

6. With the Code Editor open, choose Edit > New Menu Handler.

7. In the dialog that appears, choose EditIndent from the pop-up menu, and click OK.

8. In the browser pane of the Code Editor, click the disclosure triangle next to Menu Handlers.

9. Click EditIndent to open the EditIndent menu handler in the editor pane.

10. Enter this code in the EditIndent menu handler in the editor pane:

```
dim Lt as string
Lt = "<"
HtmlField.text = Indent(HtmlField.
→ text,Lt)
```

You've coded the Indent menu item. When the user selects it, this code will define a variable Lt, assign to it the single character <, and replace the text in HtmlField with the result returned by the Indent method. Now you can create the Indent method.

To create the Indent method:

1. With the Code Editor open, choose Edit > New Method.

2. In the New Method dialog, enter Indent for the method's name.

3. In the Parameters field, enter T as String, C as String.

4. In the Return Type field, enter String.

5. Click OK

You've created a method named Indent that takes two string parameters and returns a string value. From the way you call this method in the menu handler you created earlier, you can see what these parameters and return value are all about: You call Indent like this:

```
HtmlField.text = Indent(HtmlField.text,Lt)
```

So the first parameter will be the HTML text; the second parameter will be the < character; and the value returned will be the HTML text, properly indented. Knowing this, you can write the code for the Indent method.

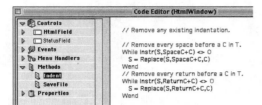

Figure 4.40 Removing leading spaces before < characters so that the indentation will be consistent.

Removing Existing Indentation

Before you can write the code that actually does the indenting, your code should remove existing spaces and return characters before tags. That way, you can be sure that existing spaces don't throw the indentation off (**Figure 4.40**).

To remove spaces:

1. Open the Code Editor.

2. Click the Indent method in the browser pane to open it in the editor pane.

3. Enter this code in the editor pane:

```
// Remove any existing indentation.


// Remove every space before a C in T.
While Instr(S,SpaceC+C) <> 0
    S = Replace(S,SpaceC+C,C)
Wend
```

To remove returns:

1. Enter this code at the end of the Indent method:

```
// Remove every return before a C in T.
While Instr(S,ReturnC+C) <> 0
    S = Replace(S,ReturnC+C,C)
Wend
```

continues on next page

2. Enter this code at the beginning of the method:

```
Dim S as String
    Dim SpaceC, ReturnC as String
Dim SlashC as String
Dim OddC, SpaceS as String
Dim IndentS as String
Dim TabLevel, TabSize as Integer
S = T
SpaceC = " "
ReturnC = Chr(13)
SlashC = "/"
OddC = Chr(255)
SpaceS = "                    "
IndentS = ""
TabLevel = 0
TabSize = 3
```

You don't need all of these variables yet, but enter them now; they'll come in handy shortly.

You should reflect on what you've learned and used in this little bit of code:

You know how to use REALbasic's `While` structure to repeat a block of code, and you've manipulated text with REALbasic's string methods `instr` and `replace`.

Your `Indent` handler removes spaces and returns from before HTML tags in the HTML text.

Now you're ready to write the code that inserts the needed spaces into the text before the tags—really just a matter of inserting a few spaces and return characters into the text in the right places. Figuring out how many spaces in what places is the tricky part, but basically, the spaces go before the < characters that mark the start of HTML tags.

Inserting Indentation Before Tags

Here's what your code will do: find the first instance of a < character, insert a return and some number of spaces before it, and repeat this procedure with all the remaining < characters. The code will indent opening HTML tags (such as `<table>`) and also closing tags (such as `</table>`). There are other cases when a < might appear in an HTML document, but for now, you'll ignore them.

You'll also ignore—but only for this set of steps—the fact that you want your indentation to show the different levels of nesting of the tags. First, you'll just get the code to indent every tag by the same amount.

If you try to follow the same procedure you used for removing spaces, you'll see a problem. That technique—looping as long as there is a particular string in the source string—works only if you delete the string you find on each step through the loop. Otherwise, you'll keep finding the same instance of the string forever.

To get around this problem, you'll write two loops. The first loop will find all the < characters, replacing them with an odd character that will never appear naturally in HTML text. You'll use the `Chr` function to get such a character. The second loop will find all these odd characters and replace each of them with a return character, a number of spaces for the indent, and the < character. The result is to replace each < character with a return character, some spaces, and the < character itself.

This trick gets around the problem: In each loop, you are eliminating the found instance of the searched-for string on each step, so that the loops won't go on forever.

To add indents:

1. Open the Indent method in the Code Editor.

2. Enter this code at the end of the method:

```
// Indent before every tag.

// Replace every C with OddChar.
While Instr(S,C) <> 0
    S = Replace(S,C,OddC)
Wend
// Replace every OddChar with return +
→ tab + C.
While Instr(S,OddC) <> 0
    IndentS = Mid(SpaceS,1,TabSize)
    S = Replace(S,OddC,ReturnC+IndentS+C)
Wend

// Add extra space before closing tabs.

// Replace every C/ with OddChar.
While Instr(S,C+SlashC) <> 0
S = Replace(S,C+SlashC,OddC)
Wend
// Replace every OddChar with tab + C/.
While Instr(S,OddC) <> 0
    IndentS = Mid(SpaceS,1,TabSize)
    S = Replace(S,OddC,IndentS+C+SlashC)
Wend

Return S
```

But you're not quite there.

```
                    Code Editor (HtmlWindow)
▽ ⛭ Controls          // Indent before every tag.
  ▷ ☐ HtmlField
  ▷ ☐ StatusField      // Replace every C with OddChar.
  ▷ ⚡ Events           While Instr(S,C) <> 0
  ▷ 🗂 Menu Handlers      S = Replace(S,C,OddC)
  ▽ 📄 Methods          Wend
     📄 Indent          // Replace every OddChar with return + tab + C.
     📄 SaveFile        While Instr(S,OddC) <> 0
  ▷ 🗂 Properties         If Mid(S,Instr(S,OddC)+1,1) = SlashC Then
                           TabLevel = TabLevel - 1
                         Else
                           TabLevel = TabLevel + 1
                         End If
                         IndentS = Mid(SpaceS,1,TabLevel*TabSize)
                         S = Replace(S,OddC,ReturnC+IndentS+C)
                       Wend

                       // Add extra space before closing tabs.

                       // Replace every C/ with OddChar.
                       While Instr(S,C+SlashC) <> 0
                         S = Replace(S,C+SlashC,OddC)
                       Wend
                       // Replace every OddChar with tab + C/.
                       While Instr(S,OddC) <> 0
                         IndentS = Mid(SpaceS,1,TabSize)
                         S = Replace(S,OddC,IndentS+C+SlashC)
                       Wend

                       Return S

                     End Function
```

Figure 4.41 Indenting the HTML code by inserting spaces before < characters.

Handling the Indent Level

This code is not how you really want to indent the HTML; you want more deeply nested tags to be indented further. To accomplish this task, you need to keep track of the level of nesting of the tags, and you can do this by noticing whether the last < found was really < or </. The < character alone marks the beginning of an HTML tag pair, whereas the </ pattern ends an HTML tag pair. Every time you come across a < character alone, you are increasing the level of nesting, entering a new tag pair, and going deeper. Every time you encounter </, you are closing off a tag pair, popping out of one level of nesting of tags. If your code keeps track of this situation, it can insert the right number of spaces to produce the nested indenting you want (**Figure 4.41**).

To handle indent level:

1. Open the Indent method handler in the Code Editor.

2. Edit the method's code to look like this:

    ```
    // Initialize some variables.

    Dim S as String
    Dim SpaceC, ReturnC as String
    Dim SlashC as String
    Dim OddC, SpaceS as String
    Dim IndentS as String
    Dim TabLevel, TabSize as Integer
    S = T
    SpaceC = " "
    ReturnC = Chr(13)
    SlashC = "/"
    OddC = Chr(255)
    SpaceS = "                          "
    ```

continues on next page

```
IndentS = ""
TabLevel = 0
TabSize = 3

// Remove any existing indentation.

// Remove every space before a C in T.
While Instr(S,SpaceC+C) <> 0
   S = Replace(S,SpaceC+C,C)
Wend
// Remove every return before a C in T.
While Instr(S,ReturnC+C) <> 0
   S = Replace(S,ReturnC+C,C)
Wend


// Indent before every tag.

// Replace every C with OddChar.
While Instr(S,C) <> 0
   S = Replace(S,C,OddC)
Wend
// Replace every OddChar with return +
→ tab + C.
While Instr(S,OddC) <> 0
   If Mid(S,Instr(S,OddC)+1,1) = SlashC
   → Then
      TabLevel = TabLevel - 1
   Else
      TabLevel = TabLevel + 1
   End If
    IndentS =
Mid(SpaceS,1,TabLevel*TabSize)
   S = Replace(S,OddC,ReturnC+IndentS+C)
Wend

// Add extra space before closing tabs.
```

```
// Replace every C/ with OddChar.
While Instr(S,C+SlashC) <> 0
    S = Replace(S,C+SlashC,OddC)
Wend
// Replace every OddChar with tab + C/.
While Instr(S,OddC) <> 0
    IndentS = Mid(SpaceS,1,TabSize)
    S = Replace(S,OddC,IndentS+C+SlashC)
Wend

Return S
```

3. Save your work, and test it.

Extending the Project

The code as written uses a fixed indent size of three characters, set in the Indent method when you set TabSize equal to 3. It would be nice to let the user set the indent size. I'll leave it as an optional challenge for you. Think about how you might present this choice to the user, and how you would code the application to accept and apply the user's chosen indent size (**Figure 4.42**).

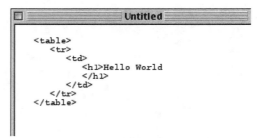

Figure 4.42 Your HTML editor now indents HTML code for readability.

WRITING OBJECT-ORIENTED CODE

The fact that REALbasic, unlike traditional Basic, is object-oriented is a Good Thing. Well-designed object-oriented code tends to be easier to read and easier to maintain than non-object-oriented code, and object-oriented programming makes it easier to reuse chunks of code in your other projects.

An *object* is an instance of a class. Object-oriented programming could just as well be called class-based programming, because classes are the key to creating object-oriented programs—not just built-in classes, such as the ListBox control class and all the other control classes that REALbasic provides, but also classes that you create.

In this chapter, you'll learn how to create and work with classes to produce well-designed object-oriented code.

Using Inheritance

Many of the benefits of object-oriented programming come from a powerful feature called inheritance.

One class of object can be a subclass of another class, inheriting all the super class's properties and methods automatically. This fact lets you reuse code that you wrote earlier, for this or another project; use code that some other programmer wrote; or use the code inherent in the built-in controls and classes of REALbasic.

You do this by creating classes that are based on existing classes, using and extending the properties and methods of the super class.

That's how REALbasic itself is structured. Essentially, all REALbasic classes are based on simpler REALbasic classes, right down to the simplest root class, which is called Object. You can see the full class hierarchy of REALbasic in the Language Reference manual and a representative part of it in **Figure 5.1**.

A class can have only one super class, but a class can have any number of subclasses, so the class hierarchy has a branching tree structure.

To see a control's super class:

1. Click an instance of the control in its window.

2. If the Properties window is not visible, choose Window > Show Properties.

   The control's super property is shown in the Properties window (**Figure 5.2**).

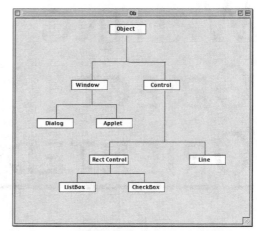

Figure 5.1 The REALbasic class hierarchy, showing which classes are subclasses of which other classes.

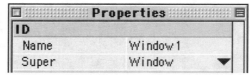

Figure 5.2 One step above a class in the class hierarchy is its super class. You can view or change the super class of a class in the class's Properties window.

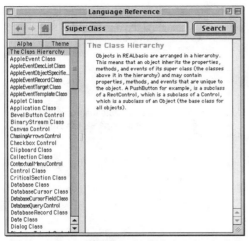

Figure 5.3 Classes inherit methods and properties from their super classes. You can investigate the inherited properties of a class by following the link to its super class in the online Language Reference manual.

To see a class's super class:

1. Click the class's icon in the Project window.

2. If the Properties window is not visible, choose Window > Show Properties.

   The class's super property is shown in the Properties window.

✔ Tip

■ You may also run across the terms *parent* and *child* in reference to OOP inheritance. These terms are equivalent to what REALbasic calls the super class and subclass, respectively.

To see all the properties and methods of a control:

1. Click the control in its window.

2. Choose Help > Language Reference.

3. Scroll the window to see all the control's properties and methods.

4. Click the control's Super property link to see the super class's properties and methods. These are all properties and methods of the selected control.

5. Repeat this procedure as long as possible. Look at the super class's super class, if there is one, and examine its properties and methods (**Figure 5.3**).

✔ Tip

■ Any instance of a subclass is a proper instance of its super class. In other words, wherever you can use the super class appropriately, you can use the subclass. A PushButton, for example, is a user interface control with certain properties and behavior; it has a screen location, height, and width. Any subclass of a PushButton that you create is still a PushButton and still has all of a PushButton's properties and behavior.

Creating Instances of Classes

As mentioned earlier in this chapter, an object is an instance of a class. For most classes, you can create as many instances in your code as you like. The process of creating an instance of a class is called *instantiation*.

To create an instance of a class:

◆ Use the new operator:

```
dim c as classname
c = new classname
```

Or let a function that knows how to instantiate a class do it for you:

```
dim f as folderitem
f = getfolderitem("fspec")
```

new is an operator. It takes a class name and returns a newly created instance of the class (**Figure 5.4**).

A control is an instance of a class, but you usually create controls in the IDE by dragging the icon for the control from the Tools palette to the window. You can create a new control in your code, but only if you have created at least one such control in the IDE. Your code uses this control as a template for creating others.

To create a new instance of a control class in code:

1. Drag an instance of the control class, such as a PushButton, from the Tools palette to the window.

2. In the control's Properties window, set its Name property to Widget and its Index property to 0.

3. In the window's Open handler, enter this code:

```
dim w1 as widget
w1 = new widget
w1.top = w1.top + 30
```

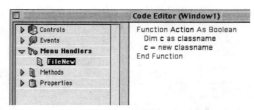

Figure 5.4 You can have multiple instances of a class in your program. Use the new operator to create a new instance of a class.

Figure 5.5 Creating a new instance of a control in your code is called cloning. The application must already contain an instance of the control, created in the IDE.

Figure 5.6 Multiple instances of a control class can form a control array.

4. Save and run your application.

   You should see two stacked instances of the control (**Figure 5.5**).

What you just did is somewhat mysterious. Notice that the `dim` statement uses the name of the control as though it were a data type or class. It would seem to make more sense to write

`dim w1 as PushButton`

or whatever control class it actually is.

What's really going on in this example is that you are creating something called a *control array*. Control arrays are, not surprisingly, arrays of controls, and you work with them the way you work with arrays of *scalar* values, such as numbers. To refer to a particular control in a control array, use the array name and the index:

`box(1).top = 30`

What made this example so mysterious was that the control array was created implicitly when you assigned a value to the `Index` parameter of the original control. Things are clearer when you create a control array explicitly.

To create an array of controls:

1. Drag an instance of a control class from the Tools palette to the window.

2. In the control's Properties window, give it a name, such as Widget.

3. Drag another instance of the same control class from the Tools palette to the window.

4. In its Properties window, give the control the same name as the first.

   A dialog appears (**Figure 5.6**), asking, "Do you want to create a new control?"

5. Click Yes.

continues on next page

CREATING INSTANCES OF CLASSES

These controls, and any subsequent controls of this class and with this name, will be assigned unique successive numbers as their Index properties. You can refer to one of these controls by its name and index, exactly as you refer to an element of an array by its name and index:

myRadioButton(1).value = true

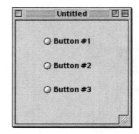

Figure 5.7 You can use a control array to manage the behavior of RadioButtons.

To create a control array of RadioButtons:

1. Drag an instance of a RadioButton control class from the Tools palette to the window.

2. In the button's Properties window, give it a name, such as myRadioButton.

3. Drag another RadioButton instance from the Tools palette to the window.

4. In its Properties window, give the control the same name as the first.

   A dialog appears, asking, "Do you want to create a control array?"

5. Click Yes.

6. Drag more RadioButton instances to the window, if desired, giving each one the same name as the first (**Figure 5.7**).

7. Double-click any of the RadioButtons to open the Code Editor for the myRadioButton control array.

8. Enter this code in the Action handler:

```
select case Index
case 0
    msgBox "You clicked button 0."
case 1
    msgBox "You clicked button 1."
case 2
    msgBox "You clicked button 2."
end select
```

   This Select Case structure assumes three buttons; modify it to match the number of buttons in your control array.

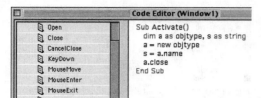

Figure 5.8 Use dot notation to refer to the properties and methods of objects.

Using Objects in Your Code

Whenever you refer to a method or property in your REALbasic code, that method or property is the method or property of some object (or possibly of the object's class). Sometimes, the object can be left unstated; at other times, the only "object" to which the method or property can be said to belong is REALbasic itself. Usually, though, you need to specify the object along with its method or property. As you saw in Chapter 3, "Programming Object Properties," you use dot notation for this purpose.

To refer to a property of an object:

◆ Specify the object by using dot notation (**Figure 5.8**):

```
dim a as objtype, s as string
a = new objecttype
s = a.name
```

To refer to a method of an object:

◆ Specify the object by using dot notation (see Figure 5.8):

```
dim a as objtype
a = new objecttype
a.close
```

References to objects

It's important to understand that objects and scalars (strings, numbers, and Booleans) are referred to differently.

When you write

```
dim s as string
```

this code creates a string variable. The variable doesn't have a value until you assign it one with

```
s = a.name
```

but it does exist.

continues on next page

On the other hand, when you write

dim a as objecttype

you are creating a reference to an object of the class objecttype. This reference, the variable a, doesn't have a value until you assign it one with

a = new objecttype

but it does exist.

The reference doesn't have a value, but the object it is going to point to doesn't even exist until you write

a = new objecttype

In other words, there is a level of indirection in referring to objects that doesn't come into play in dealing with scalars. The value of **s** *is* the string that it represents, but the value of *a* is merely a reference to the object it names.

This situation will become clearer later in this chapter when you look at comparing objects.

To refer to a object's properties or methods from within the object:

◆ You can drop the mention of the object:

controlname.prop = "yadda"

controlname.methodX()

or

prop = "yadda"

methodX()

if the code is in a handler for the control controlname (**Figure 5.9**).

✔ Tip

■ After you create an instance of a class and assign a variable name to a reference to it, you can use the variable name as you do any object reference, including dot notation.

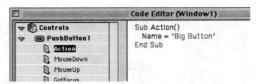

Figure 5.9 When you're referring to an object from within one of its handlers, you don't have to specify the object.

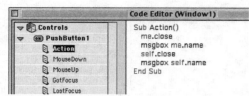

Figure 5.10 The me and self functions.

To refer to a property of a control in another window:

◆ Specify the window as well as the control by using dot notation:

`window2.editfield.text = "yadda"`

if this code is in a handler in a different window from `window2`.

In Chapter 3, you learned about the special term me. Here's what it's really about:

To refer to the control whose handler is running:

◆ Use the me function:

`me.close`

`msgbox me.name`

Placed in the handler of a control, the second line will display the control's name (**Figure 5.10**).

To refer to the window containing the control whose handler is running:

◆ Use the self function:

`self.close`

`msgbox self.name`

Placed in the handler of a control, the second line will display the name of the windows that the control is in (see Figure 5.10).

Comparing Objects

Comparing objects is different from comparing scalar values, such as strings and numbers. Typically, it is not meaningful to ask whether one instance of an object is greater than another, for example. One comparison operator *is* used with objects— the = operator— but with a different meaning from its use with strings and numbers. The = comparison applies to the *value* of the variable, and in the case of objects, the variable's value is a reference, not the object itself. So if you write

```
dim x1, x2 as objtype
dim b as boolean
x1 = new objtype
x2 = new objtype
b = (x1 = x2)
```

the result (the value of variable **b**) will always be **false**, because you have created two *distinct* instances of class **objtype**, and **x1** and **x2** refer to these distinct objects so, write the code as shown in **Figure 5.11**.

When applied to scalars, the = operator tests for equality of values. When applied to objects, it still tests for equality of value, but for equality of the values of the references. In terms of the objects themselves, this test amounts to a test of absolute identity. This test returns **true** only if the references point to exactly the same object.

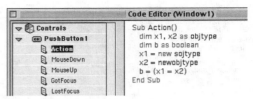

Figure 5.11 Comparing object references.

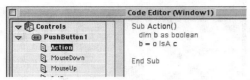

Figure 5.12 Use the `IsA` operator to determine the class of an object.

To compare two object references:

◆ Use the = operator:

```
dim x1, x2 as objtype
dim b as boolean
x1 = new objtype
[some more statements]
b = (x1 = x2)
```

You've compared two object references, x1 and x2, and stored the result in Boolean variable b—which will be **true** if, and only if, x2 got assigned to the same object as x1 in the bracketed section. One way to accomplish this would be:

```
x2 = x1
```

But there are subtler ways.

To test an object reference:

◆ Compare the object reference with the special object `nil`:

```
dim b as boolean
b = (o <> nil)
```

This reference tests whether o refers to *some* object. `nil` is a way of indicating the absence of an object. The `nil` object is what all object references refer to if they don't refer to any object.

To test the class of an object:

◆ Use the `IsA` operator:

```
dim b as boolean
b = o IsA c
```

The Boolean variable b will be **true** if, and only if, o is an object of class c or if o is an object of a subclass of class c (**Figure 5.12**).

Creating Your Own Classes

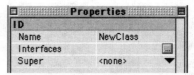

Figure 5.13 Creating a new class.

Classes are important in writing code. But when the program starts running, all the action is in the objects, the particular *instances* of which the classes are the templates or patterns. Roughly speaking, you create classes in the IDE, and objects are created while your code is running. Here's how to create classes and objects.

To create a new class:

1. Choose File > New Class.

An icon for the new class appears in the Project window.

2. Press the Tab key.

The Properties window shows the new class.

3. In the Properties window, type a name for the new class (**Figure 5.13**).

To create a new window class:

1. Choose File > New Window.

An icon for the window appears in the Project window, and the window opens.

2. Click the icon for the window in the Project window, and press the Tab key.

The Properties window shows the properties of the new window.

3. In the Properties window, type a name for the new window.

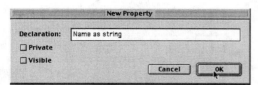

Figure 5.14 Adding a property to a created class.

To create a new class as a subclass of an existing class:

1. Choose File > New Class.

An icon for the new class appears in the Project window.

2. Press the Tab key.

The Properties window shows the new class.

3. In the Properties window, type a name for the new class.

4. In the Properties window, choose a class from the Super pop-up menu.

Your new class will inherit methods and properties from whatever class you choose as its super. Your new class becomes a special case of this super class.

5. Add any desired methods or properties (see below).

Your new class has all the methods and properties of its super class, as well as any you've added that are unique to this new subclass.

To add a property to a created class:

1. Double-click the class icon in the Project window.

The Code Editor for the class appears.

2. Choose Edit > New Property.

A property-definition dialog appears.

3. Enter the declaration for the property, giving it a name and data type, such as the following:

▲ Name as string

▲ i as integer

▲ f as folderitem

4. Click OK (**Figure 5.14**).

To add a method to a created class:

1. Double-click the class icon in the Project window.
   The Code Editor for the class appears.

2. Choose Edit > New Method.
   A method-definition dialog appears.

3. Enter the name, parameters, and return type for the method in the dialog.
   Parameters and return type are optional.

4. Click OK (**Figure 5.15**).

Your newly created class inherits event handlers along with other methods from its super class. This means that you can add code to these event handlers as well as to any new methods that you create. You can customize the behavior of the new class so that it responds to events differently than the super class does.

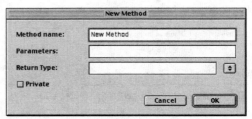

Figure 5.15 Adding a method to a created class.

To customize an event handler for a created class:

1. Open the Code Editor for the custom class, as described earlier in this chapter.

2. Click the desired handler in the left pane of the Code Editor.

3. Edit its code in the right pane.

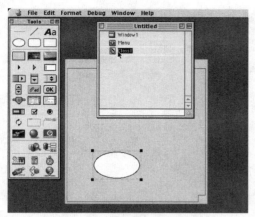

Figure 5.16 You can drag an instance of a created control class to a window much as you do with built-in controls.

Any class that can receive the focus can control menus when it has the focus. On the Macintosh platform, this capability is limited to classes based on `EditField` and `ListBox`.

To create a new class based on a control:

1. Choose File > New Class.

   An icon for the new class appears in the Project window.

2. Press the Tab key.

   The Properties window shows the new class.

3. In the Properties window, type a name for the new class.

4. In the Properties window, choose a control class from the Super pop-up menu.

   Your new class will inherit methods and properties from whatever control class you choose as its super. Your new class becomes a special case of this control class.

You can customize this new class by creating new methods or properties for it or simply by setting some of its existing properties to nondefault values. You could, for example, create a custom BevelButton control that is a 32-by-32 square with a standard icon and a distinctive caption text font.

After you create this new kind of control, you can drag instances of it into a window of your project as you would drag instances of any "real" control class—except that you drag this new kind of control from the Project window instead of from the Tools palette (**Figure 5.16**).

Constructors

Object-oriented programming provides a convenient way to initialize a newly created object's properties. Windows and controls already have such a facility, called the Open handler, which is invoked when the window or control is opened. Any initialization code goes in that handler. If you want to set certain properties of a window or control when it is first opened, for example, you put the code to do that in its Open handler.

Any new class that you create will also have an Open handler if it is based on a window or control class. Otherwise, you may want some way to initialize the instance of the class when it gets created. For this purpose, you use a constructor.

To create a constructor for a class:

1. Double-click the class icon in the Project window.
   The Code Editor for the class appears.

2. Choose Edit > New Method.
   A method-definition dialog appears.

3. Enter the name of the class as the name of the method in the dialog.

4. Click OK (**Figure 5.17**).

To invoke a class's constructor:

◆ Just create a new instance of the class, and its constructor will run:

   g = new greenhouse

   A lot is going on in this apparently simple command. The new operator creates a new instance; the = sign assigns to the variable g a reference to this instance; and the constructor, greenhouse, performs any needed initialization for the instance.

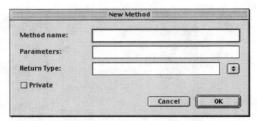

Figure 5.17 A constructor is a method that executes when a class instance is created. You can use it to set any properties the instance may need.

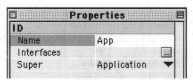

Figure 5.18 Creating a subclass of the Application class gives you a place to put code that must be available throughout your application.

The Application class

REALbasic supplies a class called Application that stands for your entire application. You encountered this class fleetingly before. You can't work with it directly, but you can subclass it, giving you a completely global class to work with. Any methods or properties defined in this class are global, too, accessible from anywhere in your application. That's chiefly what the class is good for.

Note: You should create only one subclass of Application in a given program. Because it represents your entire application, you need only one.

To create a subclass based on the Application class:

1. Choose File > New Class.

   An icon for the new class appears in the Project window.

2. Press the Tab key.

   The Properties window shows the new class.

3. In the Properties window, type **App** as the name of the new class.

4. In the Properties window, choose Application from the Super pop-up menu.

   Giving the class the name **App** is not mandatory, but it proves to be convenient because of the **App** function. This globally available function refers to your application, and it prevents confusion if it and your subclass have the same name—although you might think the opposite (**Figure 5.18**).

Removing Classes and Objects

Classes and instances don't necessarily last forever. Removing a class from a project and deleting an instance of a class from a running program, though, are two very different things.

To remove a class from your project:

1. Make sure that no part of your code is using the class.

2. Click the class icon in the Project window.

3. Press the Delete key.

   or

   Choose Edit > Clear (**Figure 5.19**).

   or

   Control-click the icon, and choose Delete from the contextual menu that appears.

To reinstate an accidentally deleted class:

◆ Immediately choose File > Undo.

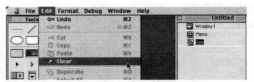

Figure 5.19 Removing a class from your project is simple, but do it only if you're sure that no part of your code uses the class.

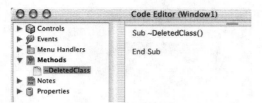

Figure 5.20 A destructor is a method that executes when a class instance is deleted. You can use it to clean up after the class.

Object deletion

REALbasic manages the deletion from memory of any instances of classes that are no longer being used. In rare cases, however, it can't do the job. In such a case, you can have your code delete an instance explicitly.

To delete an instance of a class:

◆ Set a reference to the instance to the value `nil`:

```
dim pic1 as hugePicture
pic1 = newPicture(n1,n2,n3)
...
pic1 = nil
```

Just as there are constructors to perform any needed initialization when an object is created, there are destructors to clean up when an object is deleted—either deleted explicitly in your code or deleted by REALbasic when it determines that the object is no longer being used.

To clean up when a class instance is deleted:

1. Double-click the class icon in the Project window.

   The Code Editor for the class appears.

2. Choose Edit > New Method.

   A method-definition dialog appears.

3. For the name of the method, enter a tilde character (~), followed by the name of the class (**Figure 5.20**).

4. Click OK.

Importing and Exporting Classes

One of the strengths of object-oriented programming is the increased capability it gives you to reuse code. You can create a class and reuse it in the same or another project, or make it available to others. You can find REALbasic classes online that other programmers have made available, freely or for money.

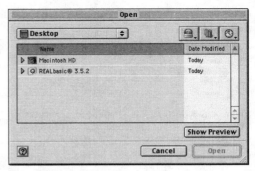

Figure 5.21 Importing a class.

To import a class from another project:

1. Locate the file icon for the class in the Finder.

2. Drag the icon to the Project window in REALbasic.

   or

1. Choose File > Import Class.

2. In the dialog that appears, select the file containing the class.

   Note: If a class is based on another class that you don't have in your project, you will need to import that class, too (**Figure 5.21**).

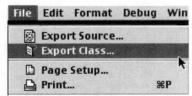

Figure 5.22 Exporting a class.

To export a class for use in other projects:

◆ Drag the class icon from the Project window to the Desktop.

   or

1. Click the class icon in the Project window.

2. Choose File > Export Class (**Figure 5.22**).

3. In the dialog that appears, give the file a name.

Figure 5.23 When you encrypt a class to hide its code, a tiny padlock appears in the lower-left corner.

Figure 5.24 Decrypting a class.

When you export a class from one of your projects and give the file to someone else, you are giving that person not only executable code, but also readable code. If you want to protect that code so that it can be used but not read or changed, you can encrypt it when you export it.

To encrypt a class to protect your code:

1. Click the class icon in the Project window.

2. Choose Edit > Encrypt.

or

1. Control-click the class icon in the Project window.

2. Choose Encrypt from the contextual menu that appears.
An encryption dialog appears.

3. Enter a password (twice).
A tiny padlock appears on the class icon to show that the class is encrypted (**Figure 5.23**).

4. Store that password in a secure place.

To decrypt a class:

1. If the class is in a file, import it into a REALbasic project as described on the previous page.

2. Click the class icon in the Project window.

3. Choose Edit > Decrypt.

or

◆ Control-click the class icon in the Project window, choose Decrypt from the contextual menu that appears, and enter the password
If you got the password right, the tiny padlock disappears from the icon to show that the class is no longer encrypted (**Figure 5.24**).

IMPORTING AND EXPORTING CLASSES

Deciding Where to Put the Code

One of the challenges of object-oriented programming is deciding where to put the code. Does this particular chunk of functionality belong in a window handler or a control handler? Should you put this code in the ListBox's CellAction handler or its CellChange handler? Thinking clearly about objects and their behavior can answer these questions and can lead to well-structured code that is easy to understand.

To decide where to put your code:

1. Decide to what object the behavior most naturally belongs.

2. Decide what event, if any, is the most appropriate to trigger the action.

3. If the code doesn't fit in any event handler naturally, create a method for it, and call that method somewhere in your code.

4. If the code should be executed one time when the object comes into existence, put it in the object's Open handler, or create a Constructor method for the object and put the code in that method.

5. If the code should be executed one time when the object ceases to exist, put it in the object's Close handler, or create a Destructor for the object and put the code there.

6. If the code needs to be available to all objects and isn't associated with any event to which any object responds, consider putting it in a module.

✔ Tips

- Deciding which object to associate a chunk of code with is a decision about naturalness. There may be more than one right answer, but one answer usually be more natural than the others. Code that sets a BevelButton's Bevel property, for example, probably should be placed in a handler of that BevelButton. Code that performs some general function may be more appropriately placed in a handler for the window.

- It is not always obvious what event handler is the right one to hold a particular chunk of code, but the answer is more likely to be obvious if you have a clear understanding of what each event for each control means. Studying the documentation for the events for each control in the online Language Reference manual will make it easier to know where to place your code.

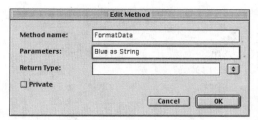

Figure 5.25 Creating a module.

Using modules

Sometimes, a chunk of code doesn't seem to have any natural object with which you can associate it. In such a case, you might consider placing the code in a module.

A *module* is a place to put any methods, properties, and constants that need to be accessible anywhere in your application. To store code in a module, first create the module and then add a method to the module, placing the code in the method.

To create a module:

1. Choose File > New Module.
   An icon for the module appears in the Project window.

2. In the Properties window for the new module, edit its name as you want.

To add a method to a module:

1. Double-click the module's icon in the Project window to open the Code Editor for it.

2. Choose Edit > New Method.
   The Method Declaration dialog appears.

3. Enter the Method name, Parameters, and Return Type (**Figure 5.25**).

4. Click OK.

Creating a Simple Spreadsheet

In the remainder of this chapter, you'll create a class named Spreadsheet and use it to implement a rudimentary spreadsheet application.

The code for this application will separate the user interface from the database and computational aspects of the spreadsheet. You'll use a multicolumn ListBox control to implement the user interface: a grid of cells that permits the entry of numbers and formulas and that displays numbers. You'll also create a Spreadsheet object that holds the numbers and formulas and performs all the calculations on them. Users of the application will see and interact with only the ListBox control, but the Spreadsheet object will be doing the heavy lifting in the background.

You'll start by creating the Spreadsheet class. An instance of this class will hold the spreadsheet data in its cells.

You'll give the class three properties: RowCount, ColumnCount, and Cell. The last of these properties will be an array for holding the spreadsheet data.

You'll also give the Spreadsheet class three methods: Spreadsheet (a constructor), Calculate, and Eval. The constructor will initialize the class; the other two methods will deal with making sense of formulas in the spreadsheet cells.

To create the Spreadsheet class:

1. Choose File > New Class.

2. Click the class icon that appears in the Project window.

   The Properties window shows the properties for the new class.

3. Set the Name property to Spreadsheet (**Figure 5.26**).

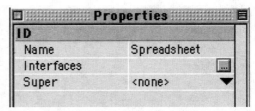

Figure 5.26 Creating the Spreadsheet class.

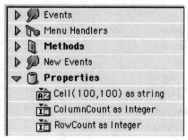

Figure 5.27 Properties of the Spreadsheet class.

To create the properties for the Spreadsheet class:

1. Double-click the Spreadsheet class icon in the Project window.

   The Code Editor for the Spreadsheet class opens.

2. Choose Edit > New Property.

   A property-definition dialog appears.

3. Enter RowCount as Integer.

4. Click OK.

5. Repeat steps 2 to 4 to create two more properties, entering the following in their respective property-definition dialogs:

   ▲ ColumnCount as Integer

   ▲ Cell(100,100) as String

   The RowCount and ColumnCount properties will keep track of the number of rows and columns actually used by the spreadsheet. The Cell property is a string array that will hold the cell data for the spreadsheet (**Figure 5.27**).

To create the methods for the Spreadsheet class:

1. Double-click the Spreadsheet class icon in the Project window.

   The Code Editor for the Spreadsheet class opens.

2. Choose Edit > New Method.

   A method-definition dialog appears.

3. Enter Calculate as the method's name.

4. For parameters, enter Row as Integer and Column as Integer.

5. Click OK.

continues on next page

CREATING A SIMPLE SPREADSHEET

6. Repeat steps 2 to 5 to create two more methods, entering the following in their respective method-definition dialogs:

▲ Name: Eval

▲ Parameters: expression as string

▲ Return type: String

and

▲ Name: Spreadsheet

▲ Parameters: numRows as Integer, numCols as Integer

The Calculate method will deal with the contents of a cell, displaying it if it is a number or, if it is a formula, displaying the result of the formula. Eval actually evaluates the formula. And the Spreadsheet method, because it has the same name as the class it belongs to, is a constructor. In this method, you will place code to initialize a newly created instance of the Spreadsheet class (**Figure 5.28**).

Figure 5.28 Methods of the Spreadsheet class.

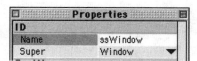

Figure 5.29 Creating the Spreadsheet window.

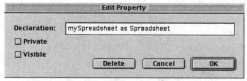

Figure 5.30 The Spreadsheet window has just one new property.

Creating an Instance of the Spreadsheet Class

Now you'll need to write code to create an instance of your Spreadsheet class when the program runs. And you'll want to create a property for that purpose.

To create the Spreadsheet window:

1. Choose File > New Window.

2. Click the new window's icon in the Project window.

3. In the Properties window, enter ssWindow as the name property (**Figure 5.29**).

To create the Spreadsheet window's one new property:

1. Click the new window's icon in the Project window.

2. Press Option-Tab.
   The Code Editor for the window opens.

3. Choose Edit > New Property.
   The property-definition dialog appears.

4. Enter mySpreadsheet as Spreadsheet (**Figure 5.30**).

5. Click OK.

To create an instance of the Spreadsheet class:

1. Click the new window's icon in the Project window.

2. Press Option-Tab.
   The Code Editor for the window opens.

3. In the left pane of the Code Editor, click the disclosure triangle next to Events to expand Events.

4. Click Open to edit the Open event's handler.

5. Enter this code in the right pane:
   mySpreadsheet = new Spreadsheet(20,6)

Using the Spreadsheet Class

When the program creates an instance of the Spreadsheet class, it's creating the object that holds the actual spreadsheet data. But as you're going to define this spreadsheet application, this Spreadsheet object is distinct from the user interface.

You'll create a multicolumn ListBox control to accept and display the spreadsheet data.

To create the ListBox user interface for the spreadsheet application:

1. Click the icon for the ssWindow window in the Project window.

   The window appears.

2. Drag a ListBox control from the Tools palette to the window.

3. If necessary, choose Window > Show Properties to show the Properties window for the ListBox control.

4. Set the control's properties as shown in **Figure 5.31**.

5. Click the Edit button next to the Initial Value property in the Properties window, and enter 13 lines, each consisting of six spaces and tabs, alternating.

   This step will seed the grid with spaces. If you didn't perform this step, you wouldn't be able to see the cells.

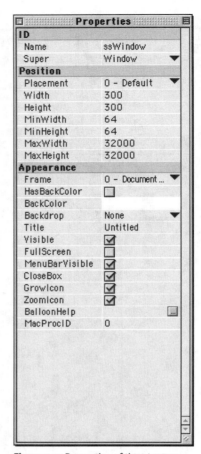

Figure 5.31 Properties of the ListBox.

To code the ListBox:

1. Double-click the ListBox in the window. The Code Editor for the ListBox opens.

2. If necessary, click the disclosure triangle next to Events.

3. Click Open to edit the ListBox's Open event handler.

4. Enter this code in the right pane:

```
dim c as Integer
for c=0 to me.columncount
    me.columnType(c) = 3
next
```

This code sets up the ListBox, making all its cells editable.

5. In the left pane, click CellAction to edit that handler.

6. Enter this code in the right pane.

```
mySpreadsheet.Cell(row,column) =
→ me.Cell(row,column)
mySpreadsheet.calculate(row,column)
```

The CellAction handler of the ListBox executes when a cell action takes place—that is, when the user edits the cell. The code you entered places the ListBox cell's data in the Spreadsheet object and then directs the Spreadsheet object to perform its calculation magic on the data.

Now you need to write the code for the Spreadsheet class.

USING THE SPREADSHEET CLASS

To code the Spreadsheet class:

1. Double-click the Spreadsheet class icon in the Project window.

   The Code Editor for the Spreadsheet class opens.

2. Click the disclosure triangle next to Methods to expand Methods.

3. Click Spreadsheet.

4. Enter this code in the right pane:

```
dim r,c as integer
RowCount = numRows
ColumnCount = numCols
for r=0 to RowCount-1
for c=0 to ColumnCount-1
    Cell(r,c) = ""
    next
next
```

   This constructor initializes the Spreadsheet object, just as the code in the ListBox's Open handler initializes the ListBox (**Figure 5.32**).

5. Click Calculate.

6. Enter this code in the right pane:

```
If left(me.Cell(Row,Column),1) = "="
→ then
    ssWindow.ssGrid.Cell(row,column) =
    → Eval(me.Cell(row,column))
Else
    ssWindow.ssGrid.Cell(row,column) =
    → me.Cell(row,column)
End if
```

   This code checks to see whether the leftmost character in the cell is an = sign. That's the signal that the cell contains a formula, not a number. If the cell contains a number, you'll put it back in the ListBox cell; if it's a formula, you'll call Eval to evaluate the formula and display the result in the ListBox cell.

```
Function Spreadsheet(numRows as integer, numCols as integer)
  dim r,c as integer
  RowCount = numRows
  ColumnCount = numCols
  for r=0 to RowCount-1
    for c=0 to ColumnCount-1
      Cell(r,c) = ""
    next
  next
End Function
```

Figure 5.32 Coding the constructor.

7. Click Eval.

8. Enter this code in the right pane:

```
// Evaluate an expression of the form
// 3,5 + 5,8
/ (the value in cell 3,5 plus the value
→ in cell 5,8)
// and return the result.
// The function will barf if it is passed
→ something other than
// [number],[number] [math operator]
→ [number],[number]

dim expr, lValue, rValue, op as string,
→ i, firstSpace, secondSpace, r, c, LV,
→ RV as integer

// Drop the = sign from the beginning of
→ the expression to be evaluated.
expr = right(expression,
→ len(expression)-1)

// Look for the two spaces that break the
→ expression into three parts.
firstSpace = instr(expr," ")
    if firstSpace > 0 then
secondSpace = firstSpace + instr(mid
→ (expr,firstSpace+1)," ")
    if secondSpace > 0 then

// Interpret the expression as a left
→ value, an operator, and a right value.
    lValue = left(expr,firstSpace-1)
    rValue =mid(expr,secondSpace+1)
    op = mid(expr,firstSpace+1,1)
```

continues on next page

```
// Interpret the left value as a
→ reference to a cell and get the cell's
→ value.
    r = val(left(lValue,instr
    → (lValue,",")-1))
    c =val(mid(lValue,instr
    → (lValue,",")+1))
    LV = val(me.Cell(r,c))


// Interpret the right value as a
→ reference to a cell and get the cell's
→ value.
    r = val(left(rValue,instr
    → (rValue,",")-1))
    c =val(mid(rValue,instr
    → (rValue,",")+1))
    RV = val(me.Cell(r,c))


// Apply the operator to the two values
→ and return the result.
    Select Case op
    Case "+"
        return str(LV + RV)
    Case "-"
        return str(LV - RV)
    Case "*"
        return str(LV * RV)
    Case "/"
        return str(LV \ RV) ' Let the user
        → enter / for division, but
        → perform integer division.
    End select
    end if
end if
return expr
```

Although this code may look daunting, all that's going on here is some text manipulation. Follow the comments to see what the code is doing; then study the code after each comment to see how it does what the comment says it does.

Figure 5.33 This is what you should see when you test the spreadsheet application.

Check the documentation on the left and the mid and instr functions to be sure you understand what each of them does.

The Eval method is perhaps the simplest possible spreadsheet-formula interpreter. It expects to see a formula of the form

= [n1],[n2] [math operator] [n3],[n4]

and it applies the math operator to the data in cells n1,n2 and n3,n4. It can't handle complicated expressions or complicated dependencies among spreadsheet cells. But it is powerful enough to implement a simple spreadsheet with formulas for row and column totals (**Figure 5.33**).

9. Save your work, and test it.

This spreadsheet application isn't usable as it stands. The user interface needs many improvements, and the Eval method doesn't do much. You might practice your REALbasic skills by trying to improve it.

WORKING WITH FILES

One thing that nearly every application needs to be able to do is work with files on disk. Your REALbasic applications will need to read and write text files, play sound or movies, or display pictures stored as files on disk. You might also want an application to manipulate files as you do in the Finder: copying or moving files, deleting or renaming them, emptying the Trash, or even processing entire folders of files. The users of your applications need to be able to choose files to open and operate on, too, so your applications need to display appropriate dialogs for this purpose, process the users' choices, and get the requested files.

This chapter will hone your REALbasic file-handling skills.

Working with File Types

Two key concepts in working with files in REALbasic are:

◆ File types

◆ The FolderItem class

To allow a user to choose a file from an Open File dialog, you need to declare the appropriate file type(s) in your application. Doing so tells REALbasic what types of files it should recognize in the dialog.

To refer to a specific file, you need to create an instance of the FolderItem class. This FolderItem object uniquely identifies the file in your application, and its methods give you ways to do things with the file.

File types

Traditionally, the Macintosh operating system has distinguished files according to two four-character codes stored in the resource fork of each file. The Type code identifies the type of the file, such as text; and the Creator code identifies the application that created the file or that should be used to open it.

REALbasic lets you create files for the traditional Mac operating system, for Mac OS X, and for Windows, but each of these operating systems handles file types differently. The File Types feature of REALbasic is an attempt to free you from having to worry about these differences. REALbasic has many predefined file types, so often, you can select a file type and ignore the details of Type and Creator codes and operating-system differences (**Figure 6.1**).

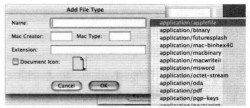

Figure 6.1 REALbasic has many predefined file types that you can use.

Figure 6.2 You use the File Types dialog to let REALbasic know what file types your application needs to deal with.

In several situations, you need to declare a file type:

◆ If your application will present an Open File dialog.

◆ If the application will open files double-clicked on the Desktop or dropped on the application's icon or in its window.

◆ If the application needs to create documents uniquely identified with itself.

Many applications will need to deal with only one of the standard file types, such as plain text.

To enable your application to work with a standard file type:

1. Choose Edit > File Types.
   The File Types dialog appears.

2. Click Add.
   The Add File Type dialog appears.

3. Choose a file type from the pop-up menu.

4. Click OK.

5. In the File Types dialog, click OK (**Figure 6.2**).

If you know the Type and Creator codes for a file type, you can enter them in the Add File Type dialog. You need to do this if you are creating a new file type for documents uniquely identified with your application.

To enable your application to work with a file type for which you know the Creator and Type codes:

1. Choose Edit > File Types.

   The File Types dialog appears.

2. Click Add.

   The Add File Type dialog appears.

3. Enter a name of your choosing, the Mac Creator, and the Mac Type for the file type.

4. Click OK.

5. In the File Types dialog, click OK.

The name that you assign or that is assigned to the file type automatically is the name by which you will refer to it in your code.

To create a new file type for documents uniquely identified with your application:

1. Choose Edit > Project Settings.

   The Project Settings dialog appears.

2. Enter a four-character code that you want to associate with your application.

   If you want to distribute your application, this code needs to be unique and should be registered with Apple, as discussed in Chapter 12, "Being a Programmer." If not, it should not duplicate any Creator code that you can find in the pop-up menu in the Add File Types dialog.

3. Click OK.

4. Choose Edit > File Types.

   The File Types dialog appears.

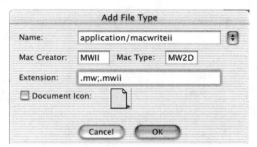

Figure 6.3 You can add your own file types...

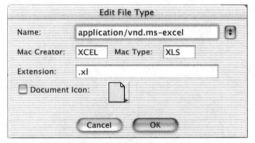

Figure 6.4 ...modify existing file types...

Figure 6.5 ...or delete file types.

5. Click Add.

The Add File Type dialog appears.

6. Enter a name of your choosing, your unique Mac Creator code, and the Mac Type code for the file type (**Figure 6.3**).

7. Click OK.

8. In the File Types dialog, click OK.

To modify an existing file type:

1. Choose Edit > File Types.

The File Types dialog appears.

2. Select a file type in the list of file types known to your application.

3. Click Edit.

The Edit File Type dialog appears.

4. Edit any of the fields (**Figure 6.4**).

5. Click OK.

6. In the File Types dialog, click OK.

To remove a file type from your application:

1. Choose Edit > File Types.

The File Types dialog appears.

2. Select a file type in the list of file types known to your application (**Figure 6.5**).

3. Click Delete.

4. Click OK.

Working with the FolderItem Class

Before you can do anything interesting with a file, such as read or rename it, you need to have a way to refer to it. REALbasic refers to volumes (disks, network servers, or your iDisk), folders, and files (documents and applications) by using objects called FolderItems. That is, *you* use FolderItems in your REALbasic code when you need to refer to a file (or a volume or folder). This section introduces the FolderItem class and describes several ways in which you can use a FolderItem to refer to a file (or folder or volume).

The FolderItem class

The FolderItem class is fully documented in the Language Reference manual. Most of the things that you do with files in REALbasic, you do through the methods and properties of an instance of the FolderItem class.

Some important properties of the FolderItem class are:

- Name. The file's name—for example, myFile.

- AbsolutePath. The file's path—for example, myDisk:myFolder:. A file is fully specified by its path and its name (such as myDisk: myFolder:myFile).

- MacType. The four-character Type code for the file as assigned in an Add File Type dialog.

- MacCreator. The four-character Creator code for the file as assigned in an Add File Type dialog.

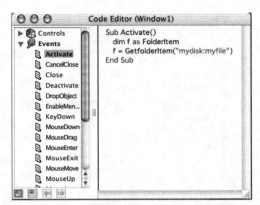

Figure 6.6 Here's how you create an instance of the FolderItem class.

A few representative methods of the FolderItem class are:

◆ **Launch.** Opens the file with the appropriate application if it is a document or launches the file if it is an application.

◆ **Delete.** Deletes the file or folder. A folder can be deleted in this way only if it is empty.

◆ **OpenAsTextFile.** Opens the file as a sequential (text) file.

◆ **CopyFileTo.** Copies the item to the location specified by the FolderItem supplied as a parameter. If the location is a folder, it copies the item to the folder. If the location is an existing file, nothing happens. Otherwise, CopyFileTo creates a copy of the item with the location and name indicated by the parameter.

To create a FolderItem instance that refers to a file in a fixed, known location:

1. Create a variable to hold the FolderItem:

Dim f as FolderItem

2. Use the GetFolderItem method to create the instance (**Figure 6.6**):

f = Getfolderitem("mydisk:myfile")

REALbasic understands Macintosh file aliases, so if the string supplied to the GetFolderItem method identifies an alias to a file (or an alias to an alias to a file), the method returns a reference to the file itself. In the rare event that you actually want to refer to the alias file (perhaps you are cleaning up by deleting unused files), use the GetTrueFolderItem method.

WORKING WITH THE FOLDERITEM CLASS

To create a FolderItem instance that refers to an alias:

1. Create a variable to hold the FolderItem:

Dim f as FolderItem

2. Use the GetFolderItem method to create the instance:

f = GetTrueFolderItem("myDisk:anAlias")

To create a FolderItem instance that refers to a folder in a fixed, known location:

1. Create a variable to hold the FolderItem:

Dim f as FolderItem

2. Use the GetFolderItem method to create the instance:

f = GetFolderItem("myDisk:myFile")

Folders and files are both FolderItems, and references to them are created in exactly the same way.

To create a FolderItem instance that refers to a special folder:

1. Create a variable to hold the FolderItem:

Dim f as FolderItem

2. Use one of the built-in functions for accessing folders, such as the System or Desktop folder (**Figure 6.7**):

f = DesktopFolder

See the Developer's Guide for a list of these functions. Note that many of the special folder names and functions are operating-system-specific and even (in the case of Mac OS 9 vs. Mac OS X) operating-system version-specific.

Figure 6.7 Here's how you access the Desktop folder.

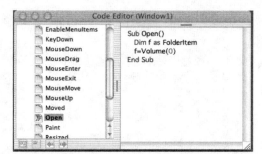

Figure 6.8 Here's how you access the boot disk.

To create a FolderItem instance that refers to the boot volume:

1. Create a variable to hold the FolderItem:

Dim f as FolderItem

2. Use the built-in Volume function (**Figure 6.8**):

f = Volume(0)

Volume(0) always refers to the boot volume.

To create a FolderItem instance that refers to a particular volume:

1. Create a variable to hold the FolderItem:

Dim f as FolderItem

2. Use the GetFolderItem method to create the instance:

f = GetFolderItem("Drive2:)"

Note the colon at the end. Without this colon, REALbasic will interpret this code as a reference to a file or folder named "Drive2".

or

If you know the volume's number, use the Volume function:

f = Volume(2)

To create a FolderItem instance that points to the parent folder of an existing file or folder:

1. Create variables to hold the FolderItems:

Dim f1,f2 as FolderItem

2. Use the GetFolderItem method to create one instance:

f1 = GetFolderItem("myDisk:myFolder: → myFile")

3. Use the Parent property of the FolderItem class to create the other instance:

f2 = f1.parent

f2 now refers to the folder myDisk:myFolder.

To create a FolderItem instance that points to a particular file or folder in an existing folder:

1. Create variables to hold the FolderItems:

   Dim f1,f2 as FolderItem

2. Use the GetFolderItem method to create one instance:

   f1 = GetFolderItem("myDisk:myFolder")

3. Use the Child method of the FolderItem class to create the other instance:

   f2 = f1.child("childFile")

   f2 now refers to the file or folder myDisk:myFolder:childFile (**Figure 6.9**).

You can rename and move files and folders easily enough in the Finder by typing and dragging. But REALbasic gives you the ability to automate the process, operating on a whole folder of files at a time.

To access every item (file or folder) in a folder:

1. Create variables to hold the FolderItems and a counter:

   Dim f,fi as FolderItem

   Dim i as integer

2. Use the Item method and Count property of the FolderItem class to loop through all the items in the folder (**Figure 6.10**):

   for i=1 to f.count

       fi = f.item(i)

       // do something with the item

   next i

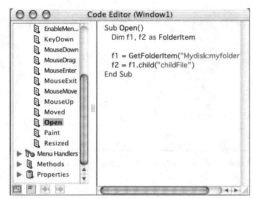

Figure 6.9 The Child method is useful for accessing a file within a folder.

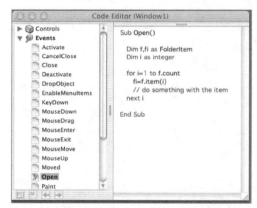

Figure 6.10 Here's how to loop through all the files in a folder.

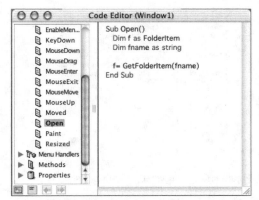

Figure 6.11 Usually, you don't know the name of a file until the program is running, so you'll use a variable to refer to it.

More often than not, your application will learn the name of a file only at run time, typically from a user response to a file dialog. In this case, you will need to store the filename in a variable or property.

To create a FolderItem instance that refers to a file whose name will be known at run time:

1. Create a variable to hold the FolderItem and one for the name of the file:

   ```
   Dim f as FolderItem
   Dim fName as string
   ```

2. Get the filename somehow, as through user input, and store it in a variable (or in a property).

3. Use the GetFolderItem method with the filename variable (or property) to create the instance (**Figure 6.11**):

   ```
   f = GetFolderItem(fname)
   ```

Working with Files and Folders

The reason to get a FolderItem instance is to have a way to refer to a file. That file, however, need not exist. You sometimes get a FolderItem instance to *create* a file. This section shows you some of the other things you can do with a file when you have a FolderItem with which to refer to it.

To determine whether a file path is valid:

◆ Test it against the value nil:

```
dim f as folderItem
dim b as boolean
f = getFolderItem("myDisk:myFile")
b = (f <> nil)
// The boolean b tests whether the
→ FolderItem is NOT nil, meaning that
→ it IS a valid file reference.
```

To determine whether a file exists:

◆ Test it by using the FolderItem method exists (**Figure 6.12**):

```
dim f as folderItem
dim b as boolean
f = getFolderItem("myDisk:myFile")
b = f.exists
// The boolean b tests if the FolderItem
→ points to a file or folder that exists.
```

✔ Tip

■ It is dangerous to mess around with files without knowing exactly what you are doing. Techniques in this section are capable of deleting important files. With great power comes great responsibility.

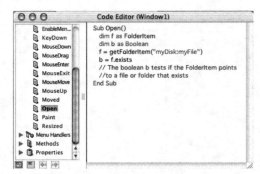

Figure 6.12 Testing whether a file exists.

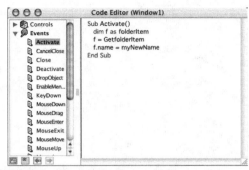

Figure 6.13 Here's how to rename a file.

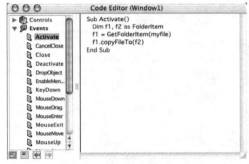

Figure 6.14 Here's how to copy a file.

Figure 6.15 Here's how to move a file.

To rename a file:

◆ Use the `Name` property of the `FolderItem` class (**Figure 6.13**):

```
dim f as folderItem
f = GetFolderItem(myFile)
f.name = myNewName
```

In Windows, you must close the file before renaming it.

To delete a file:

◆ Use the `Delete` method of the `FolderItem` class:

```
dim f as folderItem
f = GetFolderItem(myFile)
f.delete
```

This method removes the file or folder. If the `FileItem` refers to a folder, the folder can be deleted only if it is empty.

To copy a file:

◆ Use the `CopyFileTo` method of the `FolderItem` class (**Figure 6.14**):

```
dim f1,f2 as folderItem
f1 = GetFolderItem(myFile)
f1.CopyFileTo(f2)
```

This method copies the file referenced by f1 to the folder referenced by f2. If f2 refers to an existing file, nothing happens. If f2 doesn't refer to an existing file or folder, a new file is created at the location it references.

To move a file:

◆ Use the `MoveFileTo` method of the `FolderItem` class (**Figure 6.15**):

```
dim f1,f2 as folderItem
f1 = GetFolderItem(myFile)
f1.MoveFileTo(f2))
```

This method moves the file referenced by f1 to the location referenced by f2.

To create a text file:

◆ Use the `CreateTextFile` method of the `FolderItem` class:

```
dim f as folderItem
dim s as textOutputStream
f = getFolderItem("myNewFile")
s = f.CreateTextFile
```

This method creates a text file at the location specified by the `FolderItem` and returns a `TextOutputStream` object.

The `TextOutputStream` class is discussed in "Working with Sequential Files" later in this chapter.

To launch a file:

◆ Use the `Launch` property of the `FolderItem` class:

```
dim f as folderItem
f = GetFolderItem(myFile)
f.launch
```

This method launches `myFile` if it is an application or opens it with the appropriate application if it is a document.

To create a folder:

◆ Use the `CreateAsFolder` method of the `FolderItem` class:

```
dim f as folderItem
f = getFolderItem("myFolder")
f.CreateAsFolder
```

This method creates a folder at the location specified by the `FolderItem`.

To tell a file from a folder:

◆ Use the `Directory` property of the `FolderItem` class:

```
dim f as folderItem
dim IsFolder as Boolean
f = GetFolderItem(myFile)
IsFolder = f.directory
```

The `Directory` property is `true` if the `FolderItem` is a folder (in Windows, a directory).

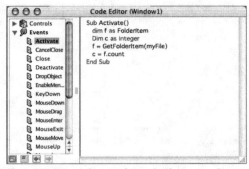

Figure 6.16 Here's how to determine how many items are in a folder.

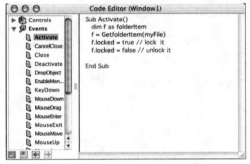

Figure 6.17 Here's how to lock or unlock a file.

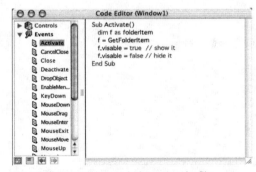

Figure 6.18 Here's how to hide or reveal a file.

To determine how many items are in a folder:

◆ Use the `Count` property of the `FolderItem` class (**Figure 6.16**):

```
dim f as folderItem
dim c as integer
f = GetFolderItem(myFile)
c = f.count
```

To test whether a file is locked:

◆ Use the `Locked` property of the `FolderItem` class:

```
dim f as folderItem
f = GetFolderItem(myFile)
if f.locked then
    // [do something]
end if
```

The `Locked` property returns `true` if a file is locked or if it resides on a locked volume.

To lock or unlock a file:

◆ Set the `Locked` property of the `FolderItem` class (**Figure 6.17**):

```
dim f as folderItem
f = GetFolderItem(myFile)
f.locked = true // lock it
f.locked = false // unlock it
```

To hide or reveal a file:

◆ Set the `Visible` property of the `FolderItem` class (**Figure 6.18**):

```
dim f as folderItem
f = GetFolderItem(myFile)
f.visible = true // show it
f.visible = false // hide it
```

WORKING WITH FILES AND FOLDERS

To determine the creation or modification date of a file:

◆ Use the CreationDate or
ModificationDate property of the
FolderItem class (**Figure 6.19**):

dim f as folderItem

dim d as date

f = GetFolderItem(myFile)

d = f.creationDate // or modificationDate

Each of these properties is of type date, so
you need a variable of that type to hold it.

To determine the size of a file:

◆ Use the Length property of the
FolderItem class:

dim f as FolderItem

dim l as Integer

f = GetFolderItem(myFile)

l = f.Length

Note that this method does *not* necessarily tell you the number of bytes that the file takes up on disk. The Length property gives only the length of the file's data fork. On Mac systems, a file's resource fork can also be substantial. The FolderItem class also has a ResourceForkLength property that tells you how much space the resource fork takes up.

Length contains 0 for a folder.

To get the pathname of a file:

◆ Use the AbsolutePath property of the
FolderItem class (**Figure 6.20**):

dim f as folderItem

dim myPath as string

f = GetFolderItem(myFile)

myPath = f.absolutePath

This method returns the path to the
FolderItem (not including its name). On
the Macintosh platform, it ends with a
colon; in Windows, there is no trailing
separator.

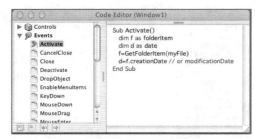

Figure 6.19 Here's how to determine the creation or modification date of a file.

Figure 6.20 Here's how to get the pathname of a file.

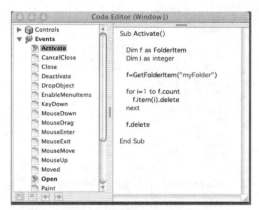

Figure 6.21 Here's how to delete all the files in a folder.

Figure 6.22 Here's how to rename all the files in a folder.

To get the file path to your application:

◆ Use the `AbsolutePath` property.

The `GetFolderItem` function defaults to the folder in which your application resides:

```
dim f as folderItem
dim myPath as string
f = GetFolderItem("")
myPath = f.absolutePath
msgBox myPath
```

To delete a folder and all the files in it:

1. Create variables to refer to the folder and a counter:

   ```
   Dim f as FolderItem
   Dim i as integer
   ```

2. Get a reference to the folder.

   ```
   f = GetFolderItem("myFolder")
   ```

3. Loop through the folder's items, using the `Item` method of the `FolderItem` class (**Figure 6.21**):

   ```
   for i=1 to f.count
       f.item(i).delete
   next
   f.delete
   ```

In this same way, you can do many other things to all the files in a folder, such as rename them.

To rename all files in a folder:

1. Create variables to refer to the folder and a counter:

   ```
   Dim f as FolderItem
   Dim i as integer
   ```

2. Get a reference to the folder:

   ```
   f = GetFolderItem("myFolder")
   ```

3. Loop through the folder's items, using the `Item` method of the `FolderItem` class as shown in **Figure 6.22**.

WORKING WITH FILES AND FOLDERS

Handling File Dialogs

So your made-with-REALbasic applications can manipulate files faster than a Brazilian football forward buzzed on the national beverage, but that's not the whole story. They also need to let your users select files to manipulate. Even if you are the only user of your applications, frequently—perhaps typically—you won't know the name or location of a file that your application needs at the time you write the application. Your applications need to have the capability to present dialogs that allow the user to select files.

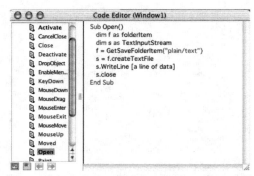

Figure 6.23 Displaying the Open File dialog for the user.

To allow the user to select a file to open:

1. Create a variable to refer to the file:

```
dim f as FolderItem
```

2. Use the GetOpenFolderItem function to present the Open File dialog:

```
f = GetOpenFolderItem(filter)
```

filter is a list of acceptable file types. When the program runs, this call to GetOpenFolderItem will cause the Open File dialog to appear. When the user closes the dialog, GetOpenFolderItem will return a FolderItem referring to the selected file or nil if the user clicked Cancel in the dialog. The assignment statement ensures that the variable f will contain this FolderItem (or perhaps nil).

3. If f now refers to something other than nil, open it:

```
f.openAsText
```

This code assumes that the file is a text file. Other possibilities, described later in this chapter, include QuickTime movie files, sound files, picture files, and binary files (**Figure 6.23**).

If the standard Open File dialog presented by the `GetOpenFolderItem` function is too restrictive, you can create your own custom dialog by using the `OpenDialog` class.

To present a custom file-opening dialog to the user:

1. Create variables to refer to the `FolderItem` and dialog:

   ```
   dim f as folderItem
   dim dlg as OpenDialog
   ```

2. Create the dialog:

   ```
   dlg = new OpenDialog
   ```

3. Set its properties as you want:

   ```
   dlg.Title = "What File?"
   ```

   See the `OpenDialog` class in the Language Reference manual for the full list of settable properties.

4. Show the dialog:

   ```
   f = dlg.ShowModal()
   ```

   `ShowModal` is the `OpenDialog` class's only method for displaying an instance of itself to the user. When the user responds to the dialog, f will contain the result—a reference to the selected file or `nil` if no file was selected.

HANDLING FILE DIALOGS

To allow the user to select a folder:

1. Create a variable to refer to the file:

```
dim f as FolderItem
```

2. Use the SelectFolder function to present the Open Folder dialog:

```
f = SelectFolder()
```

When the program runs, this call to SelectFolder will cause the Open Folder dialog to appear. When the user closes the dialog, SelectFolder will return a FolderItem referring to the selected folder or nil if the user clicked Cancel in the dialog. The assignment statement ensures that the variable f will contain this FolderItem (or perhaps nil).

3. If f now refers to something other than nil, do with it what you will (**Figure 6.24**).

To present a custom folder-opening dialog to the user:

1. Create variables to refer to the FolderItem and dialog:

```
dim f as folderItem
dim dlg as OpenDialog
```

2. Create the dialog:

```
dlg = new SelectFolderDialog
```

3. Set its properties as you want:

```
dlg.Title = "What File?"
```

See the SelectFolderDialog class in the Language Reference manual for the full list of settable properties.

4. Show the dialog:

```
f = dlg.ShowModal()
```

ShowModal is the SelectFolderDialog class's only method for displaying an instance of itself to the user. When the user responds to the dialog, f will contain the result—a reference to the selected folder or nil if no folder was selected.

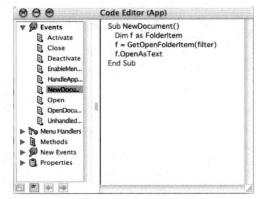

Figure 6.24 Displaying the Open Folder dialog for the user.

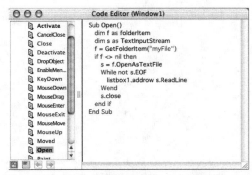

Figure 6.25 Displaying the Save As dialog for the user.

To allow the user to choose where to save a file:

1. Create a variable to refer to the file:

   `dim f as FolderItem`

2. Use the `GetSaveFolderItem` function to present the Save As dialog (**Figure 6.25**):

   `f = GetSaveFolderItem(filter)`

   `filter` is the single appropriate file type. When you offer the user the chance to save some data, you presumably have some particular data in mind, so only one file type will be appropriate for it.

   When the program runs, this call to `GetSaveFolderItem` will cause the Save As dialog to appear. When the user closes the dialog, `GetSaveFolderItem` will return a `FolderItem` referring to the selected file or `nil` if the user clicked Cancel in the dialog. The assignment statement ensures that the variable `f` will contain this `FolderItem` (or perhaps `nil`).

3. If `f` now refers to something other than `nil`, save to it.

   Exactly what you need to do to respond to the user's selection of a file depends on what you had in mind when you offered her that option. A typical case would be writing the contents of an `EditField` to the file, discussed later in this chapter.

✔ Tip

■ If a specified file does not exist, a folderItem function will return a value of nil rather than the desired folderItem. Failing to test for nil is probably the most common programming error REALbasic users make. Always test for nil like this:

   `f = [some folderItem function]`

   `if f = nil then [use the folderItem]`

   `else [tell user it was not found]`

   `End if`

To present a custom file-save dialog:

1. Create variables to refer to the FolderItem and dialog:

```
dim f as folderItem
dim dlg as OpenDialog
```

2. Create the dialog:

```
dlg = new SaveAsDialog
```

3. Set its properties as you choose:

```
dlg.Title = "What File?"
```

See the SaveAsDialog class in the Language Reference manual for the full list of settable properties.

4. Show the dialog:

```
f = dlg.ShowModal()
```

ShowModal is the SaveAsDialog class's only method for displaying an instance of itself to the user. When the user responds to the dialog, f will contain the result—a reference to the selected file or nil if no file was selected.

Implicit file opening

If your application creates and works with files of a custom type unique to your application, you can add capability that allows a user to launch your application by double-clicking one of these files or by dragging and dropping such a file on your application's icon in the Finder. In fact, you can enable your application to be launched by the user's dragging *any* file onto its Finder icon.

To allow the user to launch your application by dropping a file on it:

1. Choose Edit > Project Settings.
The Project Settings dialog appears.

2. Enter a unique four-character code that you want to associate with your application.

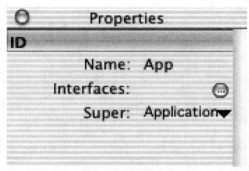

Figure 6.26 Choosing Application from the new class's Super pop-up menu.

3. Click OK.

4. Choose Edit > File Types.
The File Types dialog appears.

5. Click Add.
The Add File Type dialog appears.

6. Enter a name of your choosing, your unique Mac Creator code, and the Mac Type code for the file type.

7. Check the Document Icon check box.

8. Click OK.

9. In the File Types dialog, click OK.

10. If your project doesn't already have an App class, choose File > New Class.

11. In the Properties window for the new class, type App as the name, and choose Application from the Super pop-up menu (**Figure 6.26**).
Now when the user drops a document of the specified type on your application's icon, the application will launch, and the App class will receive the OpenDocument event.

12. Open the Code Editor for the App class, and place the code that opens the file in the OpenDocument event handler.

To allow the user to launch your application by double-clicking a document on the Desktop

◆ See "To allow the user to launch your application by dropping a file on it" on page 206.

The procedure is identical. Only the user's action is different.

Another kind of implicit file opening often occurs when an application is launched in the usual way. If your application is document-centric, it probably should create a new default document when it is launched.

To create a default document when your application launches:

1. If your project doesn't already have an App class, choose File > New Class.

2. In the Properties window for the new class, type App as the name, and choose Application from the Super pop-up menu.

3. Place the code that actually opens the file in the App class's NewDocument handler (**Figure 6.27**).

   Note: That's the NewDocument event handler—not, as with the other forms of implicit file opening, the OpenDocument event handler. When an application that has a class based on the Application class is launched without a document's being opened, REALbasic causes the NewDocument event of that class to execute. Placing your document-creating code there ensures that a new document will be created when your application is launched.

Now you know how to manipulate files and to present file dialogs to the user. But the process of actually reading and writing data to files depends on the type of data and the type of files involved. The remaining sections of this chapter deal with how to read and write data to various types of files.

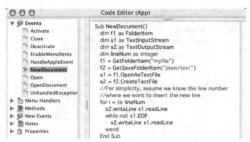

Figure 6.27 Placing this code in the App class's NewDocument handler ensures that the application will create a new default document when it is launched.

Working with Sequential Files

The REALbasic documentation refers to sequential files as text files, but they can contain any kind of data consisting of a sequence of characters, including text documents, tab-delimited spreadsheet and database files, and many other kinds of files. The defining feature of these files is that they are read and written sequentially. You can get to the 1,000th character only by passing over the first 999. REALbasic provides several methods and classes for dealing with sequential files.

Text streams

REALbasic provides the `TextInputStream` and `TextOutputStream` classes as an object-oriented way to deal with the process of reading and writing to sequential files. The `TextInputStream` and `TextOutputStream` objects that you create in reading and writing to sequential files are distinct from the `FolderItems` that you create to refer to the files themselves. Think of the `TextInputStream` and `TextOutputStream` objects as being pipes through which the data will flow.

To read a sequential file one line at a time:

1. Create variables to refer to the `FolderItem` and `TextInputStream` objects:

   ```
   dim f as FolderItem
   dim s as TextInputStream
   ```

2. Get a `FolderItem` object:

   ```
   f = GetFolderItem("myFile")
   ```

continues on next page

3. Use a `TextInputStream` object and its `EOF`
(end of file) property to read data into a
`ListBox`, for example (**Figure 6.28**):

```
if f <> nil then
    s = f.OpenTextFile
    While not s.EOF
        listbox1.addrow s.readline
    Wend
    s.close
End if
```

The key line is

`s = f.OpenTextFile.`

The `FolderItem` class's `OpenTextFile`
method opens the file and returns a
`TextInputStream` object to use in reading
from it.

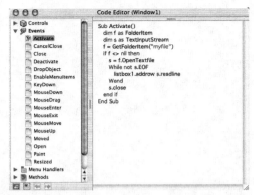

Figure 6.28 Here's how to read a sequential file one line at a time.

To read a sequential file in one gulp:

1. Create variables to refer to the
`FolderItem` and `TextInputStream` objects:

```
dim f as FolderItem
dim s as TextInputStream
```

2. Get a `FolderItem` object:

```
f = GetFolderItem(myFile)
```

3. Use a `TextInputStream` object and its
`ReadAll` method to read all the data in
the file:

```
if f <> nil then
...s = f.OpenTextFile
    EditField1.text = s.ReadAll
End if
```

The `ReadAll` method reads the entire file,
which can be a lot of data, so be sure that
you have some place to put it. This
example loads the file directly into an
`EditField` without first storing it in a
variable, which would eat up a lot of
memory.

The next example shows how to read tab-delimited data into a `ListBox`. It assumes the existence of a `ListBox` called `ListBox1` and a file of data in which return characters separate rows and tab characters separate cells within the rows.

To read tabular data:

1. Create variables to hold a `FolderItem` and `TextInputStream`, as well as variables to hold one row and one cell of data, plus a counter variable:

```
dim f as FolderItem
dim s as TextInputStream
dim rowData, cellData as string
dim i as integer
```

2. Get a `FolderItem` object:

```
f = GetFolderItem("text/plain")
```

3. Open the file, and get a `TextInputStream` object:

```
s = f.OpenAsTextFile
```

4. Read one line from the file, which represents one row of data:

```
rowData = s.ReadLine
```

5. Make sure that the `ListBox` has enough columns to accommodate the cells in this row:

```
if ListBox1.ColumnCount < CountFields
→ (rowData,Chr(9)) then
    ListBox.ColumnCount = CountFields
    → (rowData,Chr(9))
End if
```

continues on next page

6. Add the row of data to the ListBox:

```
// add the first cell ListBox1.AddRow
→ NthField(rowData,Chr(9),1)
// add the rest of the cells
For i = 1 to CountFields(rowData,Chr(9))
    cellData = NthField(rowData,
    → Chr(9),i)
    ListBox1.Cell(ListBox1.ListCount-1,
    → i-1) = cellData
next
```

7. Wrap most of this code in a Do...Loop structure to repeat the process for all rows, and use the TextInputStream class's EOF property to determine when you've read all the data:

```
Do
    // add the first cell
    ListBox1.AddRow NthField(rowData,
    → Chr(9),1)
    // add the rest of the cells
    For i = 1 to
CountFields(rowData,Chr(9))
        cellData = NthField(rowData,
        → Chr(9),i)
        ListBox1.Cell(ListBox1.
        → ListCount-1,i-1) = cellData
    next
Loop until s.EOF
```

8. Close the file:

```
s.Close
```

9. Make sure that the `FolderItem` refers to a real file by wrapping most of the code in an `If` structure:

```
dim f as FolderItem
dim s as TextInputStream
dim rowData, cellData as string
dim i as integer
if f <> nil then
    Do
        // add the first cell
    ListBox1.AddRow NthField(rowData,
    → Chr(9),1)
        // add the rest of the cells
        For i = 1 to CountFields(rowData,
        → Chr(9))
            cellData = NthField(rowData,
            → Chr(9),i)
            ListBox1.Cell(ListBox1.
            → ListCount-1,i-1) = cellData
        next
    Loop until s.EOF
End if
```

Two functions in this code are unfamiliar: `CountFields` and `NthField`. These functions do what their names indicate: `CountFields` returns a count of the number of fields in a string of data, in which fields are separated by a specified delimiter character. `NthField` returns the contents of the `Nth` field and expects to be given a string, a delimiter character, and the number of the field that you seek.

To write to a sequential file one line at a time:

1. Create variables to refer to the FolderItem and TextOutputStream objects:

   dim f as FolderItem

   dim s as TextInputStream

2. Get a FolderItem object:

   f = GetSaveFolderItem("plain/text", → "whatever")

3. Use a TextOutputStream object and its WriteLine method to write the data (**Figure 6.29**):

   s = f.CreateTextFile

   s.WriteLine [a line of data]

   s.close

To write an arbitrary chunk of data to a sequential file:

1. Create variables to refer to the FolderItem and TextOutputStream objects:

   dim f as FolderItem

   dim s as TextInputStream

2. Get a FolderItem object:

   f = GetSaveFolderItem("plain/text", → "whatever")

3. Use a TextOutputStream object and its Write method to write the data:

   s = f.CreateTextFile

   s.Write [a chunk of data]

   s.close

The WriteLine and Write methods differ only in that the WriteLine method appends a return character to the data written. Technically, WriteLine appends a delimiter, which by default is a return character but can be anything you want to use.

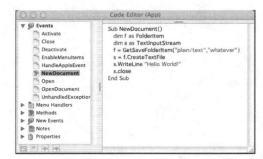

Figure 6.29 Here's how to write lines to a sequential file.

Figure 6.30 Here's how to insert a line into the middle of a sequential file.

To change the delimiter character for a sequential file:

◆ Set the `delimiter` property of its TextOutputStream object:

`theStream.delimiter = chr(9)`

The delimiter is not a fixed property of the file but of aTextOutputStream associated with it. Different delimiters can be used with the same file on different occasions.

To insert a line into the middle of a sequential file:

1. Create variables to refer to the FolderItems and TextInputStream and TextOutputStream objects, as well as a counter variable:

   ```
   dim f1, f2 as FolderItem
   dim s1 as TextInputStream
   dim s2 as TextOutputStream
   dim lineNum as integer
   ```

2. Read each line of the file until you reach the spot where you want to insert the line, writing the line to a scratch file:

   ```
   f1 = GetFolderItem(myFile)
   f2 = GetSaveFolderItem("plain/text",
   → "whatever")
   s1 = f1.OpenAsTextFile
   s2 = f2.CreateTextFile
   // Assuming that lineNum is a global
   → property
   For i = 1 to lineNum
       s2.WriteLine s1.ReadLine
   Next
   ```

3. Write the line you want to insert:

   ```
   // Assuming that the LineToInsert is
   → a globalproperty
   s2.WriteLine theLineToInsert
   ```

4. Write the rest of the lines, and rename the files (**Figure 6.30**):

   ```
   While not s1.EOF
       s2.WriteLine s1.ReadLine
   next
   ```

WORKING WITH SEQUENTIAL FILES

215

Styled text files

REALbasic has different means for dealing with styled text files, such as are produced by TextEdit or any word processor—or, for that matter, by a REALbasic application.

To read styled text from a file:

◆ Use the `OpenStyledEditField` method of the `FolderItem` class (**Figure 6.31**):

```
dim f as FolderItem
f = GetFolderItem("Styled Text Files")
If f <> nil then
    f.OpenStyledEditField myEditField
end if
```

You must have an `EditField` in which to place the styled text, and its `Styled` property must be `true`.

To write styled text to a file:

◆ Use the `SaveStyledEditField` method of the `FolderItem` class (**Figure 6.32**):

```
dim f as FolderItem
f = GetSaveFolderItem("plain/text",
→ "Untitled")
If f <> nil then
    f.SaveStyledEditField myEditField
end if
```

You must have an `EditField` from which to get the styled text, and its `Styled` property must be `true`.

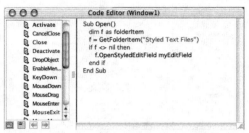

Figure 6.31 Here's the special technique for reading styled text from a file.

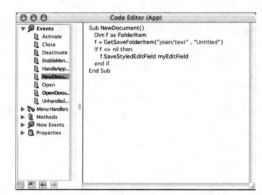

Figure 6.32 And here's how you write styled text to a file.

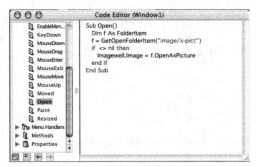

Figure 6.33 This code opens a picture file and displays the picture by using an `ImageWell` control.

Working with Picture, Sound, and Media Files

Sometimes, the data that you want your application to deal with is not in the form of simple sequences of characters but is in some more elaborate format. Pictures, sounds, and QuickTime movies are examples of file formats that need special handling. REALbasic supplies tools for dealing with such structured data.

Picture files

REALbasic understands the PICT file type and can read and write PICT files. It also provides some support for other picture-file types, such as JPEG.

To read a picture from a file:

1. Create a place to hold the picture in your application (in a `Canvas` or `ImageWell` control, for example).

2. Use the `OpenAsPicture` method of the `FolderItem` class (**Figure 6.33**):

```
dim f as folderItem
f = GetOpenFolderItem("image/x-pict")
if f <> nil then
    ImageWell.Image = f.OpenAsPicture
end if
```

To save a picture to a file:

◆ Assuming that your picture is in the backdrop property of a `Canvas` control named `Canvas1`, use the `FolderItem` class's `SaveAsPicture` method:

```
dim f as folderItem
f = GetSaveFolderItem("image/x-pict",
→ "Untitled"
if f <> nil then
    f.SaveAsPicture Canvas1.backdrop
end if
```

To save a picture in a different format:

◆ Follow the procedure in "To save a picture to a file" earlier in this chapter, but change the file type in the call to GetSaveFolderItem (**Figure 6.34**):

```
dim f as folderItem
f = GetSaveFolderItem("image/jpeg",
→ "untitled"
if f <> nil then
    f.SaveAsPicture Canvas1.backdrop
end if
```

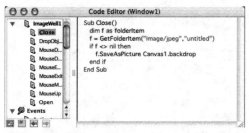

Figure 6.34 Here's how you save a picture as a JPEG file.

You'll find more information on working with pictures and graphics in Chapter 7.

Sound files

REALbasic lets you read sounds into your application, but you can't create or write to a sound file. Supported sound files are those whose Kind field in the file's Get Info dialog (in the Classic Mac OS) is Sound. These files are Macintosh System 7 sounds. In Windows, MP3, MIDI, and MPEG are supported. You can also import sounds into your application by dragging the sound file's icon into your Project window. In addition, a sound can be part (or all) of a movie; see "Movie files" later in this chapter.

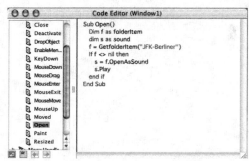

Figure 6.35 This code reads a sound from a file and plays it.

To read a sound from a file:

1. Create variables to hold the FolderItem and the sound:

```
dim f as folderItem
dim s as sound
```

2. Read the sound, using the OpenAsSound method of the FolderItem class (**Figure 6.35**):

```
f = GetFolderItem("JFK-Berliner")
if f <> nil then
    s = f.OpenAsSound
    s.Play
end if
```

You'll find more information on working with sounds in Chapter 8.

Figure 6.36 This code reads a QuickTime movie from a file and uses the MoviePlayer control to play it.

Movie files

REALbasic lets you read movies into your applications from files, but you can't write movies to files. You can also get a movie into your application by dragging the movie file's icon to your project folder. The supported movie type is QuickTime.

To read a movie from a file:

1. Create variables to hold the FolderItem and the movie:

   ```
   dim f as folderItem
   dim m as movie
   ```

2. Read the movie, using the OpenAsMovie method of the FolderItem class, and play it, using a MoviePlayer control (**Figure 6.36**):

   ```
   f = GetFolderItem("Madonna")
   if f <> nil then
       m = f.OpenAsMovie
       MoviePlayer1.movie = m
       MoviePlayer1.Play
   end if
   ```

You'll find more information on working with movies in Chapter 8, "Working with Animations and Movies."

WORKING WITH PICTURE, SOUND, AND MEDIA FILES

Working with Binary Files

Binary files are the most general case of file encoding. No assumption is made about the structure of the data, which can be accessed at any position. REALbasic provides several classes and methods for reading a chunk of data from a binary file and interpreting it either as a number or as an arbitrary string of characters.

Binary streams

Like the TextInputStream and TextOutputStream classes, the BinaryStream class provides an object-oriented way to deal with the process of reading and writing to files. Unlike their sequential stream analogs, BinaryStreams come in only one flavor; you use the same object for input or output. The BinaryStream objects that you create in reading and writing to binary files are distinct from the FolderItems that you create to refer to the files themselves. Think of the BinaryStream objects as being pipes through which the data will flow.

To read from a binary file:

1. Create variables to hold the FolderItem and BinaryStream objects:

    dim f as FolderItem

    dim s as BinaryStream

2. Read the file, using the OpenAsBinaryFile method of the FolderItem class and the EOF property of the BinaryStream class (**Figure 6.37**):

    f = GetFolderItem("myFile")

    if f <> nil then

        s = f.OpenAsBinaryFile(false)

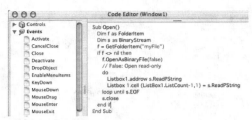

Figure 6.37 Here's how to read from a binary file...

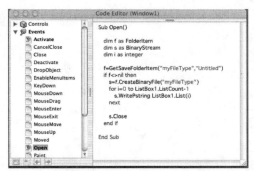

Figure 6.38 ...and how to write to a binary file.

```
// false: open read-only
    do
        Listbox1.addrow s.ReadPstring
        Listbox1.cell(ListBox1.
        → ListCount-1,1) = s.ReadPstring
    loop until s.EOF
    s.close
end if
```

To write to a binary file:

1. Create variables to hold the FolderItem and BinaryStream objects, plus a counter:
   ```
   dim f as FolderItem
   dim s as BinaryStream
   dim i as integer
   ```

2. Write the file, using the CreateBinaryFile method of the FolderItem class (**Figure 6.38**):
   ```
   f = GetSaveFolderItem("myFileType",
   → "Untitled")
   if f <> nil then
       s = f.CreateBinaryFile("myFileType")
       for i = 0 to ListBox1.ListCount-1
           s.WritePstring ListBox1.List(i)
       next
       s.Close
   end if
   ```

Binary files are especially efficient for storing numeric data.

To read or write numeric data from or to a binary file:

◆ Use any of the `BinaryStream` class's numeric methods.

ReadShort, ReadLong, WriteShort, and WriteLong handle integers; ReadSingle, ReadDouble, WriteSingle, and WriteDouble deal with floating-point singles and doubles.

Now you know the basics of manipulating files in REALbasic and of moving data between files and your application. You also see the centrality of the `FolderItem` class to this process; most of the methods used to read or write data are methods of the `FolderItem` class. You will often find the answer to a question about how to read or write files in the documentation for that class.

Having learned how to get data into your application, it's time to see how to do something interesting with that data. In the next chapter, you'll learn how to work with picture and graphics data in your REALbasic applications.

WORKING WITH PICTURES

This chapter is all about pictures and graphics. For many programmers, this is The Good Stuff. Your REALbasic applications can be colorful and richly endowed with graphical pizzazz. REALbasic has many tools and techniques for adding graphical flair to your programs, from displaying pictures to creating new drawings with REALbasic code.

In this chapter, you'll learn how to exploit REALbasic's graphics capabilities, and you'll write a complete graphics application called TurtleDraw.

Creating Graphics with Graphical Controls

The REALbasic Tools palette has several graphics-savvy controls that you can use to create simple graphics by doing little more than dragging them into your application's window. Although these controls are not intended for creating complex graphical objects or graphical effects such as drop shadows, masking, and transparency, other tools (discussed later in this chapter) are designed for these things; you can do more with them than it might appear at first. These controls (**Figure 7.1**) include:

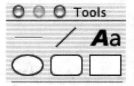

Figure 7.1 Several of the Controls in REALbasic's Tools palette are graphical objects that you can use to construct simple pictures.

◆ The Line control

◆ The Oval control

◆ The Rectangle control

◆ The RoundRectangle control

◆ The ImageWell control

Each of these controls inherits all the properties, methods, and events of the Control class, including:

◆ The MouseX and MouseY properties, which are the coordinates of the mouse within the window.

◆ The AcceptPictureDrop and NewDragItem methods and the DropObject event, which allow a picture to be dropped on any control and some action to be taken as a result.

All of them except the Line control are also based on the RectControl class and inherit all its properties, methods, and events, including the Top, Left, Height, and Width and the LockTop, LockLeft, LockBottom, and LockRight properties, which define the control's location and size, and the MouseEnter, MouseExit, and MouseMove events, which recognize and let you deal with mouse actions within the perimeter of the control.

Figure 7.2 The Line control.

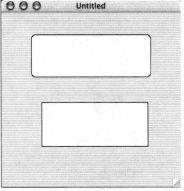

Figure 7.3 The RoundRectangle and Rectangle controls.

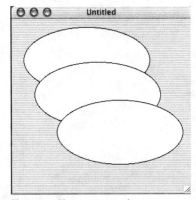

Figure 7.4 The Oval control.

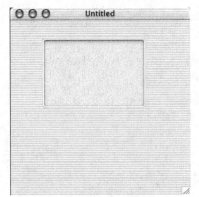

Figure 7.5 The ImageWell is a simple picture-display tool.

Each of these controls has its own unique properties, methods, and events as well.

The Line control draws a line (**Figure 7.2**). You can specify the line's color, its thickness, and its starting and ending points. You can also make a line invisible.

The Rectangle and RoundRectangle controls draw rectangles with right-angled or rounded corners, respectively (**Figure 7.3**). You can specify the border thickness and the color of the interior. For the Rectangle control, the TopLeftColor and BottomRightColor properties let you give the button a 3D look, and the RoundRectangle control lets you specify the curvature of the corners.

The Oval control draws an oval or circle (**Figure 7.4**). You can set its border color and width and its interior color.

The ImageWell control has only one property: Image. It displays a picture (**Figure 7.5**).

CREATING GRAPHICS WITH GRAPHICAL CONTROLS

To produce a drop shadow with the Rectangle control:

1. In the IDE, drag a ListBox (or any control to which you want to add a drop shadow) from the Tools palette to the window.

2. Drag a Rectangle control to the window. This control will be your drop shadow— a gray rectangle behind and offset slightly from the ListBox.

3. In the Rectangle control's Properties window, set its Height and Width properties to those of the ListBox.

4. Set the control's Left and Top properties to 4 more than the Left and Top properties of the ListBox to offset its position.

5. Set its BorderWidth property to 0. (Shadows don't have borders.)

6. Set its FillColor property to a medium gray.

7. Click the Rectangle control in the window.

8. Choose Format > Move to Back. The rectangle now has a drop shadow like the one in **Figure 7.6**.

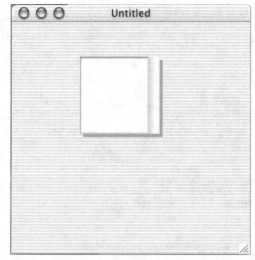

Figure 7.6 Using the Rectangle control to produce a drop shadow.

Creating graphics with the basic graphical controls is fairly limiting; you can draw ovals with these controls but not curves, for example. Sometimes, though, you can work around the limitations.

To use one graphical object to mask part of another:

1. Drag an Oval control from the Tools palette to the window.

2. In its Properties window, set the control's properties as follows:

Left: 64   Height: 132

Top: 62   BorderWidth: 2

Width: 132   BorderColor: gray

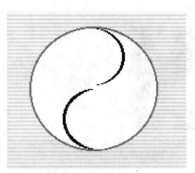

Figure 7.7 Using overlapping Oval controls to produce curves.

3. Drag two more Oval controls to the window, each about half the diameter of the first one, and place them inside the first Oval.

4. Set the new controls' properties thus:

Left: 98	Height: 64
Top: 64	BorderWidth: 3
Width: 64	BorderColor: gray

and

Left: 94	Height: 64
Top: 128	BorderWidth: 3
Width: 64	BorderColor: gray

5. Now drag two more Oval controls to the window, and set their properties as follows to mask, or hide, parts of the previous two Ovals:

Left: 94	Height: 64
Top: 64	BorderWidth: 0
Width: 64	

and

Left: 98	Height: 64
Top: 128	BorderWidth: 0
Width: 64	

It's not a perfect yin-yang symbol, but it does show how you can mask off parts of figures for different effects. (You could add two more Ovals, as shown in **Figure 7.7**, to make the symbol a little more authentic. The red and cyan colors are chosen for their yin-yang relationship, as described in the next section.)

CREATING GRAPHICS WITH GRAPHICAL CONTROLS

To display alternating pictures by using the ImageWell control:

1. Drag two related pictures (such as images of a button in a clicked and an unclicked state or day and night pictures of the same scene) to the Project window.

   The pictures must be of type Pict, which is the only data type that the ImageWell control accepts. In the following code, it's assumed that you have unimaginatively named these pictures Image1 and Image2.

2. Drag an ImageWell control to the window.

3. Double-click the ImageWell to open its Code Editor.

4. Enter this code in the ImageWell's MouseEnter handler:

   ```
   me.image = Image1
   ```

5. Enter this code in the ImageWell's MouseExit handler:

   ```
   me.image = Image2
   ```

6. Resize the ImageWell to accommodate the image.

   You can use this technique to produce buttons with the mouseOver effect used on many Web sites (**Figure 7.8**).

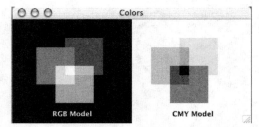

Figure 7.8 Using the ImageWell control to reproduce the common mouseOver effect used on Web sites.

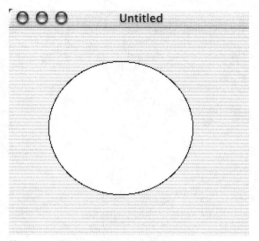

Figure 7.9 Although there is no `Circle` control, you can use inheritance to create your own.

Although these basic graphical controls are limited, you can customize them somewhat.

To create custom graphical controls:

1. Drag a `Rectangle` control from the Tools palette to your window.

2. In its Properties window, set its name to `Square` and its `Index` property to `0`.

   Setting a control's `Index` property to `0` creates a control array, so that you can create new instances of this same control in your code and refer to them as you would elements of any array: `Square(1)`, `Square(2)`, and so on.

   Note: Control arrays are covered in more detail in Chapter 5, "Writing Object-Oriented Code."

3. Double-click this `Rectangle` control in your window to open its Code Editor.

4. Enter this code in the control's `Open` handler:

   `me.height = me.width`

   This code, executed when a new instance of the `Rectangle` (or `Square`) is created, forces its height to match its width, making it a square indeed.

   The same code in an `Oval` object's `Open` handler will produce circles. Slightly different code will produce so-called Golden Rectangles, which have the classical proportions of the Parthenon (**Figure 7.9**):

   `me.height = me.width * 0.618`

Working with Color

You work with colors in REALbasic via the Color data type. Although Color is not a class (it's an intrinsic data type, stored internally as an integer), it does have properties and associated functions. A color's properties are:

- Red: the amount of red in the color
- Green: the amount of green in the color
- Blue: the amount of blue in the color
- Cyan: the amount of cyan in the color
- Magenta: the amount of magenta in the color
- Yellow: the amount of yellow in the color
- Hue: the color's position in the hue dimension
- Saturation: how saturated the color is
- Value: how dark or light the color is

The properties are read-only. To set a color's value, you use one of three functions: RGB, CMY, or HSV. Each function sets the color's values according to one of the three supported color models (described in the following section).

Color models

Even though a color has nine properties, it takes only three of them to specify the color fully: Red, Green, and Blue; Cyan, Magenta, and Yellow; or Hue, Saturation, and Value. These sets of three colors comprise the three color models.

Color models are different ways that have been developed for representing the multidimensional information in a color. Any color can be defined by any of REALbasic's three models and its appropriately named functions: RGB, CMY, and HSV.

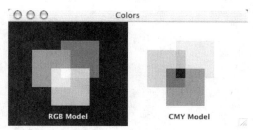

Figure 7.10 The RGB and CMY color models.

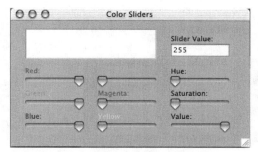

Figure 7.11 A Color Sliders tool for exploring color models.

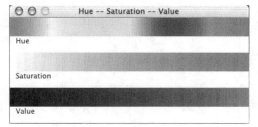

Figure 7.12 The HSV color model.

The RGB model (**Figure 7.10**) is based on the colors red, green, and blue—the so-called *additive primaries*. When you combine two of these colors, the effect is like shining two colored lights on a surface: The combination is lighter than either of the components. Combining the maximum amounts of red, green, and blue produces white.

The CMY model, which is closely related to the CMYK model used in the printing industry, is based on the *subtractive primaries*: cyan, magenta, and yellow (see Figure 7.10). Combining these colors is like layering watercolors: The combination is darker. A maximum mix of cyan, magenta, and yellow produces black.

The RGB and CMY models are in a sense mirror images of each other. **Figure 7.11** shows a tool for examining the relationships among the three color models. One example of what it shows is that increasing the red component of a color decreases cyan, and vice versa. Instructions for building this color-model tool appear in the "Building the Color Sliders" section on page 255.

The HSV model (**Figure 7.12**) represents the same information as the other models but breaks it down differently. Hue is the color's position along a spectrum of colors. Saturation and Value, respectively, can be thought of as measuring the amount of white or black added to the basic hue.

To convert between one color model and another:

◆ Create the color in the first color model, and access any of its properties in another model.

Keep in mind that the RGB model's Red, Green, and Blue properties are integers in the range 0 to 255 and that the other models' properties are doubles in the range 0 to 1:

```
dim c as color
dim y as double
c = RGB(127,127,0)
y = c.Yellow
```

Although the CMY and HSV color models use doubles and the RGB model uses integers to represent color values, each color property can take on only one of 256 values. You can specify any value between 0 and 1 for Yellow, for example, but it will be rounded to the nearest 1/256th.

The REALbasic IDE provides a Colors window as an aid to colorizing elements of your application's user interface. Initially, though, the window has no colors in it. It's up to you to populate the window with the colors you use most frequently. These colors will be specific to the current project; other projects can populate the Colors window with their own sets of colors.

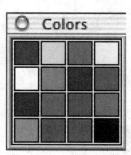

Figure 7.13
The Colors window.

To set up the Colors window:

1. Choose Window > Show Colors.

The Colors window appears.

2. Click any of the 16 cells in the Colors window.

The Color Picker appears.

3. Select a color, using any of the color-choosing methods the Color Picker provides.

The selected color appears in the selected cell of the Colors window.

4. Repeat steps 2 and 3 to populate all 16 cells with colors (**Figure 7.13**).

To use the Colors window in developing your application, drag from a cell of the Colors window to any place in the IDE that can accept a color, such as the `FillColor` property in the main window's Properties window.

✔ Tip

- A quick way to get colors from your project into the Colors window is to drag them there from, for example, a control's Properties window.

To allow the user to choose colors:

◆ Use the `SelectColor` function to display a Color Picker (**Figure 7.14**):

```
dim c as color
dim b as boolean
c = RGB(255,255,255)
b = SelectColor(c,"Choose a color")
if b then
  Window1.BackColor = c
End if
```

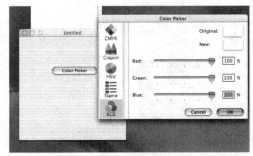

Figure 7.14 Using the `SelectColor` function to display a Color Picker.

The `SelectColor` function takes two parameters: a default color and a prompt string to display to the user. The function returns a Boolean value: `true` if the user selected a color; `false` otherwise. Surprisingly, it doesn't return the selected color. Rather, the function uses the user's selection to change the color passed to it. Methods usually don't modify the values of the parameters passed to them, but they can if the definition of the method identifies the parameter as a `"By Reference"` parameter, as is the case with the first parameter of the `SelectColor` function. The effect is that the chosen color is available to you in the variable c in the sixth line above.

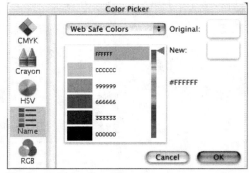

Figure 7.15 Web-safe colors.

The `RGB`, `CMY`, and `HSV` functions would seem to be enough ways to get the value of a color, but in some cases, you might want to define your own color methods. One such case is what are called *Web-safe colors*. This set of 216 colors is supposed to represent those colors that you can expect to display consistently in all Web browsers. If you wanted to restrict your color choices to these 216 values, you could write a `WebColor` method and use it, rather than `RGB` or one of the other built-in functions, to get all your color values (**Figure 7.15**).

To create your own custom Color function:

1. With the Code Editor open, choose Edit > New Method.

2. In the Method Declaration dialog that appears, enter `WebColor` as the method name, enter `Color` as the return value, and put the following in the Parameters field:

   `R as Integer, G as Integer, B as Integer`

   The `WebColor` method will take three integer values representing the RGB values of a color and return the nearest Web-safe color.

3. Open the Code Editor for the `WebColor` method, and enter this code:

   `dim Rsafe, Gsafe, Bsafe as integer`

4. Next, you'll create three variables to hold the modified values of `R`, `G`, and `B` by entering this code:

   `Rsafe = R`

   `Gsafe = G`

   `Bsafe = B`

   This code is obviously wrong, but you'll be transforming each of these color components to produce the Web-safe version, so you'll start with the identity transformation and refine it as you figure out how.

   continues on next page

5. End the handler with this code:

```
return RGB(Rsafe,Gsafe,Bsafe)
```

You use the transformed values to return an RGB color from the restricted set of Web-safe colors.

6. Change each of the middle lines of this handler thus:

```
Rsafe = 51 * (R \ 51)
Gsafe = 51 * (G \ 51)
Bsafe = 51 * (B \ 51)
```

This code is the needed transformation. Every 51st RGB value is a Web-safe color. This bit of integer arithmetic maps each of the next 50 RGB colors to the previous Web-safe one.

But you can make Web-safe color a little safer.

7. Control for values larger than 255:

```
Rsafe = min(255, 51 * (R \ 51))
Gsafe = min(255, 51 * (G \ 51))
Bsafe = min(255, 51 * (B \ 51))
```

8. Finally, control for values less than zero:

```
Rsafe = max(0, min(255, 51 * (R \ 51)))
Gsafe = max(0, min(255, 51 * (G \ 51)))
Bsafe = max(0, min(255, 51 * (B \ 51)))
```

9. Type Cmd-S to save your work.

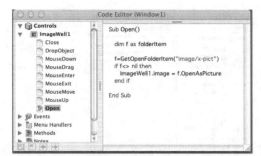

Figure 7.16 Reading a picture from a file.

Working with Graphics File Types and File I/O

Some of the material in this section was also covered in Chapter 6, "Working with Files."

To read a picture from a file:

1. Create a place to hold the picture in your application (in a Canvas or ImageWell control, for example).

2. Use the OpenAsPicture method of the FolderItem class, specifying the file type of the picture (**Figure 7.16**):

   ```
   dim f as folderItem
   f = GetOpenFolderItem("image/x-pict")
   if f <> nil then
     ImageWell1.image = f.OpenAsPicture
   end if
   ```

To import a picture into a project:

◆ Drag the icon of the picture file to the Project window.

   The picture file is not copied into the project, so if the project moves, the picture file must move with it. The picture *is* copied into the compiled stand-alone application, however, so the separate picture file is no longer needed at that point.

To let the user choose a picture file:

1. Create variables to refer to the FolderItem and dialog:

```
dim f as folderItem
dim dlg as OpenDialog
```

2. Create the dialog:

```
dlg = new OpenDialog
```

3. Set its properties:

```
dlg.Title = "What File?"
```

See the OpenDialog class in the Language Reference manual for the full list of settable properties.

4. Show the dialog:

```
f = dlg.ShowModal
```

When the user responds to the dialog, f will contain the result—either a reference to the selected file or nil if none was selected (**Figure 7.17**).

To save a picture to a file:

◆ Assuming that your picture is in the image property of an ImageWell control named ImageWell1, use the FolderItem class's SaveAsPicture method.

```
dim f as folderItem
f = GetSaveFolderItem("image/x-pict",
→ "Untitled"
if f <> nil then
  f.SaveAsPicture ImageWell1.image
end if
```

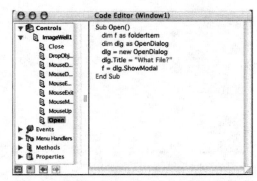

Figure 7.17 Allowing the user to select a picture to open.

Figure 7.18 Allowing the user to save a picture to a file.

Figure 7.19 Converting between picture-file formats.

To let the user choose a folder and file type for saving a picture to a file:

◆ Call the `ExportPicture` function (**Figure 7.18**):

```
dim p as picture
dim f as folderItem
dim b as boolean
p = ImageWell1.image
b = exportPicture(p)
if not b then
msgbox "Picture was not saved."
end if
```

`ExportPicture` displays a Save File dialog that lets the user choose any QuickTime-supported file type and a folder in which to save it. Currently supported types are BMP, PICT, PhotoShop, JPEG, PNG, SGI, TGA, TIFF, and QuickTime image. `ExportPicture` returns a Boolean value indicating whether the file was saved successfully.

To convert a picture file from one format to another:

◆ Use the `OpenAsPicture` and `SaveAsPicture` methods of the `FolderItem` class, calling them with different image-file types (**Figure 7.19**):

```
dim f1,f2 as folderItem
dim p as picture
f1 = GetOpenFolderItem("image/x-pict")
if f1 <> nil then
  p = f1.OpenAsPicture
  f2 = GetSaveFolderItem("image/jpeg",
  → "Untitled"
  if f2 <> nil then
    f2.SaveAsPicture p
  end if
end if
```

Using the Picture and Graphics Classes

REALbasic gives you a lot of control over pictures, especially pictures that you create. You can draw your own pictures, manipulate a picture's transparency, change any pixel, and change colors. You do all these things through the `Picture` and `Graphics` classes. Many examples of their use will be given in the following sections, but it is important to understand their methods and properties, as well as their responsibilities.

The Picture class

You create a new instance of the `Picture` class from a file—by importing the file into your project or reading the file via code—or by means of the `NewPicture` function. An instance of the `Picture` class gives REALbasic a place to hold a picture, whether or not it is being displayed. When the picture is displayed in the image property of an `ImageWell` control, for example, the property holds a pointer to the `Picture` instance.

A `Picture` object has no methods, only properties. Its properties include:

- `Height`, `Width`: dimensions of the picture, in pixels

- `IndexCount`, `IndexedImage`: used to get image from the indexed image picture (QuickTime 4 or later)

- `Transparency`, `Mask`: used to control the transparency of the picture

- `RGBSurface`: used to access individual pixels of the picture

- `Graphics`: provides broad capability to draw and modify pictures

You work with a picture object through these properties (**Figure 7.20**).

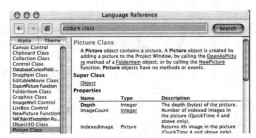

Figure 7.20 The `Picture` class is fundamental to graphics in REALbasic. You can explore its properties by using the online Language Reference manual.

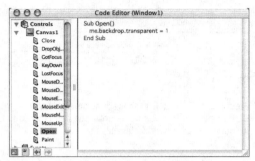

Figure 7.21 Making a picture transparent.

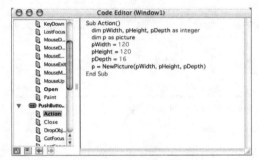

Figure 7.22 Creating a new Picture object.

To make a picture transparent:

1. Open a new window.

2. Do *not* check the BackColor property.

3. Drag a Canvas control from the Tools palette to the window.

4. Drag a picture file to the Project window.

5. In the Canvas's Properties window, select the picture as the Canvas's Backdrop property.

6. Open the Canvas's Code Editor.

7. In the Canvas's Open handler, put the following code (**Figure 7.21**):

   ```
   me.backdrop.transparent = 1
   ```

   When you run the application, you will see the picture's white pixels rendered transparent. The default window background should show through.

To create a picture:

◆ Use the NewPicture function (**Figure 7.22**):

   ```
   dim pWidth, pHeight, pDepth as integer
   dim p as picture
   pWidth = 120
   pHeight = 120
   pDepth = 16
   p = NewPicture(pWidth, pHeight, pDepth)
   ```

   The third parameter is the picture depth: 1 = black and white, 2 = four colors, 4 = 16 colors, and so on.

But the most important of a picture's properties is its Graphics property—an automatically generated instance of the Graphics class.

The Graphics class

The Graphics class is what gives you control of your drawing. Every picture has a Graphics property. Unless the picture was created via the NewPicture function, however, the Graphics property will be nil. This means that the drawing capabilities of the Graphics class are not available for pictures from files.

The Graphics class has many properties and methods for drawing text, as well as standard icons and polygons for the control of printing (**Figure 7.23**).

Properties of the Graphics class include:

◆ Bold, Underline, Italic, TextFont, and other properties for working with text

◆ Copies, FirstPage, LastPage: properties for controlling print jobs

◆ Pixel: for getting and setting individual pixels of the picture

Methods of the Graphics class include:

◆ DrawLine, DrawPicture, DrawString, DrawPolygon, and similar methods for drawing your own pictures

◆ FillPolygon and other space-filling methods

◆ StringWidth: returns the pixel width of a string of text

To crop a picture to fit:

◆ Adjust the *source* X, Y, Height, and Width parameters in the DrawPicture method of the Graphics object (**Figure 7.24**):

```
// If g is a Graphics object, p is a
→ picture, the rest of these values are
→ integers, and sW and sH are the Width
→ and Height of the picture, this method
→ will strip 4 pixels off all the way
→ around the picture.
g.DrawPicture p,dX,dY,dW,dH,4,4,sW-8,
→ sH-8
```

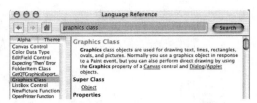

Figure 7.23 The Graphics class controls drawing in REALbasic. You can explore its properties and methods in the online Language Reference manual.

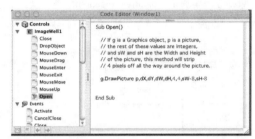

Figure 7.24 Cropping a picture.

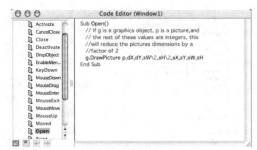

Figure 7.25 Scaling a picture.

Figure 7.26 Drawing a standard icon.

To scale a picture:

◆ Set the *destination* `Height` and `Width` parameters in the `DrawPicture` method of the `Graphics` object to a multiple of the *source* parameters (**Figure 7.25**):

```
// If g is a Graphics object, p is a
→ picture, and the rest of these values
→ are integers, this will reduce the
→ picture's dimensions by a factor of 2.
g.DrawPicture p,dX,dY,sW\2,sH\2,sX,
→ sY,sW,sH
```

Use the same multiple if you don't want to distort the image.

To display the Caution icon:

◆ Use the `DrawCautionIcon` method of the `Graphics` object (**Figure 7.26**):

```
g.DrawCautionIcon X,Y
```

At the end of this chapter is a full application that allows the user to draw lines to create linear patterns and drawings. The application uses the `Line` control for pedagogical purposes, but the powerful methods of the `Graphics` class offer another way to implement the same program.

The photo op: when things get updated

All controls in a window are redrawn whenever REALbasic perceives the necessity—such as when a dialog or other object moves, revealing a previously obscured part of the window or a control. But REALbasic may not recognize when your code makes it necessary to redraw the window or some part of it. For these occasions, you have the `Refresh` and `RefreshRect` methods. These methods erase the window's (or control's) `Graphics` property, so if it is to be maintained, it must be redrawn. The methods also send the `Paint` message, so the `Paint` handler of the object is where this redrawing is done. For more information on this topic, see "Using the `Canvas` Control" on page 246.

Using Graphics-Savvy Objects

The most graphics-savvy object is the Canvas control, which is discussed in some depth later in this chapter. But many objects have some graphics-displaying capability, including windows and Canvas, ImageWell, ListBox, Clipboard, and BevelButton.

Indeed, you can even drop a picture on a Rectangle control, because like all controls, it has an AcceptPictureDrop method and a DropObject event handler. But the Rectangle control has no place to put a picture.

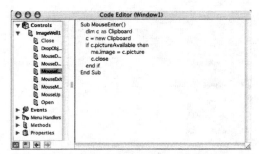

Figure 7.27 Getting a picture from the Clipboard.

To place a picture from the Clipboard in an ImageWell:

1. Create an instance of the Clipboard object:

   ```
   dim c as Clipboard
   c = new Clipboard
   ```

2. Capture its picture, if any, in the ImageWell's image property:

   ```
   if c.pictureAvailable then
     me.image = c.picture
     c.close
   End if
   ```

   This code could appear in the ImageWell's MouseEnter handler (**Figure 7.27**).

To create a picture picker:

1. Create a one-column ListBox by dragging the ListBox control from the Tools palette to the main window.

2. Drag several small pictures, such as icons, to the Project window.

3. Open the Code Editor, and select the ListBox's Open event.

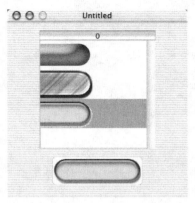

Figure 7.28 Creating a picture picker.

Figure 7.29 Creating a button with an icon.

4. Enter this code in the right pane of the Code Editor:

```
me.AddRow("")
// repeat for as many pictures as you
→ want to display
me.RowPicture(0) = picture0
// and similarly for each other picture
→ you want to display
```

5. Adjust the ListBox to accommodate the pictures by dragging to resize it and by tweaking the TextHeight property.

6. In the ListBox's CellClick handler, enter this code to display the user-selected picture in the ImageWell (**Figure 7.28**):

```
ImageWell1.image = me.RowPicture(row)
```

To create a button with an icon:

1. Drag a BevelButton control from the Tools palette to the main window.

2. Drag a PICT file to the Project window.

3. In the BevelButton's Properties window, set its icon property to the picture (**Figure 7.29**).

To set a window's background color:

◆ Set the HasBackColor and BackColor properties of the window:

```
Window1.HasBackColor = true
Window1.BackColor = RGB(255,0,0)
```

To set a window's background picture:

◆ Assuming that the picture has been imported into the project, set the window's BackDrop property to its name:

```
Window1.BackDrop = myPicture
```

The most useful tool for displaying pictures, though, is the Canvas control.

USING GRAPHICS-SAVVY OBJECTS

Using the Canvas Control

The Canvas control is the most powerful and flexible of the graphics-savvy controls. It is powerful enough that you can use it to develop your own custom controls. Like the ImageWell control, the Canvas control can display an existing image. But it can also respond to a variety of events and user actions; it can interact in clever ways with other controls; it gives you a great deal of power over pictures displayed in its two graphical layers; and it lets you draw your own pictures.

A Canvas is a RectControl, so it inherits all the properties of a RectControl and of *its* parent, the Control class. The Canvas class adds only two new properties that are unique to itself, but both are powerful and important:

♦ The Backdrop property holds a picture to be drawn within the Canvas's boundaries, much like the Image property of an ImageWell.

♦ The Graphics property provides a separate visual layer and a tool kit of drawing techniques that let you layer rich drawings on top of the background image.

The Backdrop layer contains a single object of the Picture class. The Graphics layer can contain many objects of the Picture class drawn in different locations within the bounds of the Canvas control. The Paint and Graphics classes were discussed earlier in this chapter, but it is in working with the Canvas control that you really begin to see what they can do.

Figure 7.30 Displaying a picture by using the Canvas control.

A Canvas control can respond to MouseDown, MouseUp, and MouseDrag events, as well as to the very important Paint event. The Paint event occurs when the Canvas area needs to be redrawn, and its handler is where you should place code that updates graphics produced by the control's Graphics property. REALbasic itself will take care of redrawing the picture in the Backdrop layer when necessary.

To display an image in a Canvas control:

◆ Place this code in the Canvas's Open handler after dragging Picture1 to the Project window:

```
me.BackDrop = Picture1
```

or

◆ Enter this code to display a picture from a file on disk:

```
me.BackDrop = myPath.myFile
```

or

◆ Enter this code after dragging Picture1 to the Project window:

```
me.BackDrop = newPicture(me.width,
→ me.height,32)
me.BackDrop.Graphics.DrawPicture
→ Picture1, 0, 0
```

Whatever method you use, the result should display your picture, as in **Figure 7.30**.

Using the power of the pen

To do something more than display a fixed image in a Canvas, you usually draw in the Graphics layer, using the Graphics property of the control and the various Draw methods that any object of the Graphics class has.

To draw a grid:

1. Drag a Canvas control from the Tools palette to the main window.

2. Open the control's Paint handler.

   Always use the Paint handler for any drawing in the Graphics layer that you want to persist.

3. Define the needed variables (**Figure 7.31**):

   dim c,r,gW,gH,gL,gT,gR,gB as integer

   // Assign values to the grid width
   → (gW), grid height (gH), grid left (gL),
   → grid top (gT), grid right (gR), and
   → grid bottom (gB).

4. Draw the columns of the grid:

   for c=0 to 7

     g.drawline c*gW+gL, gT, c*gw+gl, gB

   next

5. Draw the rows:

   for r=0 to 6

     g.drawLine gL, r*gH+gT, gR, r*gH+gT

   next

   The grid of lines transparently overlays any picture placed in the Backdrop.

Although the easiest way to display text in your applications is to place it in an EditField or a StaticText control, the most flexible way is to *draw* the text in a Canvas, using the DrawString method of the Graphics class. You can draw text and then rotate it, for example.

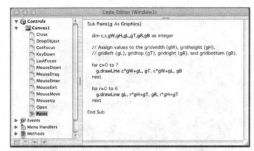

Figure 7.31 Using the Canvas control to draw grid lines.

Figure 7.32 Using the Canvas control to rotate text.

To rotate text:

1. Drag a Canvas control to the main window.

2. With the Code Editor open, choose Edit > New Property.

3. In the Property Declaration dialog that appears, enter:

   TempPict as Picture

4. Click OK.

5. In the Code Editor, select the Canvas control's Open handler.

6. Create a new Picture instance, and assign it to TempPict (**Figure 7.32**):

   TempPict = newPicture(me.width,
   → me.height,32)

7. Create another new Picture instance, and assign it to the Canvas's Backdrop:

   me.backdrop = newPicture(me.width,
   → me.height,32)

   You'll need the additional Picture to hold the rotated image while it is being constructed and before it is redrawn to the Backdrop.

8. Set the text properties, and draw the text:

   me.backdrop.graphics.textFont =
   → "Apple Chancery"

   me.backdrop.graphics.textSize = 72

   me.backdrop.graphics.drawString
   → "Hello!", 2, me.height\2

   continues on next page

USING THE CANVAS CONTROL

9. Copy each pixel of the Backdrop image to TempPict, with the x and y coordinates swapped:

```
for x=1 to me.width-1
  for y=1 to me.height-1
    TempPict.graphics.pixel(x,y) =
    → me.backdrop.graphics.pixel
    → (me.height-y,x)
// Swapping x and y rotates the text by
→ 90 degrees, and subtracting the y
→ coordinate from the height makes the
→ text read from bottom to top rather
→ than top to bottom.
  next
next
```

10. Copy TempPict to Backdrop:

```
for x=1 to me.width-1
  for y=1 to me.height-1
    me.backdrop.graphics.pixel(x,y) =
    → TempPict.graphics.pixel(x,y)
  next
next
```

11. Complete the handler by adding this declaration at the top:

```
dim x,y as integer
```

Notice that you're using the Backdrop here, not the Canvas control's Graphics property. Despite what I said earlier—that the Backdrop property "merely" contains a picture—every Picture object has a Graphics property, so you can do these Graphics manipulations in the Backdrop layer as well as in the Graphics layer. If you intend to create the image and leave it alone, the Backdrop probably is the place for it. If you want to layer images, or if you expect to modify the image after it is created, consider using the Graphics layer.

As you can tell if you try to use these techniques with large images, they are not very fast. There are ways to speed your graphics code significantly, discussed in the "Handling performance anxiety" section on page 254.

Controlling the Canvas control

As you can tell from the preceding example, you can manipulate pictures right down to the level of the individual pixels. You can get or set the value of a single pixel, and you can manipulate all the pixels to transform the picture in many interesting ways. You've seen how to scale, crop, and rotate pictures. Here is a general technique for changing the colors in a picture for many effects, from posterization to brightening a dull image or turning a richly colored image into a sepia-tone picture.

To transform the colors of a picture:

1. Drag a Canvas control to the main window.

2. Drag a picture to the Project window, and name it Picture 1.

3. In the Code Editor, open the Canvas control's Open handler.

4. Enter this code:

```
dim x,y as integer
dim c as color
dim g as graphics
me.backdrop = newPicture(100,100,32)
g = me.backdrop.graphics
// just creating a synonym for this long
→ expression so you don't have to keep
→ typing it
g.drawPicture Picture1,0,0,100,100
for x=1 to g.width-1
  for y=1 to g.height-1
    c = pixel(x,y)
    g.pixel(x,y) = CMY(morph(c.cyan),
    → c.magenta,c.yellow)
  next
next
```

continues on next page

5. With the Code Editor still open, choose Edit > New Method.

6. In the Method Declaration dialog that appears, enter `Morph` as the name of the method.

7. Enter `Double` as in the Return Value filed and `"d as Double"` in the Parameters field.

8. Click OK.

9. In the Code Editor, select your new `Morph` method, and enter this code:

```
return pow(d,1.5)
```

Figure 7.33 You can write your own methods to transform pictures pixel by pixel.

`Morph` changes the value of a color according to a formula. The formula in this example raises the color value to a power. This formula will produce inappropriate values if `Morph` gets an RGB color value, but it will produce interesting effects if it is given various powers and applied to CMY or HSV values, which are in the range 0 to 1.

Specifically, raising CMY color values to the 1.5 power makes small numbers very small and large numbers slightly smaller. Applying this transformation to the cyan values throughout the image shifts all values away from cyan but has the greatest effect where there is the least cyan. Because of the duality of cyan and red, the eye will perceive this transformation as increasing the red values of image, with colors containing only a little red being slightly affected and really red areas being most affected.

You can explore many effects by substituting different mathematical functions in `Morph`; by applying `Morph` to one, two, or all components of a color; and by using it with HSV values as well as CMY values (**Figure 7.33**).

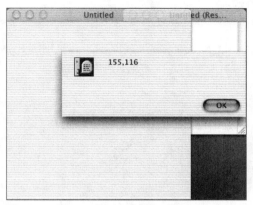

Figure 7.34 Responding to clicks at different locations in a picture.

Making your Canvas control—and, hence, the pictures in it—responsive to user input is a large subject, but the essence of it is to take the appropriate action in response to the right event, as the following example shows.

To respond to clicks in different parts of an image:

1. Drag a Canvas control to the main window.

2. In the Code Editor, open the Canvas control's MouseDown handler, and enter this code:

   ```
   return true
   ```

   The MouseDown handler must return a value of true for mouse actions to be handled in your code.

3. Open the Canvas control's MouseUp handler, and enter this code:

   ```
   msgBox str(x) + "," + str(y)
   ```

   All this text does is demonstrate that your code is handling the MouseUp event when the user clicks in the control and that the code knows where the click occurred. Anything that you want to happen in response to the click should be placed in the MouseUp handler (**Figure 7.34**).

This chapter could run twice its length if it discussed all the things that you can do with the Canvas control. Some untouched topics that you can explore on your own by creating a Canvas control and playing around with its properties and methods are scrolling, transparency, and drag-and-drop capability.

Handling performance anxiety

The examples in this chapter make no attempt to produce efficiency or speed. But graphics manipulations use up a lot of memory and processing power quickly, and you will often find it desirable to fine-tune your graphics for speed or memory use. Here are a few strategies for improving graphics performance:

◆ Leave off excess parameters in the Graphics class's DrawPicture method. If you supply all the parameters, including both the source height and width and the destination height and width, DrawPicture will attempt to change the size of the picture. Leaving off those parameters will speed the drawing.

◆ Never create the same image twice. When you're drawing to a Canvas, save the picture to a user property if you will be displaying it more than once. Or put the picture in a Canvas and hide that Canvas off-screen when it is not to be seen by setting its left property to a sufficiently negative number.

◆ Use RGBSurface rather than the Pixel property. The Pixel property is a property of the Graphics class, whereas the RGBSurface property is a property of the Picture class, so they are not directly interchangeable, but RGBSurface is enough faster than Pixel to justify thinking about how to redesign your code to use it.

◆ Move calculations out of loops wherever possible. This guideline doesn't apply just to graphics. If your code is performing a calculation inside a For...Next or other kind of loop, and if that calculation is going to produce the same result every time it is performed, move it outside the loop and use just the *result* of the calculation inside the loop.

But wait—there's more

As Apple's CEO is fond of saying, there's one more thing.

In version 4.5 of REALbasic, REAL Software introduced vector-graphics classes that extend the graphics capabilities of the product and make some tasks easier to accomplish. The yin-yang symbol (see page 227) is easier to draw when you use the curve-drawing capabilities of the new classes (although the point about using one object to mask part of another is still valid). These features, and some others added in version 4.5 and later, are discussed in Chapter 12, "Being A Programmer."

The remainder of this chapter presents two projects: the Color Sliders tool and the TurtleDraw application.

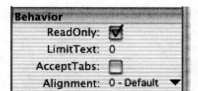

Figure 7.35 Creating a component of the Color Sliders tool.

Building the Color Sliders Tool

Although you can do anything you want to do with colors by using just the RGB model, working in a different model is handy sometimes. The Color Sliders tool (see Figure 7.11) is helpful for seeing just how changing a value in one of the models affects values in the others. The following exercises show you how to build it.

To create the Color Sliders window:

1. Launch a new project, and double-click the Window icon in the Project window to open the main window.

2. In the Properties window, set the main window's Title to Color Sliders, its Width and Height to 410 and 224, and its BackColor to a middle shade of gray.

To create the ColorStrip to display the selected color:

1. Drag a Rectangle control from the Tools palette to the main window.

2. Set the control's Left, Top, Width, and Height properties to 25, 14, 225, and 54; its BorderWidth to 2; its TopLeftCorner to darkish gray (Aluminum); and its BottomRightCorner to light gray (Silver).

To create the Meter to display the latest slider setting:

1. Drag an EditField control to the main window.

2. Set the control's Name to Meter; set its Left, Top, Width, and Height to 275, 41, 100, and 22; and check the check box for its ReadOnly property (**Figure 7.35**).

To create the color sliders:

1. Drag nine Slider controls to the main window.

2. Set all the controls' Width properties to 100 and their Heights to 16.

3. Lay out the controls in a 3 x 3 array by setting their Left and Top properties as follows:

25, 100	150, 180
25, 140	275, 100
25, 180	275, 140
150, 100	275, 180
150, 140	

4. Set the Minimum, Value, and Maximum of the three controls on the left to 0, 255, and 255.

5. Set the Minimum, Value, and Maximum of the middle three controls to 0, 0, and 100.

6. Set the Minimum, Value, and Maximum of the control at the top right to 0, 0, and 100.

7. Set the Minimum, Value, and Maximum of the two controls on the right to 0, 100, and 100.

To create the labels for everything:

1. Drag 10 StaticText controls to the main window.

2. Position the controls by setting their Left and Top properties as follows:

275, 22	150, 120
25, 80	275, 120
150, 80	25, 160
275, 80	150, 160
25, 120	275, 160

3. Set the Caption of each StaticText to match **Figure 7.36**.

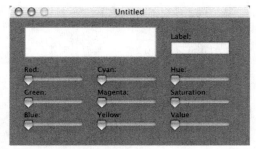

Figure 7.36 Labeling the sliders.

To code the sliders:

1. In the left pane of the Code Editor, click the `SliderRed` control, click its `ValueChanged` method, and enter this code in the right pane:

   ```
   setRGB
   meter.text = str(me.value)
   ```

2. Enter the same code in the `SliderGreen` and `SliderBlue` controls' `ValueChanged` handlers.

3. Enter this code in the `ValueChanged` handlers of the `SliderCyan`, `SliderMagenta`, and `SliderYellow` controls:

   ```
   setCMY
   meter.text = str(me.value)
   ```

4. Enter this code in the `ValueChanged` handlers of the `SliderHue`, `SliderSaturation`, and `SliderValue` controls:

   ```
   setHSV
   meter.text = str(me.value)
   ```

   Each of these handlers calls a method (which you haven't written yet) to set the values of all the sliders, and the handlers display their own values in the `Meter` control.

To create the slider-setting methods:

1. With the Code Editor open, choose Edit > New Method.

2. In the Method Declaration dialog that appears, enter `SetRGB`.

3. Click OK.

4. Repeat steps 1 through 3 to create the `SetCMY` and `SetHSV` methods.

continues on next page

BUILDING THE COLOR SLIDERS TOOL

5. In the Code Editor, select the SetRGB method, and enter this code in the right pane:

```
// Color the ColorStrip according to the
→ settings of the sliders for this color
→ model.

ColorStrip.fillColor =
→ RGB(SliderRed.value,
→ SliderGreen.value,
→ SliderBlue.value)

// Set the other sliders for the other
→ color models based on the color of the
→ ColorStrip.

SliderCyan.value =
→ ColorStrip.fillColor.cyan*100

SliderMagenta.value =
→ ColorStrip.fillColor.magenta*100

SliderYellow.value =
→ ColorStrip.fillColor.yellow*100

SliderHue.value =
→ ColorStrip.fillColor.hue*100

SliderSaturation.value =
→ ColorStrip.fillColor.saturation*100

SliderValue.value =
→ ColorStrip.fillColor.value*100
```

6. In the Code Editor, select the SetCMY method, and enter this code in the right pane:

```
// Color the ColorStrip according to the
→ settings of the sliders for this color
→ model.

ColorStrip.fillColor =
→ CMY(SliderCyan.value/100,
→ SliderMagenta.value/100,
→ SliderYellow.value/100)

// Set the other sliders for the other
→ color models based on the color of the
→ ColorStrip.

SliderRed.value =
→ ColorStrip.fillColor.red

SliderGreen.value =
→ ColorStrip.fillColor.green
```

```
SliderBlue.value =
→ ColorStrip.fillColor.blue

SliderHue.value =
→ ColorStrip.fillColor.hue*100

SliderSaturation.value =
→ ColorStrip.fillColor.saturation*100

SliderValue.value =
→ ColorStrip.fillColor.value*100
```

7. In the Code Editor, select the SetHSV method, and enter this code in the right pane:

```
// Color the ColorStrip according to the
→ settings of the sliders for this color
→ model.

ColorStrip.fillColor =
→ HSV(SliderHue.value/100,
→ SliderSaturation.value/100,
→ SliderValue.value/100)

// Set the other sliders for the other
→ color models based on the color of the
→ ColorStrip.

SliderRed.value =
→ ColorStrip.fillColor.red

SliderGreen.value =
→ ColorStrip.fillColor.green

SliderBlue.value =
→ ColorStrip.fillColor.blue

SliderCyan.value =
→ ColorStrip.fillColor.cyan*100

SliderMagenta.value =
→ ColorStrip.fillColor.magenta*100

SliderYellow.value =
→ ColorStrip.fillColor.yellow*100
```

To prevent changes from repeating forever:

1. With the Code Editor open, choose Edit > New Property.

2. In the Property Declaration dialog that appears, enter the following:

   `LockChanges as Boolean`

3. Click OK.

4. Enter this line in the window's `Open` handler:

   `LockChanges = false`

5. In the `ValueChanged` handler for each of the nine sliders, add this line just *before* the first line:

   `if not lockChanges then`

6. Add this line just after the line you added in step 5:

   `End if`

7. In each of the three methods `SetRGB`, `SetCMY`, and `SetHSV`, add this line after the first line of the code:

   `LockChanges = true`

8. Add this line at the end of the code:

   `LockChanges = false`

   You're allowing a change in any one of the sliders to effect a change in all the others. To prevent these subsequent changes from triggering yet more changes in an infinite loop, you've created this `LockChanges` property, which you can use to turn this triggering on and off.

9. Save your work, and test it.

   You should be able to see the relationships among values in the three color models as you move the sliders (**Figure 7.37**).

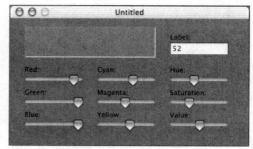

Figure 7.37 The Color Sliders tool.

Table 7.1

Properties of the TurtleDraw Window	
PROPERTY	VALUE
Width	633
Height	420
MinWidth	512
MinHeight	420
HasBackColor	Checked
BackColor	<white>
GrowIcon	Checked
ZoomIcon	Checked

Building the TurtleDraw Application

In the remainder of this chapter, you'll develop a turtle-graphics application. In turtle graphics, all drawing is done via a few simple controls or commands that tell the drawing pen (referred to as a *turtle* for historical reasons that need not distract you here) to move forward or turn left or right. In your variation on the turtle theme, you'll implement four buttons to move left, right, up, and down a fixed distance in a defined drawing area. Same idea.

Turtle graphics will be familiar to anyone who knows the Logo programming language or who has used an Etch-a-Sketch. Turtle-graphics techniques have also been used in sophisticated systems for creating lifelike botanical forms based on fractals. But your application will be designed for a child, with large type, primary colors, and simple instructions.

The application will be a complete one, as well as a lesson in many of the graphics techniques discussed in this chapter.

To start the project:

1. Choose File > New to create a new project.

2. In the Project window, click the icon for the default window, and in the Properties window that appears, set its properties as shown in **Table 7.1**.

3. Choose File > Save As, and save the project with the name TurtleDraw.rb.

To create the navigation buttons and drawing area:

1. Drag four PushButton controls from the Tools palette to the window.

2. In the Properties window for each control, set its properties as shown in **Table 7.2**.

   Each of these buttons will move the turtle one step in one of four directions. You'll set some combination of the LockLeft, LockTop, LockRight, and LockBottom properties for every control you place in the window, because you gave the window a GrowIcon and a ZoomIcon when you set its properties. As a result, the user can resize the window, and you need to keep in charge of what happens to the controls in the window when this happens.

3. Drag a Rectangle control from the Tools palette to the window, and name it Page. This control will be your drawing area.

Table 7.2

Properties of the Navigation PushButtons

PROPERTY	UPBUTTON	DOWNBUTTON	LEFTBUTTON	RIGHTBUTTON
Name	UpButton	DownButton	LeftButton	RightButton
Left	52	52	30	74
Top	24	112	68	68
Width	32	32	32	32
Height	32	32	32	32
LockLeft	Checked	Checked	Checked	Checked
LockTop	Checked	Checked	Checked	Checked
Caption	U	D	L	R
TextSize	14	14	14	14

Table 7.3

Properties of the Drawing Area	
PROPERTY	VALUE
Name	Page
Left	132
Top	14
Width	487
Height	392
LockLeft	Checked
LockTop	Checked
LockWidth	Checked
LockHeight	Checked
FIllColor	<white>
BorderWidth	2
TopLeftCorner	Aluminum
BottomRightCorner	Silver

4. Set the drawing area's properties as shown in **Table 7.3**.

Turning on all four of the locking properties will ensure that the drawing area grows and shrinks when the user resizes the window. Chances are that she's enlarging it to get more room to draw.

5. Save your work, and test it.

The application doesn't do anything yet, but the main elements are in place: a place for the drawing to happen and four buttons to drive the drawing process.

The next question is how to draw. You have many ways to put lines on the screen with REALbasic, but for this application, you'll use the Line control.

This situation raises a problem: You'll need a lot of lines, produced as needed during the running of the program, but you can't create controls except in the IDE. You can create instances of a control array, however, as you saw in Chapter 5. That's what does the trick here; each new line drawn will be another item in an array of lines.

To create an array of Line control objects:

1. Drag a Line control from the Tools palette to your window.

Put the control where it won't be in your way as you continue to design your user interface. When the program runs, this first line will be invisible.

2. Set the control's Name property to Line and its Index property to 0 to make it the first item of a control array.

Now you can create new items in this array in your code, each referred to by its index: TurtleLine(10) will be the 10th line drawn. Your drawing method—when you write it—will create a new item of this array when and where you need it.

To define the properties needed by the application:

1. Press Option-Tab to open the Code Editor.

2. Choose Edit > New Property.

3. In the Property Declaration dialog that appears, enter TurtleX as integer, and click OK.

4. In the same way, create three other integer properties named TurtleY, TurtleNextX, and TurtleNextY.

   These properties will keep track of the X and Y coordinates of the points where the next line should start and end.

5. Create additional properties as shown in **Table 7.4**.

Because your lines are instances of the Line control, they have the properties of that control, including BorderWidth, LineColor, and the Visible property (as well as a length that is not a property but that can be deduced from the beginning and ending coordinates of the line, which are properties). You might want to change these properties during the running of the program. These global properties will keep track of the currently preferred value for each Line property.

The four integer properties named PageL, PageR, PageT, and PageB will hold the boundaries of your drawing area, which you named Page. Your drawing method will need to check these boundaries to be sure of staying inside the drawing area. Also, because you're allowing the user to resize the window and the drawing area along with it, you'll need to keep track of these boundaries and update them.

Table 7.4

User-Created Properties	
PROPERTY	DATA TYPE
TurtleX	Integer
TurtleY	Integer
TurtleNextX	Integer
TurtleNextY	Integer
TurtleWidth	Integer
TurtleStep	Integer
TurtleColor	Color
TurtleVisible	Boolean
PageL	Integer
PageT	Integer
PageR	Integer
PageB	Integer

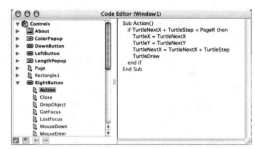

Figure 7.38 Coding the R button of the TurtleDraw application.

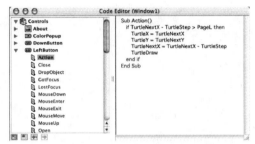

Figure 7.39 Coding the L button of the TurtleDraw application.

```
Sub Action()
    if TurtleNextX - TurtleStep > PageL then
        TurtleX = TurtleNextX
        TurtleY = TurtleNextY
        TurtleNextY = TurtleNextY + TurtleStep
        TurtleDraw
    end if
End Sub
```

Figure 7.40 Coding the D button of the TurtleDraw application.

```
Sub Action()
    if TurtleNextX - TurtleStep > PageL then
        TurtleX = TurtleNextX
        TurtleY = TurtleNextY
        TurtleNextY = TurtleNextY - TurtleStep
        TurtleDraw
    end if
End Sub
```

Figure 7.41 Coding the U button of the TurtleDraw application.

The need for some of these properties is not yet evident, but it's convenient to get them all created at the same time. When you're developing an application from scratch, you create properties when you see the need for them.

To code the navigation buttons:

1. Double-click the R button to open its Code Editor.

2. In the right pane, enter the following code:

   `TurtleX = TurtleNextX`

   `TurtleY = TurtleNextY`

   The starting coordinates for the next drawing step are the ending coordinates for the preceding step.

3. Increment the next X coordinate by one step, leaving the next Y coordinate alone:

   `TurtleNextX = TurtleNextX + TurtleStep`

4. Draw the line:

   `TurtleDraw`

   The TurtleDraw method, if it existed, would draw the next line based on the global properties. For now, assume that the method exists, and write it later.

5. Wrap this code in an If structure to make sure you aren't drawing outside the drawing area (**Figure 7.38**).

6. Code the L button exactly the same way, but this time, you *decrement* the next X coordinate (**Figure 7.39**).

7. Code the D button like the R button, but this time, you increment the next Y coordinate (**Figure 7.40**).

8. Code the U button like the D button, decrementing the next Y coordinate (**Figure 7.41**).

Now it's time to face the music and write the method that does the drawing. As it turns out, that's not very hard.

To create the TurtleDraw method:

1. Press Option-Tab to open the Code Editor.

2. Choose Edit > New Method.

3. In the Method Declaration dialog, enter TurtleDraw as the name of the method, and click OK.

4. In the Code Editor, click the disclosure triangle next to Methods to expand it, and click the TurtleDraw method.

5. In the right pane, enter code to create a new item of that TurtleLine array that you created:

```
dim T as TurtleLine
T = new TurtleLine
```

6. Set the line's properties, using the global properties you created:

```
T.visible = TurtleVisible
T.BorderWidth = TurtleWidth
T.LineColor = TurtleColor
```

7. Set the line's coordinates, using these properties:

```
T.X1 = TurtleX
T.Y1 = TurtleY
T.X2 = TurtleNextX
T.Y2 = TurtleNextY
```

8. Save your work, and test it.

What about those properties that you so foresightedly created? You could make some of them user-modifiable by adding some user customization buttons.

To create the customization buttons:

1. Drag three PopupButtons and one CheckBox to the main window.

2. Set the controls' properties as shown in **Table 7.5**.

3. Set the InitialValue properties of these buttons as follows:

   LengthPopup: 1 2 3 4 5 6 7 8 16 32 64

   WidthPopup: 1 2 3 4 5 6 7 8

   ColorPopup: Black White Red Yellow Blue
   → Green Purple Orange Cyan Magenta Pink

   VisibleCheckBox: Visible

   For the three pop-ups, you should enter each item on a separate line in the InitialValue field—not all on one line as I show them here.

4. Set the Value property of the VisibleCheckBox to Checked.

To code the Width and Length buttons:

◆ Enter this code in each of these buttons' Change handlers:

```
TurtleWidth = val(me.text)
```

Table 7.5

Properties of the Customization Buttons

PROPERTY	LENGTHPOPUP	WIDTHPOPUP	COLORPOPUP	VISIBLECHECKBOX
Name	LengthPopup	WidthPopup	ColorPopup	VisibleClickBox
Left	20	20	20	20
Top	224	196	252	168
Width	100	100	100	100
Height	20	20	20	20
LockLeft	val	Checked	Checked	Checked
LockTop	val	Checked	Checked	Checked
TextSize	val	14	14	14

To code the Visible button:

◆ Enter this code in the button's Action
handler:

```
me.value = not TurtleVisible
TurtleVisible = me.value
```

To code the Color button:

◆ Enter this code in the button's Change
handler:

```
Select Case me.text
Case "Black"
  TurtleColor = RGB(0,0,0)
Case "White"
  TurtleColor = RGB(255,255,255)
Case "Red"
  TurtleColor = RGB(255,0,0)
Case "Yellow"
  TurtleColor = RGB(255,255,0)
Case "Blue"
  TurtleColor = RGB(0,0,255)
Case "Green"
  TurtleColor = RGB(0,255,0)
Case "Purple"
  TurtleColor = RGB(127,0,127)
Case "Orange"
  TurtleColor = RGB(255,127,0)
Case "Cyan"
  TurtleColor = RGB(0,255,255)
Case "Magenta"
  TurtleColor = RGB(255,0,255)
Case "Pink"
  TurtleColor = RGB(255,127,127)
Else
// No change
End Select
```

Save your work, and test it. It may be evident
that you need to initialize a few things.

To initialize the application:

1. Assign a default value to every user-defined property by placing this code in the window's `Open` handler:

```
PageT = Page.top
PageL = Page.left
PageR = PageL + Page.width - 1
PageB = PageT + Page.height - 1
TurtleX = (PageL + PageR) \ 2
TurtleY = (PageT + PageB) \ 2
TurtleNextX = TurtleX
TurtleNextY = TurtleY
TurtleVisible = true
TurtleStep = 8
TurtleWidth = 1
TurtleColor = RGB(0,0,0)
```

2. Save your work, and test it.

You'll need to reassess `PageR`, `PageL`, and so on when the window is resized.

To keep track of the drawing area's boundaries:

◆ Copy from the window's `Open` handler to its `Paint` handler the four lines that set the `PageT`, `PageL`, `PageR`, and `PageB` properties.

The `Paint` handler is invoked whenever the window is resized.

This method is not a complete solution to keeping the drawing within bounds. If the user draws in the drawing area and then resizes the window so as to place some of the drawing outside the area, the program won't fix this problem; in fact, the program will probably start misbehaving. Moral: Your users shouldn't resize the window so as to place some of the drawing outside the drawing area.

BUILDING THE TURTLEDRAW APPLICATION

It would be nice to have a background picture behind all this stuff.

To create a background picture:

1. Drag a nice picture to the Project window.

   To get the picture in the illustrations, grab the first beach scene in the screen-saver files that came with OS X.

2. In the Properties window of the main window, select this picture for the Backdrop property.

You also need some way of presenting instructions to the user on the use of the program. Because this application is intended to be accessible to very young children, it might be best to put the instructions right out front, rather than in a Help menu, and to make them brief.

For this task, you'll use a Canvas control, which is the most flexible of graphical controls. It will allow you to float white text over that blue beach scene, like foam on the sea.

To create the About Canvas control:

1. Drag a Canvas control from the Tools palette to the main window.

2. Position the control roughly in the bottom-left corner of the window, and set its properties as follows:

   Name: About   Height: 108

   Left: 12   LockLeft: checked

   Top: 292   LockTop: checked

   Width: 115

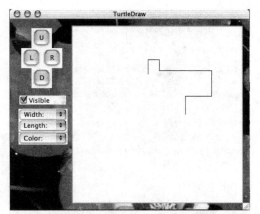

Figure 7.42 The TurtleDraw application, not quite finished.

To code the About Canvas control:

1. Open the About control's Paint handler. The Canvas control will display a string.

2. Define the string:
   dim s as string

3. Put your instructional text in the string:
   s = "• U, D, L, and R draw lines up, down,
   → left, and right." + chr(13) +
   → "Visible, Width, Length, and Color
   → change the way the line looks."

4. Because the Graphics property does the work, use its properties to set the text characteristics:
   g.bold = true
   g.foreColor = RGB(255,255,255)
   g.textSize = 10

5. Draw the string via the Graphics property's DrawString method:
   g.drawString(s,4,12,107)

6. Save your work, and test it (**Figure 7.42**).

BUILDING THE TURTLEDRAW APPLICATION

The application is not quite complete. Those buttons don't look so nice against that busy background. You need to apply some cosmetics.

To frame the navigation buttons:

1. Drag two RoundRectangle controls to the main window.

2. Set the properties of one of the controls as follows:

   Left: 44   LockLeft: checked

   Top: 114   LockTop: checked

   Width: 48   BorderWidth: 2

   Height: 142   BorderColor: Silver

3. Set the properties of the other control as follows:

   Left: 20   LockLeft: checked

   Top: 60   LockTop: checked

   Width: 96   BorderWidth: 2

   Height: 48   BorderColor: Silver

4. Click each control in turn, and choose Format > Move to Back (**Figure 7.43**).

To frame the customization buttons:

1. Drag a Rectangle control to the main window.

2. Set the control's properties as follows:

   Left: 12   LockLeft: checked

   Top: 160   LockTop: checked

   Width: 115   BorderWidth: 2

   Height: 120   TopLeftCorner: Aluminum

                     BottomRightCorner: Silver

3. Click this Rectangle control, and choose Format > Move to Back.

4. Save your work, and test it (**Figure 7.44**).

Figure 7.43 Some cosmetic enhancements for the TurtleDraw application.

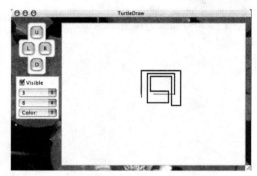

Figure 7.44 The buttons are framed.

That could be the end, but one thing that you don't have is an Erase option. Well, you do: It's called White. Painting over a line with white erases it because the background is white. But that solution is a little unsatisfactory. Why not change the background color and add a line color that matches the new background color, so you can have a real, visible white line in addition to an eraser?

To set the color of the drawing area:

1. Click in the drawing area in the main window.

2. In the Properties window, click FillColor.

3. In the left pane of the Color Picker that appears, examine the different color models.

   You've set the colors with the RGB model, so try that one. But there's a problem: When you specify RGB values in code, you use integers in the range 0 to 255, but here in the Color Picker, RGB values are expressed as percentages. Do you have to do the math to match your background color and the color of the line you'll use to erase?

   You could, but maybe you can prevent the problem. REALbasic supports different color models, and there are different models here in the Color Picker. Do some models work together better?

   There are—REALbasic's CMY and the Color Picker's CMYK models, for example.

4. Choose the CMYK model in the left pane of the Color Picker.

5. Set the sliders to read as follows:

   Cyan: 0   Yellow: 3

   Magenta: 0   Black: 0

6. Click OK.

continues on next page

7. Double-click the ColorPopup button.

8. In the Code Editor, select the ColorPopup's Change handler.

9. Add this code before the line that contains just the word Else:

```
Case "Erase"
    TurtleColor = CMY(0.00,0.00,0.03)
```

10. Close the Code Editor, and double-click the ColorPopup button again.

11. In the button's Properties window, add one line to its InitialValue property:

```
Erase
```

12. Save your work, and test it.

Choose a White line color from the pop-up menu, and draw a line. You should see a faint white line. Now choose Erase as the line color, and draw over the line to erase it. You should see a perfect match to the background (**Figure 7.45**).

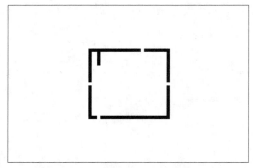

Figure 7.45 Now the application can erase as well as draw.

To build the application:

1. Choose File > Build Settings.

2. Enter TurtleDraw as the application's name.

3. Adjust any other setting you want to change.

4. Click OK.

5. Choose File > Build Application.

You can do many more things with pictures in REALbasic. In Chapter 8, "Working with Animations," you'll learn how to make pictures move.

Working with Animations and Movies

8

One way to animate an image in REALbasic is to draw a picture in a `Canvas` control and then do it again—and again and again, changing the image on each iteration. But that process gets tedious quickly, so REALbasic provides several tools that help you incorporate animations and movies into your applications.

The `MoviePlayer` control makes it easy to play existing QuickTime movies in your REALbasic applications and even develop your own movies, adding effects and editing down to the level of the individual frame. (Movies can also contain sounds, and REALbasic has tools for working with sounds in your applications.)

The `RB3DSpace` control lets you display and rotate 3D graphics created with QuickDraw 3D or Questa.

And the sprite-animation tools let you develop your own animations for creating games or other animated applications.

In this chapter, you'll learn how to use these tools to make pictures move.

Sprite Animation

REALbasic lets you create and run animations by using sprite animation. In sprite animation, objects move against a backdrop, like cartoon figures against a still background picture or actors against the backdrop of a stage set. The objects are created as instances of the Sprite class, and the backdrop is an instance of the SpriteSurface control.

Sprites and SpriteSurfaces

A Sprite is basically a picture that belongs to some SpriteSurface control, which does all the work (**Figure 8.1**). After it has been created, all that a Sprite can do on its own is disappear when its time on stage is over. The SpriteSurface manages the movement of the Sprite—of all the Sprites under its control. It also monitors and responds to mouse and keyboard actions by the user, and it detects and deals with collisions between the sprites as they move about the SpriteSurface.

A Sprite has properties that indicate its position and its relationship to other Sprites in its SpriteSurface. It also has an Image property, which is its picture.

A SpriteSurface also has a property that is a picture: its Backdrop property. Other properties control its position and dimensions, bit depth, and frame speed. It has methods that allow it to scroll its Backdrop image; start, stop, and single-step the animation; check for keyboard events; and create new Sprites or attach existing ones to itself (**Figure 8.2**).

The actual animation of the Sprites consists of changing the position of one or more Sprites or swapping one picture for another in the Sprite's Image property. You write code to carry out this task and cause it to be executed whenever the SpriteSurface gets the NextFrame event, which occurs at a rate dictated by the FrameRate property of the SpriteSurface.

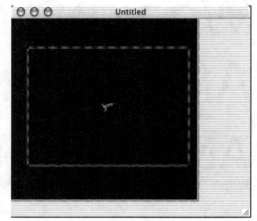

Figure 8.1 A SpriteSurface is like a stage on which animations play.

Figure 8.2 A SpriteSurface's Backdrop property is a picture that serves as the backdrop for the animation.

The mechanics of sprite animation, then, are pretty simple: create some Sprites and a SpriteSurface, associate them with the desired pictures, and write some code to move them around. Professional animators do some planning before they get to the mechanics of the operation, though, and so should you.

To create a simple Sprite animation:

1. Drag a SpriteSurface to the main window, and name it SpriteSurface1.

2. Locate a picture to serve as the backdrop of your animation, drag it to the Project window, and name it Backdrop1.

3. In the SpriteSurface's Properties window, set its Backdrop property to this picture.

4. With the Code Editor open, choose Edit > New Property.

5. In the dialog that appears, enter:

   mySprite as Sprite

   You've created a new property of the main window to hold your Sprite. This property will allow both the SpriteSurface and a button to refer to this same Sprite.

6. Locate a small picture that you want to animate, drag it to the Project window, and name it SpritePic1.

   This picture will be your Sprite's image.

7. Drag a PushButton from the Tools palette to the main window.

8. In the PushButton's Properties window, name it Run.

continues on next page

9. Open the Code Editor for the
PushButton, and enter this code in its
Action handler (**Figure 8.3**):

```
mySprite = new Sprite
mySprite.image = SpritePic1
SpriteSurface1.attach mySprite
SpriteSurface1.clickToStop = true
SpriteSurface1.frameSpeed = 2
SpriteSurface1.run
```

This code creates a new Sprite, assigns
it an image, attaches it to the
SpriteSurface, sets some properties of
the SpriteSurface, and starts the animation running. The clickToStop property
of the SpriteSurface ensures that when
the user clicks, the animation stops.
Even if you don't intend to keep this
capability in your animation, it makes
testing easier.

10. Open the NextFrame handler of the
SpriteSurface1 control, and enter
this code:

```
mySprite.x = mySprite.x+rnd*4
mySprite.y = mySprite.y+rnd*3
```

This code is where the animation takes
place. The frameSpeed property that you
set in the button handler controls how
often the NextFrame event occurs, and
each time it occurs, this code is executed.
All that this example does is move the
Sprite on a drunken diagonal downward
and rightward over the SpriteSurface.

11. Save your work, and test it.

By clicking to stop the animation and
clicking the button again, you can send
a stream of Sprites staggering across
the SpriteSurface (**Figure 8.4**).

Figure 8.3 Driving Sprite animation via a PushButton.

Figure 8.4 Is this how Trey Parker and Matt Stone
got started?

SPRITE ANIMATION

Figure 8.5 You can freeze animations or step through them one frame at a time.

To single-step a Sprite animation:

1. Create a `SpriteSurface`, `PushButton`, and `mySprite` property as described in the previous step.

2. In the Code Editor, open the window's `Open` event handler, and enter this code:

```
mySprite = new Sprite
mySprite.image = SpritePic1
SpriteSurface1.attach mySprite
SpriteSurface1.clickToStop = true
SpriteSurface1.frameSpeed = 2
```

3. In the `PushButton`'s `Action` handler, enter this code:

```
SpriteSurface1.update
```

4. In the `SpriteSurface`'s `NextFrame` handler, enter this code:

```
mySprite.x = mySprite.x+rnd*4
mySprite.y = mySprite.y+rnd*3
```

When you save and run this project, you must click the button repeatedly to move the `Sprite` across the `SpriteSurface`, because unlike the run method, the update method advances the animation only one frame.

This project produces only one `Sprite`, because the code that creates the `Sprite` resides in the window's `Open` handler.

Single-stepping an animation is useful for testing purposes, but you can also use this technique to control the speed of the animation, because the frame advances only when you tell it to (**Figure 8.5**).

To change a Sprite's image:

1. Create a SpriteSurface, PushButton, and mySprite property as described on pages 277-8.

2. Enter code in the PushButton's Action handler and the SpriteSurface's NextFrame handler as described on pages 277-8.

3. Drag a second small picture to the Project window to serve as the alternate image for the Sprites, and name it SpritePic2.

4. Modify the Action code as follows:

```
mySprite = new Sprite
if rnd > 0.5 then
  mySprite.image = SpritePic1
else
  mySprite.image = SpritePic2
end if
SpriteSurface1.attach mySprite
SpriteSurface1.clickToStop = true
SpriteSurface1.frameSpeed = 2
SpriteSurface1.run
```

5. Save your work, and test it (**Figure 8.6**). Notice that the Sprite images change randomly, and the movement continues as in the first example in this chapter. You can modify both a Sprite's image and its position on each step of the animation. You might try modifying the example in "To single-step a Sprite animation" on page 279. to see clearly how one Sprite can change in both ways in one step.

Figure 8.6 You can animate the Sprite both by moving it around the SpriteSurface and by changing the Sprite's image.

The next example requires some simple drawing on your part, which you can do with AppleWorks or any drawing program.

To animate a walking figure:

1. Create a `SpriteSurface`, `PushButton`, and `mySprite` property as described in steps 1, 5, 7, and 8 on page 277.

2. Drag three pictures to the Project window.

   One of these pictures should be something appropriate for a backdrop for your walking figure. Name it `Backdrop1`, and assign it as the `Backdrop` property of the `SpriteSurface`.

   The other two pictures will be two views of your walking figure, created with any drawing program. They should be identical except for the position of the feet. In one picture, the left foot is advanced, and in the other, the right foot is. Name these two pictures `SpritePic1` and `SpritePic2`.

3. With the Code Editor open, choose Edit > New Property.

4. In the dialog that appears, enter:

   `leftFoot as Boolean`

   You'll use this window property to keep track of which foot your figure should advance, changing the property's value after each step.

5. In the Code Editor, open the window's `Open` event handler, and enter this code:

```
mySprite = new Sprite
mySprite.image = SpritePic1
SpriteSurface1.attach mySprite
SpriteSurface1.clickToStop = true
SpriteSurface1.frameSpeed = 0
leftFoot = true
```

continues on next page

6. In the PushButton's Action handler, enter this code:

```
if leftFoot then
  mySprite.image = SpritePic1
else
  mySprite.image = SpritePic2
end if
SpriteSurface1.update
leftFoot = not leftFoot
```

7. In the SpriteSurface's NextFrame handler, enter this code:

```
mySprite.x = mySprite.x+12
```

8. Save your work, and test it (**Figure 8.7**).

You'll want to alter the x-coordinate increment in the NextFrame handler to make your figure move the right distance, and you may want to adjust the FrameSpeed.

Figure 8.7 You need both techniques to produce the effect of walking.

To change the speed of an animation:

◆ Set the SpriteSurface's FrameSpeed property higher for slower animation and lower to speed things up. A setting of 0 gets you the maximum speed your machine can deliver.

Technically, FrameSpeed is the number of vertical retraces per frame.

To change the bit depth of an animation:

◆ Change the SpriteSurface's Depth property.

This property can take the values 0, 8, 16, or 32 and can even be changed in the NextFrame event handler for an unsettling effect. A setting of 0 chooses the bit depth of the monitor at the time when the SpriteSurface was opened (**Figure 8.8**).

Figure 8.8 Some properties of a SpriteSurface that can be set in the IDE.

Figure 8.9 Scrolling the SpriteSurface itself, which is what you need to do if you want to hold the character in the center of the frame as she walks.

To scroll the SpriteSurface:

1. Drag a SpriteSurface to the main window, and name it SpriteSurface1.

2. Assign a picture to its Backdrop property as described on pages 277-8.

3. With the Code Editor open, choose Edit > New Property.

4. In the dialog that appears, enter:
   mySprite as Sprite

5. Drag another picture to the Project window, and name it SpritePic1.

6. In the window's Open handler, enter this code to create your Sprite and run your animation:
   ```
   mySprite = new Sprite
   mySprite.image = SpritePic1
   SpriteSurface1.attach mySprite
   SpriteSurface1.clickToStop = true
   SpriteSurface1.frameSpeed = 2
   ```

7. In the SpriteSurface's MouseEnter handler, place this code:
   ```
   SpriteSurface1.run
   ```

8. Drag a PushButton to the main window, and name it Scroll.

9. In the Scroll button's Action handler, enter this code (**Figure 8.9**):
   ```
   SpriteSurface1.scroll 1,0
   ```
   This code will scroll the SpriteSurface 1 pixel to the right. If you change the second parameter to something other than 0, you'll scroll in the y direction. Technically, this is a pan, not a scroll, as REALbasic author and developer Matt Neuburg has pointed out. It is as though the SpriteSurface is a window onto its Backdrop and is sliding over the backdrop.

   continues on next page

Unfortunately, the SpriteSurface is taking all the Sprites with it, which probably isn't what you want. To keep the Sprites in position in the overall window, you need to adjust the positions of the Sprites.

10. Add this code to the Scroll button's Action handler:

```
mySprite.x = mySprite.x + 1
```

This code will undo the movement of the Sprite caused by scrolling. If you scroll in the y direction, you need to adjust mySprite.y appropriately.

The SpriteSurface's Backdrop image is repainted automatically as you scroll. If you want to modify anything when this happens, put that code in the SpriteSurface's PaintTile event handler, which runs every time scrolling takes place.

In games (a typical application of animation techniques), users often press keys rather than buttons to control the game action. A SpriteSurface has the capability to respond to any key press, but it uses key codes that are platform-specific.

To let an animation respond to key presses:

1. Following the procedure on pages 277-8, create a SpriteSurface named SpriteSurface1 and a Sprite property named mySprite, and import pictures for both.

2. Enter this code in the window's Open handler to create the new Sprite:

```
mySprite = SpriteSurface1.newSprite
→ (SpritePic1,200,200)
SpriteSurface1.attach mySprite
SpriteSurface1.clickToStop = true
```

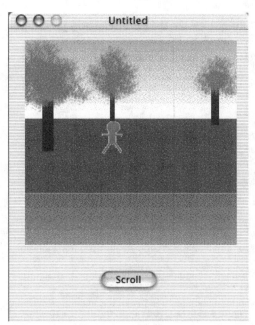

Scroll

Figure 8.10 You can also put scrolling under user control.

3. In the SpriteSurface's MouseEnter handler, place this code:

```
SpriteSurface1.run
```

4. Enter this code in the SpriteSurface's NextFrame event:

```
// Left
if SpriteSurface1.keyTest(&h7B) then
  me.scroll -1,0
// Right
elseif SpriteSurface1.keyTest(&h7C)
→ then
  me.scroll 1,0
// Up
elseif SpriteSurface1.keyTest(&h7E)
→ then
  me.scroll 0,-1
// Down
elseif SpriteSurface1.keyTest(&h7D)
→ then
  me.scroll 0,1
End if
```

This code lets the user scroll the SpriteSurface by using the arrow keys (**Figure 8.10**).

To create new Sprites on the fly:

1. Following the procedure on pages 277-8, create a SpriteSurface named SpriteSurface1, import a picture for your SpriteSurface and one for your Sprites, and assign the first picture to the SpriteSurface as its Backdrop property.

2. Drag a PushButton to the main window, and enter this code in its Action handler:

   ```
   SpriteSurface1.run
   ```

3. With the Code Editor open, choose Edit > New Property.

4. In the Property Declaration dialog that appears, enter:

   ```
   mySprite(100) as Sprite
   ```

   This code creates a property that is a 100-element array of items whose type is Sprite. You'll also need a way to keep track of how many of these Sprites there are.

5. With the Code Editor open, choose Edit > New Property.

6. In the Property Declaration dialog that appears, enter:

   ```
   SpriteCount as Integer
   ```

7. In the window's Open handler, enter this code:

   ```
   SpriteCount = 0
   ```

8. In the SpriteSurface's NextFrame handler, enter this code:

   ```
   if me.keyTest(&h2D) then
     mySprite(spriteCount) = me.newSprite
   → (SpritePic1,100+SpriteCount*32,
   → 100+SpriteCount*32)
   me.attach mySprite(spriteCount)
   SpriteCount = SpriteCount + 1
   end if
   ```

   This code allows the user to create new Sprites by pressing the N key (**Figure 8.11**).

Figure 8.11 In fact, you can let the user create new Sprites.

SPRITE ANIMATION

When you create new Sprites on the fly this way, you have to keep track of how many Sprites you have, as well as their properties, and you have to set properties initially. One way to get this situation under control, particularly if you create several similar Sprites, is to create your own Sprite classes. Following are two examples.

To create a Sprite class without movement:

1. Drag a SpriteSurface to the main window, and name it SpriteSurface1.

2. Locate a picture to serve as the backdrop of your animation, drag it to the Project window, and name it Backdrop1.

3. Drag a small picture to the Project window, and name it WallPict.

4. In the SpriteSurface's Properties window, set its Backdrop property to the Backdrop1 picture.

5. Choose File > New Class.

6. In the new class's Properties window, set its Name property to Wall and its Super to Sprite.

   This new class is a subclass of the Sprite class. Now you can add properties to make it distinctive.

7. Double-click the Wall class's icon in the Project window to open its Code Editor.

8. Choose Edit > New Property.

9. In the Property Declaration dialog that appears, enter Orientation as String, and click OK.

continues on next page

SPRITE ANIMATION

This step gives your Wall Sprite a unique property, but you might also want to customize some of the standard Sprite properties, such as the Image. This process falls under the heading of initialization of a class and is just what Constructor functions are for. (You learned about Constructors in Chapter 5, "Writing Object-Oriented Code.")

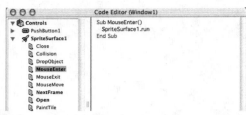

Figure 8.12 Animation can be triggered by many events, including the action of the user moving the mouse pointer over the SpriteSurface.

10. Choose Edit > New Method.

11. In the Method Declaration dialog that appears, enter Wall as the name of the method, and click OK.

12. In the Code Editor for the Wall method, enter this code:

```
me.image = WallPict
me.x = 100 * rnd
me.y = 100 * rnd
if me.image.height > me.image.width
then
  Orientation = "Vertical"
else
  Orientation = "Horizontal"
end if
```

Having created a new class of Sprite with its own distinguishing properties, you can create instances of the class.

13. Click the main window's icon in the Project window, and press Option-Tab to open the Code Editor for the window.

14. In the SpriteSurface's NextFrame handler, enter this code:

```
dim w as Wall
if SpriteSurface1.keyTest(&h2D) then
  w = new Wall
  SpriteSurface1.attach w
end if
```

15. In the SpriteSurface's MouseEnter handler, place this code (**Figure 8.12**):

```
SpriteSurface1.run
```

To create a Sprite class with movement:

1. Drag a SpriteSurface to the main window, and name it SpriteSurface1.

2. Locate a picture to serve as the backdrop of your animation, drag it to the Project window, and name it Backdrop1.

3. Drag a small picture to the Project window, and name it BallPict.

4. In the SpriteSurface's Properties window, set its Backdrop property to the Backdrop1 picture.

5. Choose File > New Class.

6. In the new class's Properties window, set its Name property to Ball and its Super to Sprite.

   This new class is a subclass of the Sprite class. Now you can add properties to make it distinctive.

7. Double-click the Ball class's icon in the Project window to open its Code Editor.

8. Choose Edit > New Property.

9. In the Property Declaration dialog that appears, enter Speed as Integer, and click OK.

10. Repeat steps 8 and 9 to create two more properties for the Ball class:

    Xdirection as Integer

    Ydirection as Integer

    This code gives your Ball Sprite three unique properties. You can initialize these properties for each new Ball with a Constructor.

11. Choose Edit > New Method.

continues on next page

12. In the Method Declaration dialog that appears, enter Ball as the name of the method, and click OK.

13. In the Code Editor for the Ball method, enter this code:

```
me.image = BallPict
me.x = 100 * rnd
me.y = 100 * rnd
Speed = 1
Xdirection = 1
Ydirection = 1
```

14. Choose Edit > New Method again.

15. In the Method Declaration dialog that appears, enter Move as the name of the method, and click OK.

16. In the Code Editor for the Move method, enter this code:

```
me.x = me.x + Xdirection * Speed
me.y = me.y + Ydirection * Speed
```

This handler will move the Ball one step. It uses the parameters you defined for this class.

Having created a new class of Sprite with its own distinguishing properties and behavior, you can create instances of the class.

17. With the Code Editor open for the main window, choose Edit > New Property.

18. In the Property Declaration dialog that appears, enter Ball1 as Ball.

This step gives you a property in which to store a Ball Sprite so that it can be referred to by more than one handler.

19. Click the main window's icon in the Project window, and press Option-Tab to open the Code Editor for the window.

20. In the SpriteSurface's NextFrame handler, enter this code:

```
Ball1.move
```

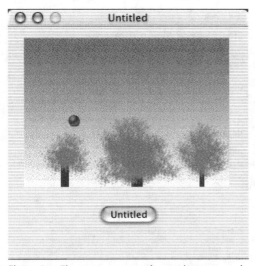

Untitled

Untitled

Figure 8.13 The most common element in games and sports: a moving ball. Getting it to move right takes some coding.

21. Drag a PushButton to the main window, and in its Action handler, enter this code:

```
SpriteSurface1.attach Ball1
```

22. In the SpriteSurface's MouseEnter handler, place this code:

```
SpriteSurface1.run
```

23. Save and test your work (**Figure 8.13**).

In the preceding examples, you defined different classes of Sprites with different properties and behavior, as well as mechanisms for creating new instances of these Sprites and ways of dealing with user input. When you have more than one Sprite moving around the SpriteSurface, though, you need to consider the interaction among the Sprites.

Sprite interaction

Sprite interaction chiefly involves three things: collisions, groups, and priorities.

When any portion of the rectangle bounding one Sprite intersects with the rectangle bounding another Sprite, this situation is (potentially) a collision. When a collision occurs, the SpriteSurface receives a Collision event, to which it can respond.

Every Sprite has a Group property, which is an integer. You can use this integer for any purpose you dream up, but a SpriteSurface checks the Group properties of intersecting Sprites to decide whether to trigger a collision event.

Depending on what Sprites represent, it may be perfectly reasonable for one to pass through the bounding rectangle of another. Two Sprites can represent cars, for example, with one passing in front of the other. In this case, you want the Sprite that is supposed to be in front to occlude the other as it passes through or over it. The Priority property controls this interaction.

SPRITE ANIMATION

To manage Sprite interaction by using Groups:

◆ Assign a number to the Group property of every Sprite in the SpriteSurface.

Table 8.2 shows the effects of different combinations of Group values.

To handle Sprite collisions:

◆ Place the code in the SpriteSurface's Collision handler:

```
if s1.group = 1 then
  s1.close
elseif s2.group = 1 then
  s2.close
end if
```

The Collision handler gives you references to the two colliding Sprites (s1 and s2). Here, the Sprite that belongs to Group 1 doesn't survive the collision (**Figure 8.14**).

To cause one Sprite to appear in front of another:

◆ Set the Priority property of the Sprite you want to pass in front to a higher value.

The SpriteSurface's NextFrame handler causes the Sprites to be drawn in the order of their Priority settings, so a Sprite with a higher Priority will be drawn over a Sprite with a lower Priority if their bounding rectangles overlap (**Figure 8.15**).

Those are the basics of REALbasic animation. At the end of this chapter is a simple game that puts many of these things together.

Table 8.2

Effect of the Group Property on Sprite Collisions

SPRITE 1	SPRITE 2	COLLISION?
0	0	No
0	Negative number	No
0	Positive number	No
Negative number	Negative number	Yes
Negative number	Positive number	Yes
Positive number	Different positive number	Yes
Positive number	Same positive number	No

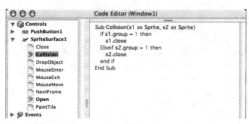

Figure 8.14 What happens when two Sprites collide depends on their Group properties.

Figure 8.15 When noncolliding Sprites pass, which one goes in front? The outcome is decided on the basis of their Priority properties.

SPRITE ANIMATION

Creating Time-Aware Applications

Many kinds of applications need to know the time, such as programs that alert you about appointments. Animations may not need to know the time of day, but they may need to run for a set number of seconds. REALbasic provides several tools for working with time in your applications, including the Ticks and Microseconds functions, the Date class, and the Timer control.

To make an action time-dependent:

1. With the Code Editor open, choose Edit > New Property.

2. In the Property Declaration dialog that appears, enter:
   ```
   StartTime as Double
   ```

3. In the main window's Open handler, enter this code:
   ```
   StartTime = Microseconds
   ```

4. Test the elapsed time, and take the appropriate action.
   Place this code in a SpriteSurface's NextFrame handler, for exmaple:
   ```
   if Microseconds - StartTime > 60 *
   → 1000000 then
     me.stop
   End if
   ```

You can use this technique with any repeating event handler, not just in animation.

The Microseconds and Ticks functions return a measure of the time since the last system startup, but they do so only when they are called. They depend on some recurring event such as NextFrame in animation to keep checking in. If you want to monitor the time continuously even when no recurring event is occurring or to take more-resolute control of the timing of the application or animation, you need to use the Timer control.

The Timer control

The Timer is an invisible control that constantly watches the time and executes its Action handler when a specified time has elapsed (**Figure 8.16**). It will even execute its Action handler if the window containing it is invisible or behind another window.

A Timer has two interesting properties and one event handler:

◆ Period. This property represents the time (in milliseconds) for which the Timer runs.

◆ Mode. 0, 1, or 2. 0 means that the Timer is turned off. 1 means that the Timer counts down once, executes its Action handler, and quits. 2 means that the Timer restarts its countdown after executing its Action handler.

To create a digital clock:

1. Drag three EditField controls from the Tools palette to the main window.

2. Set the controls' Name properties to HourField, MinuteField, and SecondField. These fields will hold the hour, minute, and second of the time: one or two digits.

3. Decide how large you want your clock to be, and set all three fields' TextSize properties to appropriate values.

4. Resize the fields to be just large enough to hold two digits at that TextSize, and line them up in a row, with a few pixels between them.

5. Drag two StaticText controls to the window, and set the Text property of each to a single character: a colon (:).

Figure 8.16 The key to time-dependent actions is the Timer control.

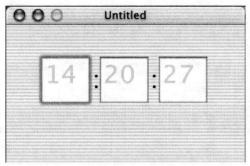

Figure 8.17 A digital clock created from a Timer control, three EditFields, and a dozen lines of code.

6. Set the TextSize properties to the same values as those of the EditFields, and drag the fields to the gaps between the EditFields, resizing them as needed.

7. Drag a Timer control to the window.

8. Set its Mode property to 2 and its Period to 100.

   The Period is measured in milliseconds, so the Timer will run for a tenth of a second, execute its Action handler, and then (because its Mode is 2) start again.

9. With the Code Editor open, choose Edit > New Property.

10. In the Property Declaration dialog that appears, enter:

    CurrentTime as Date

11. Code the Timer's Action handler:

```
dim s as string
CurrentTime = New Date
HourField.text = str(CurrentTime.hour)
s = str(CurrentTime.minute)
if len(s) = 1 then
  s = "0" + s
End if
MinuteField.text = s
s = str(CurrentTime.second)
if len(s) = 1 then
  s = "0" + s
End if
SecondField.text = s
```

The Timer just reads off the hour, minutes, and seconds from the current time (which the Date object returns) and displays the values in the fields (**Figure 8.17**). A slight complication: You need to convert the numbers to text and add a leading 0 into the minutes and seconds if they don't have two characters after conversion to text.

Displaying 3D Animations

In addition to Sprite animation, REALbasic supports the display and manipulation of 3D objects via the RB3DSpace control. 3D animation has no connection with Sprite animation, and neither of these animation systems has any connection with REALbasic's facilities for playing QuickTime video, which are discussed on pages 300-306. You can't incorporate Sprites into a movie or a movie into a SpriteSurface, and you can't mix the effects of either of these with 3D animation.

To make things even more interesting, REALbasic's 3D capabilities are based on QuickDraw 3D, a technology that Apple decided to drop in 1999 in favor of OpenGL. QuickDraw 3D has been re-created independently, however, in an Open Source project called Quesa (pronounced as in *quesadilla*). REALbasic supports Quesa 3D models, and Quesa runs on Mac OS 8/9, Mac OS X, Windows, and other operating systems, so REALbasic hasn't exactly hitched its 3D wagon to a dead horse.

The RB3DSpace control displays objects of class Object3D. To use the RB3DSpace control to display 3D objects, you need to have a source of 3D objects and models. You (or someone else) will have created these objects or models by using QuickDraw3D or Quesa. For the purposes of this section, you can download QuickDraw 3D or Quesa models from several sites, such as the Quesa site (www.quesa.org) or Joseph Strout's REALbasic programming site (www.strout.net/info/coding/rb/intro.html). A Web search will turn up many other sources of models that you can play with (**Figure 8.18**).

Figure 8.18 REALbasic will help you run 3D animations, not create them. But you can find 3D animation files to experiment with on the Web.

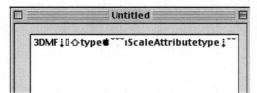

Figure 8.19 3D object files are machine-readable text descriptions of objects or scenes.

To set up for 3D modeling:

◆ For the Classic Mac OS, check to see whether QuickDraw3D is installed and enabled.

   If so, you'll see QD3D files in your Extensions folder inside the System folder, and the Extensions Manager Control Panel will indicate that the files are enabled. If not, use the Extensions Manager to enable it or the QuickTime Installer to install it.

   or

   For Mac OS X or Windows use, install OpenGL (which should already be installed) and Quesa, which you can download from the Quesa site (www.quesa.org).

To view a 3D object file as text:

1. Drag an `EditField` control to the main window, and name it `EditField1`.

2. Choose Edit > File Types.

3. In the dialog that appears, click Add.

4. In the next dialog, enter ???? as the Mac Creator, 3DMF as the Mac Type, and 3DMF as the Name.

5. Click OK; then click OK again to dismiss both dialogs.

6. Enter this code in the window's `Open` event handler:

```
dim f as folderItem
f = getOpenFolderItem("3DMF")
editfield1.text =
→ f.openAsTextFile.readAll
```

3D object files are machine-readable text descriptions of 3D objects or scenes. By reading an object file as text, you can tell something about what the file is, as well as determine whether the file is corrupted (**Figure 8.19**).

To load a 3D object file into an RB3DSpace control:

1. Choose Edit > File Types.

2. In the dialog that appears, click Add.

3. In the next dialog, enter ???? as the Mac Creator, 3DMF as the Mac Type, and 3DMF as the Name.

4. Click OK; then click OK again to dismiss both dialogs.

5. Drag an RB3DSpace control to the main window, and name it RB3DSpace1.

6. Enter this code in the window's Open event handler:

```
dim f as folderItem
dim o as Object3D
f = getOpenFolderItem("3DMF")
o = new Object3D
o.addShapeFromString
→ f.openAsTextFile.readAll
RB3DSpace1.objects.append o
```

When you have a 3D scene in your RB3DSpace control, you can manipulate the properties of the control and those of the objects in the scene. One of those objects is always the Camera. Although the Camera is never visible (how would it see itself?), it is implemented as a 3D object, so it can be manipulated just like the real objects in the scene. An Object3D instance has a position, orientation, and scale, and it has methods to rotate it in three dimensions.

Initial State	
Hither	5
Yon	5000
FieldOfView	50
SkyColor	
AmbientLight	30
FloodLight	90
Wireframe	☑
DebugCube	☐

Figure 8.20 The ability to render any 3D scene or object as a wireframe is useful for debugging.

To change a 3D scene's lighting:

◆ Adjust either of the RB3DSpace's AmbientLight and FloodLight properties.

Each property is an integer in the range 0 to 100, with 0 being total darkness.

To change the field of view of a 3D scene:

◆ Adjust the RB3DSpace's FieldOfView property.

The property is an integer representing the number of degrees (not radians) for the field of view.

To change the camera angle or position in a 3D scene:

◆ Adjust the Camera's Position property, or invoke its Roll, Pitch, or Yaw method.

Position is a list of the x, y, and z coordinates of the object. Roll, Pitch, and Yaw take a double as a parameter, representing the number of radians (not degrees) to rotate the object:

Camera.Roll(3.14)

To rotate an object in a 3D scene:

◆ Call its Roll, Pitch, or Yaw method:

TallGuy.Yaw(3.14)

To render a 3D scene as a wireframe:

◆ Set the RB3DSpace's WireFrame property to true (**Figure 8.20**).

Movies

REALbasic supports the playing of QuickTime video via its MoviePlayer control. Using the MoviePlayer control is delightfully simple compared with working with the RB3DSpace control. But for those who want a little more challenge, REALbasic also lets you build movies, break movies into their constituent parts, and put them back together again by using the EditableMovie class.

Using video tools

The tools with which you need to be familiar to master REALbasic video are:

◆ MoviePlayer **control.** Gives you a space in which a movie can play and provides the properties, events, methods, and visible controls for managing the movie (**Figure 8.21**).

◆ Movie **class.** A reference to a QuickTime movie. To play a movie, you assign an instance of the Movie class to the Movie property of a MoviePlayer control.

◆ EditableMovie **class.** Used to create, edit, and save QuickTime movies. Opening a QuickTime movie as an EditableMovie gives you access to many properties of the movie but does not allow the movie to be played.

◆ **Effects.** Several REALbasic classes and functions allow you to add visual effects such as cross-fades and wipes to your videos.

◆ **Movie file I/O.** The FolderItem methods for opening and saving movies were covered in Chapter 6, "Working with Files"; other techniques are presented in this chapter.

Figure 8.21 The MoviePlayer control gives you a place for the movie to play and the controls to manage its playing.

Figure 8.22 If you choose, you can give the user all the familiar QuickTime movie controls.

To set up a movie to be played:

1. Drag a QuickTime movie file to the Project window, and give it the name `Movie1`.

2. Drag a MoviePlayer control from the Tools palette to the main window, and name it `MoviePlayer1`.

3. In the window's `Open` event handler, enter this code:

```
MoviePlayer1.movie = Movie1
```

When you run the program, the user can start the movie, stop the movie, and adjust the sound by using the standard QuickTime controls (**Figure 8.22**). You might have noticed, too, that the `MovieController` control resizes itself to fit the movie.

To load a movie from a disk file:

1. Drag a `MoviePlayer` control from the Tools palette to the main window, and name it `MoviePlayer1`.

2. In the window's `Open` event handler, enter this code:

```
dim f as folderItem
f = getFolderItem("Movie1")
MoviePlayer1.movie = f.openAsMovie
```

You can even play movies right off the Web.

To load a movie from the Web:

1. Drag a `MoviePlayer` control from the Tools palette to the main window, and name it `MoviePlayer1`.

2. In the window's `Open` event handler, enter this code:

```
dim trailer as string
trailer = "http://yaddayadda/
→ TheTwoTowers.240.mov"
MoviePlayer1.movie =
→ openUrlMovie(trailer)
MoviePlayer1.play
```

Sorry—the preceding URL won't really work. Because of the way WebObjects serves up movies, I wasn't able to supply a fixed URL for the movie trailer. But you can substitute between those quotation marks any valid URL for a QuickTime movie file (identified by .mov at the end of the URL).

To let the user choose a movie to play:

1. Choose Edit > File Types.

2. In the dialog that appears, click Add.

3. In the resulting dialog, choose video/quicktime from the Name pop-up menu.

4. Click OK twice to dismiss both dialogs.

5. Drag a `MoviePlayer` control from the Tools palette to the main window, and name it `MoviePlayer1`.

6. In the window's `Open` event handler, enter this code:

```
dim f as folderItem
f = getOpenFolderItem
→ ("video/quicktime")
MoviePlayer1.movie = f.openAsMovie
```

That's all that's required to create a simple movie viewer (**Figure 8.23**).

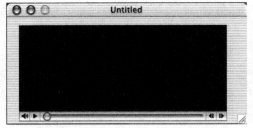

Figure 8.23 It takes only three lines of code to give the user a simple movie viewer that will play QuickTime movies of the user's choosing.

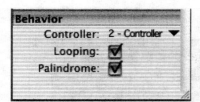

Figure 8.24 You can retain control of movies yourself, making a movie loop repeatedly, for example.

To hide the QuickTime controls:

◆ Set the MoviePlayer's Controller property to 0.

This setting will give the user no way to start the movie and no way to stop it except by quitting the application, so you'll need to provide some means for the user to do these things or do them yourself in code.

To control the start or stop time of a movie:

◆ Use the MovieController's Play and Stop methods.

You can use a Timer control to start or stop the movie after a set time (see the section on the Timer control earlier in this chapter). The movie will stop itself when it gets to the end unless you have set it to loop. Set the Position property of the MovieController to something other than 0 to set the number of seconds into the movie to start.

To loop a movie:

◆ Set the MovieController's Looping property to true (check the check box in the IDE).

To make the movie play alternately forward and backward (although I don't know why you'd want to do this), check the Looping and Palindrome properties (**Figure 8.24**).

Editing movies

You use the EditableMovie class to edit movies, building up tracks from collections of pictures and adding effects (**Figure 8.25**).

To turn two pictures into a movie by using a video effect:

1. Drag a MoviePlayer control to the main window, and name it MoviePlayer1.

2. Drag two pictures to the Project window, and name them Pic1 and Pic2.

3. Place this code in the window's Open handler:

```
dim p1,p2 as picture
dim f as folderItem
dim m as editableMovie
dim effect as QtEffect
dim sequence as QtEffectSequence
dim track as QtVideoTrack
dim i as integer
p1 = pic1
p2 = pic2
// Create an editablemovie
f = getFolderItem("myMovie")
m = f.createMovie
// Select an effect and create the frame
→ sequence
effect = getQtSmpteEffect(122)
sequence = new QtEffectSequence
→ (effect,p1,p2,20)
// Build the track
track = m.newVideoTrack
→ (p1.width,p1.height,5)
track.appendPicture(p1)
for i = 1 to 20
  sequence.frame = i
  track.appendPicture sequence.image
next
// Load it into the MoviePlayer
  MoviePlayer1.movie = m
```

See the Language Reference manual for the full list of effects.

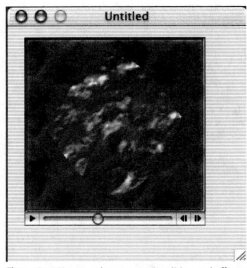

Figure 8.25 You can also use movie editing and effects tools within REALbasic to create your own movies.

Working with Sound

A QuickTime movie doesn't have to contain any video; it can be all sound, or you can just hide the video and play the sound. Two other ways to make noise with REALbasic are the NotePlayer control and the Sound class.

To play just the sound from a QuickTime movie:

1. Drag a QuickTime movie file to the Project window, and give it the name Movie1.

2. Drag a MoviePlayer control from the Tools palette to the main window, and name it MoviePlayer1.

3. Uncheck its Visible property.

4. In the window's Open event handler, enter this code:
   ```
   MoviePlayer1.movie = Movie1
   MoviePlayer1.play
   ```

To play a Sound for a specified duration:

1. Drag a PushButton to the main window, and name it Sound Test.

2. Drag a Timer control to the main window.

3. In the Timer's Properties window, set its Name to Timer1, its Mode to 0, and its Duration to 3000 (for 3 seconds).

4. In the Sound Test button's Action handler, enter this code:
   ```
   dim f as folderItem
   f = getFolderItem("SomeSound")
   Timer1.mode = 1
   Sound1 = f.openAsSound
   Sound1.playLooping
   ```

continues on next page

5. In the Timer's Action handler, enter this code:

```
Sound1.stop
```

6. Choose Edit > New Property.

7. In the Property Declaration dialog that appears, enter:

Sound1 as Sound

When you run the program and click the button, the sound will play for 3 seconds and then stop.

To play a musical note for a specified duration:

1. Drag a PushButton to the main window, and name it NotePlayer Test.

2. Drag a Timer control to the main window.

3. In the Timer's Properties window, set its Name to Timer2, its Mode to 0, and its Duration to 3000 (for 3 seconds).

4. In the NotePlayer Test button's Action handler, enter this code:

```
Timer2.mode = 1
NotePlayer1.instrument = 66
NotePlayer1.playNote(60,127)
```

5. In the Timer's Action handler, enter this code:

```
NotePlayer1.playNote(60,0)
```

6. Drag a NotePlayer control to the main window, and name it NotePlayer1.

When you run the program and click the button, you should hear the sound of middle C played on an alto sax for 3 seconds (**Figure 8.26**).

Figure 8.26
REALbasic provides tools for playing simulated musical instruments, sound files, or QuickTime audio tracks. The examples show how to create a button script to experiment with these effects.

Rediscovering a Classic Video Game

People were building custom hardware to play ping-pong (or tennis) on television screens at least as far back as 1958. The most famous electronic implementation of the game, though, was Pong, released in 1972. Pong was so popular that it allowed Nolan Bushnell to start a company to create video games. He called it Atari.

In a time when every byte of memory was precious, Pong was famous for its succinct, six-word instructions: "Avoid missing ball for high score." Today, it takes 16 pages to explain how to change the drum kit in a printer. I'll try to explain how to write your own version of Pong in fewer pages than that.

To create the game window:

1. Open a new project.

2. In the main window's Properties window, set the `Name` to `Game Window`, its `MinWidth` to `400`, its `MinHeight` to `200`, and its `Title` to `Avoid Missing Ball For High Score`.

3. Check the check boxes for the `GrowIcon` and `ZoomIcon` properties.

Modifying the size of the window will be one of the tools the user has to adjust the difficulty of the game.

To gather the pictures:

1. Locate or create the pictures you'll need for the game:

   ▲ PaddleImage: a rectangle, 2 to 8 pixels wide and 20 to 40 pixels tall

   ▲ BackgroundImage: a large solid-color rectangle

   ▲ BallImage: a circle or ball, about 8 pixels in diameter

   ▲ WallImage: a large rectangle, 600 pixels or more on a side

2. Drag these images to the Project window, and name them as indicated in step 1 (Figure 8.27).

The pictures will be associated with custom Sprites, which you'll create next.

Figure 8.27 Building the classic video game. First, find or create some graphics.

To create the Paddle class:

1. Choose File > New Class.

2. In the new class's Properties window, set its Name to Paddle and its Super to Sprite.

   This step gives you a new class that is a subclass of Sprite—a particular kind of Sprite called a Paddle. You'll do the same for the game's Ball, Walls, and Goals. The players move their Paddles up and down to block the Ball as it caroms off the Walls and Paddles until it eventually hits a Goal.

3. In the Project window, double-click the icon for the Paddle class to open its Code Editor.

4. Choose Edit > New Method.

5. In the Method Declaration dialog that appears, enter Move as the name of the method, and click OK.

6. Enter this code for the Move method:

```
// Move the Paddle
dim bottom as integer
bottom = me.y + me.image.height
if me.y + speed > 1 and bottom + speed <
→ GameWindow.SpriteSurface1.height - 1
→ then
  me.y = me.y + speed
End if
```

7. Choose Edit > New Property.

8. In the Property Declaration dialog that appears, enter:

```
Speed as Integer
```

To create the Ball class:

1. Choose File > New Class.

2. In the new class's Properties window, set its Name to Ball and its Super to Sprite.

The Ball and the Paddles are the only ones of these custom Sprites that move. The Paddles just move up and down, but the Ball can go anywhere in the SpriteSurface, possibly colliding with Paddles, Walls, and Goals.

3. In the Project window, double-click the icon for the Ball class to open its Code Editor.

4. Choose Edit > New Method.

5. In the Method Declaration dialog that appears, enter Move as the name of the method, and click OK.

6. Enter this code for the Move method:

```
// Move the Ball
me.x = me.x + Xdirection * Speed
me.y = me.y + Ydirection * Speed
```

7. Choose Edit > New Property.

continues on next page

REDISCOVERING A CLASSIC VIDEO GAME

8. In the Property Declaration dialog that appears, enter:

Speed as Integer

9. Repeat steps 7 and 8 to create two other properties:

Xdimension as Integer

Ydimension as Integer

To create the Wall class:

1. Choose File > New Class.

2. In the new class's Properties window, set its Name to Wall and its Super to Sprite.

The Walls are the edges of the screen that the Ball will bounce off.

To create the Goal class:

1. Choose File > New Class.

2. In the new class's Properties window, set its Name to Goal and its Super to Sprite.

The Goals are the edges of the screen behind the Paddles. If the Ball gets to one of the Goals, one player or the other scores a point.

To set up the SpriteSurface:

1. Drag a SpriteSurface to the main window.

2. Set its properties as follows:

Name: SpriteSurface1

Left: 4

Top: 4

Width: 392

Height: 276

LockLeft, LockTop, LockRight, LockBottom: checked

Backdrop: BackgroundImage

ClickToStop: checked

3. Double-click the SpriteSurface to open its Code Editor.

4. Enter this code in its `NextFrame` handler:

```
// Interpret keypresses and move Paddle
if me.keyTest(&h00) then
  Paddle1.speed = -1 * abs(Paddle1.speed)
  Paddle1.move
End if
if me.keyTest(&h27) then
  Paddle2.speed = -1 * abs(Paddle2.speed)
  Paddle2.move
End if
if me.keyTest(&h2C) then
  Paddle2.speed = abs(Paddle2.speed)
  Paddle2.move
End if
if me.keyTest(&h06) then
  Paddle1.speed = abs(Paddle1.speed)
  Paddle1.move
End if
ball1.move
```

5. Enter this code in the `SpriteSurface`'s `Collision` handler:

```
// There was a sprite collision.
// Was one of the sprites a Ball?
if s1.group = 2 or s2.group = 2 then
// Ball hit Paddle
  if s1.group = 1 then
    Ball(s2).Xdirection = Ball(s2).Xdirection * -1
  elseif s2.group = 1 then
    Ball(s1).Xdirection = Ball(s1).Xdirection * -1
// Ball hit Wall
  elseif s1.group = 3 then
    Ball(s2).Ydirection = Ball(s2).Ydirection * -1
  elseif s2.group = 3 then
    Ball(s1).Ydirection = Ball(s1).Ydirection * -1
// Ball hit Goal
  elseif s1.group = 4 then
    if s1.x > 10 then
      Player1Score.text = str(val(Player1Score.text)+1)
```

continues on next page

```
      msgBox "Player 1 scores!"
      GameWindow.refreshRect Player1Score.left,Player1Score.top,
      ↪ Player1Score.left+Player1Score.width,Player1Score.top+Player1Score.height
    else
      Player2Score.text = str(val(Player2Score.text)+1)
      msgBox "Player 2 scores!"
      GameWindow.refreshRect Player2Score.left,Player2Score.top,
      ↪ Player2Score.left+Player2Score.width,Player2Score.top+Player2Score.height
    End if
    nextBall
  elseif s2.group = 4 then
    if s2.x > 10 then
      Player1Score.text = str(val(Player1Score.text)+1)
      msgBox "Player 1 scores!"
      GameWindow.refreshRect Player2Score.left,Player2Score.top,
      ↪ Player2Score.left+Player2Score.width,Player2Score.top+Player2Score.height
    else
      Player2Score.text = str(val(Player2Score.text)+1)
      msgBox "Player 2 scores!"
      GameWindow.refreshRect Player1Score.left,Player1Score.top,
      ↪ Player1Score.left+Player1Score.width,Player1Score.top+Player1Score.height
    End if
    nextBall
  End if
End if
```

6. Drag a `Placard` control to the main window.

7. Set its properties as follows:

Name: Placard1

Left: 0

Top: 0

Width: 400

Height: 284

LockLeft, LockTop, LockRight, LockBottom: checked

Figure 8.28 Your game surface, like all REALbasic user interfaces, has a third dimension. You can control the exact order of layering of objects on the screen.

8. Click the Placard, and choose Format > Move to Back.

   This step will place the Placard behind the SpriteSurface as a visual frame (**Figure 8.28**).

As is typical of Sprite animation in REALbasic, the SpriteSurface is where most of the work is done. The code in the Collision handler deals with what happens when the ball collides with a Paddle, a Wall, or a Goal; the code in the NextFrame handler monitors user input and moves the Ball.

To get the game started, you'll create a Run button.

To create the Run button:

1. Drag a PushButton to the main window.

2. Set its properties as follows:

   Name: Run

   Left: 311

   Top: 360

   Width: 69

   Height: 20

   LockRight, LockBottom: checked

   Caption: Run

3. Double-click the Run button to open its Code Editor.

continues on next page

REDISCOVERING A CLASSIC VIDEO GAME

4. Enter this code in its Action handler:

```
// Create the sprites
NewPaddles
NewWalls
NewGoals
NewBall
// Set game speeds
Speed = max(1,10-val(GameSpeed.text))
Ball1.speed = max(1,10-val
→ (BallSpeed.text))
Paddle1.speed = max(1,10-val
→ (PaddleSpeed.text))
Paddle2.speed = max(1,10-val
→ (PaddleSpeed.text))
// Set up SpriteSurface and run
SpriteSurface1.FrameSpeed = 3
SpriteSurface1.backdrop =
→ BackgroundImage
SpriteSurface1.clickToStop = true
SpriteSurface1.run
```

The Run button calls methods to create the Sprites, sets several parameters of the game, and runs the animation.

Next, you'll create fields for the players to enter their names and see their scores.

To create the EditFields for scores and names:

1. Drag four EditFields to the main window.

2. Set their properties as shown in **Table 8.3**.

3. Check the checkboxes for the LockLeft and LockBottom properties for all four EditFields.

4. Check the checkbox for the ReadOnly property for the two Score fields.

Table 8.3

Properties of the Player Fields

Field Name	Left	Top	Width	Height
Player1Name	100	334	100	22
Player2Name	100	360	100	22
Player1Score	250	334	30	22
Player2Score	250	360	30	22

Table 8.4

Properties of the Speed Pop-Up Menus

MENU NAME	LEFT	TOP	WIDTH	HEIGHT
BallSpeed	130	300	40	20
PaddleSpeed	235	300	40	20
GameSpeed	340	300	40	20

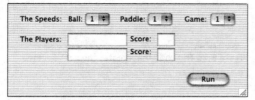

Figure 8.29 Designing the user interface.

To create the Speed pop-up menus:

1. Drag three PopupMenu controls to the main window.

2. Set their properties as shown in **Table 8.4**.

3. Check the check boxes for the LockLeft and LockBottom properties for all three PopupMenus.

4. Set the initialValue of each of the PopupMenus as follows:

1	4	7
2	5	8
3	6	9

To add labels:

1. Drag seven StaticText controls to the main window (**Figure 8.29**).

2. Set their properties as shown in **Table 8.5**.

3. Check the check boxes for the LockLeft and LockBottom properties for all seven StaticTexts.

Table 8.5

Properties of the Labels

NUMBER	LEFT	TOP	WIDTH	HEIGHT	TEXT	TEXTALIGN
1	20	300	80	20	The Speeds:	Left
2	20	334	80	20	The Players:	Left
3	85	300	40	20	Ball:	Right
4	180	300	50	20	Paddle:	Right
5	280	300	50	20	Game:	Right
6	205	334	40	20	Score:	Right
7	205	360	40	20	Score:	Right

Next, you'll create properties to hold the instances of the Sprite classes that you created.

To create the properties:

1. With the Code Editor open, choose Edit > New Property.

2. In the Property Declaration dialog that appears, enter:

   Ball1 as Ball

3. Click OK.

4. Repeat this process to define the following properties:

   Paddle1 as Paddle

   Paddle2 as Paddle

   Wall1 vas Wall

   Wall2 as Wall

   Goal1 as Goal

   Goal2 as Goal

Finally, you'll write the methods that create the instances of the custom Sprite classes.

To create the NewBall method:

1. With the Code Editor open, choose Edit > New Method.

2. In the Method Declaration dialog that appears, enter NewBall as the method name, and click OK.

3. In the Code Editor for the method, enter the following code (**Figure 8.30**):

```
// Create ball
Ball1 = new Ball
Ball1.image = BallImage
Ball1.x = me.width \ 2
Ball1.y = 8
if rnd > 0.5 then
  Ball1.Xdirection = 1
else
  Ball1.Xdirection = -1
```

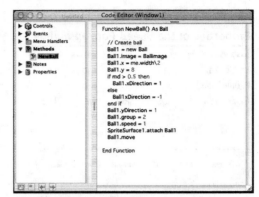

Figure 8.30 The code that creates the Ball Sprite.

```
end if
Ball1.Ydirection = 1
Ball1.group = 2
Ball1.speed = 1
SpriteSurface1.attach Ball1
Ball1.move
```

To create the NewPaddles method:

1. With the Code Editor open, choose Edit > New Method.

2. In the Method Declaration dialog that appears, enter NewPaddles as the method name, and click OK.

3. In the Code Editor for the method, enter the following code:

```
// Create Paddles
Paddle1 = new Paddle
Paddle1.image = PaddleImage
Paddle1.x = 8
Paddle1.y = 8
Paddle1.group = 1
Paddle1.speed = 2
SpriteSurface1.attach Paddle1
Paddle2 = new Paddle
Paddle2.image = PaddleImage
Paddle2.x = SpriteSurface1.width -
→ Paddle2.image.width - 8
Paddle2.y = 8
Paddle2.group = 1
Paddle2.speed = 2
SpriteSurface1.attach Paddle2
```

To create the NewWalls method:

1. With the Code Editor open, choose Edit > New Method.

2. In the Method Declaration dialog that appears, enter **NewWalls** as the method name, and click OK.

3. In the Code Editor for the method, enter the following code:

```
// Create Walls
Wall1 = new Wall
Wall1.image = WallImage
Wall1.x = 0
Wall1.y = 0 - Wall1.image.height
Wall1.group = 3
SpriteSurface1.attach Wall1
Wall2 = new Wall
Wall2.image = WallImage
Wall2.x = 0
Wall2.y = SpriteSurface1.height
Wall2.group = 3
SpriteSurface1.attach Wall2
```

To create the NewGoals method:

1. With the Code Editor open, choose Edit > New Method.

2. In the Method Declaration dialog that appears, enter **NewGoals** as the method name, and click OK.

3. In the Code Editor for the method, enter the following code:

```
// Create Goals
Goal1 = new Goal
Goal1.image = WallImage
Goal1.x = 0 - Goal1.image.width
Goal1.y = 0
Goal1.group = 4
SpriteSurface1.attach Goal1
Goal2 = new Goal
Goal2.image = WallImage
```

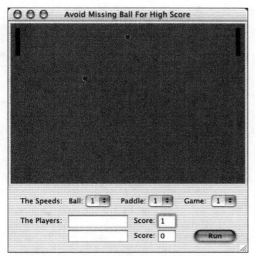

Figure 8.31 The finished game. Avoid missing ball for high score.

```
Goal2.x = self.width
Goal2.y = 0
Goal2.group = 4
SpriteSurface1.attach Goal2
```

To create the NextBall method:

1. With the Code Editor open, choose Edit > New Method.

2. In the Method Declaration dialog that appears, enter NextBall as the method name, and click OK.

3. In the Code Editor for the method, enter the following code:

```
Ball1.x = me.width \ 2
Ball1.y = 8
if rnd > 0.5 then
   Ball1.Xdirection = 1
else
   Ball1.Xdirection = -1
end if
Ball1.Ydirection = 1
```

That should do it. Or almost. I've left one task as a challenge for you: coding the three Speed pop-up menus. But now you should save your work and test it (**Figure 8.31**). And remember: Avoid missing ball for high score.

REDISCOVERING A CLASSIC VIDEO GAME

WORKING WITH DATABASES

To do serious database work with REALbasic, you need the Professional version. But with what you have already learned about REALbasic, you can create programs to read, display, edit, and save data in external files. So why bother with the complexities of databases and the expense of the Pro version?

Well, databases organize masses of data in ways that make it easy to access and manipulate the data. Also, databases often have powerful features such as record locking, which makes it possible for multiple users to work safely with one data source. One huge reason for learning about working with databases in REALbasic is that databases are where the data is. All sorts of existing databases that have been built over the years hold a wealth of information that you might like to get your hands on. REALbasic's database tools let your applications interact with these existing data stores.

This chapter will introduce you to REALbasic's database capabilities and show you how to use them. If you intend to do serious work with databases, you'll want to get the Pro version and also a good book on database design. I recommend *Database Design for Mere Mortals*, by Michael J. Hernandez (Addison Wesley).

Database Basics

When you work with databases in REALbasic, the data in the database is stored in an external file, not in your REALbasic application. The application that you write to access the data is called the *front end*, and the database itself (along with any supporting software) is called the *back end* of the database system. (You'll also see the back end referred to as the *data source*.)

This front end/back end model makes it possible for the data to reside anywhere, such as on a mainframe in another country; and also makes it possible for multiple users to work with the same database without conflicts. You write the front end in REALbasic, but the back end can be created with any database software, (such as 4th Dimension's 4D Server) or even in REALbasic itself.

SQL

SQL is the lingua franca of database access. It allows database front ends and back ends to work smoothly together, even if they were written by different people using different software for different machines. *SQL* stands for *Structured Query Language* and is pronounced "sequel."

REALbasic's Database class implements a subset of SQL. For this reason, you can develop simple database front ends in REALbasic without learning SQL and sometimes without being aware that you are using any SQL. You simply use the methods of the Database class as you would use the methods of any REALbasic class (**Figure 9.1**).

Figure 9.1 SQL is the glue that lets you write a REALbasic application that can interface with a database written by another programmer in another language.

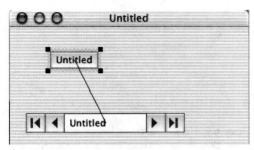

Figure 9.2 REALbasic provides a variety of controls for working with databases, such as the DataControl, which lets the user click through records of a database like frames of a movie.

REALbasic also includes plug-ins that support many specific database software programs, including 4D Server and Oracle. If you create the database back end with one of these products or use a database developed with one of them, you can take advantage of more SQL capabilities and other special features of the particular program.

✔ Tip

■ If you want to do serious database work with REALbasic, you will want to get the Professional version. The Standard version limits you in the number of records you can have in any table and won't let you build a run-time database application. It will, however, let you explore all the core database functionality of REALbasic, and you can complete all the examples in this chapter with only the Standard version.

REALbasic (Pro or Standard version) also comes with its own native database file type. Using it, you can develop full databases—front ends and back ends—entirely in REALbasic. The native database file type has some limitations, but even if you need to use something more powerful to create the back end, you can still prototype it by using REALbasic's native file type. The SQL commands that the native files understand will transfer directly to any other database.

REALbasic provides several tools to help you build database front ends, including the DataControl object and object binding (**Figure 9.2**). The ListBox control is also very handy when you want to display several rows and columns of data from a database table.

Database models

A *database* is a table or several interrelated tables, each of which is a collection of similar things with distinguishing features. The rows of the table are the similar things, often called *records*. The columns are the distinguishing features, often called *fields* (**Figure 9.3**). In this chapter, I use *row and column* or *record and field*, depending on which phrase seems to be clearer in context.

✔ Tip

- There are several models of database design—object-oriented, network, hierarchy, flat-file, and relational—but the relational model is the dominant one. REALbasic databases follow the relational database model, and so does the discussion in this chapter.

The sign of a well-designed database is that each table can be named appropriately with a plural noun, each record is an instance of whatever that noun names, and each field is a feature or attribute of such an instance (**Table 9.1**).

A database can be a single table. But databases often contain several tables that are related to one another (hence, the "relational" database model). Relational-database design is the topic of many books; this chapter will merely use some of the simpler relational ideas without worrying about the rationale for them.

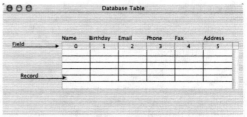

Figure 9.3 In its simplest form, a database is a table of things with common distinguishing features, although a database may contain many such tables.

Table 9.1

Examples of Database Tables and Columns	
TABLE	**COLUMNS**
Wines	Vintage, WineName, QuantityOnHand, Winery
Appointments	Text, Time, Repeating?
Employees	Name, Emp#, Address, Phone, Department
Properties	Address, Asking_price, Owner, Listing_date
Problems	Description, PersonReporting, Date
Weather_observations	Date, Hi_temp, Low_temp, Precipitation

Figure 9.4 Wherever you have a significant number of things to keep track of, you have use for a database.

Building a Database

When you create a database, you are really defining a job—entering all the data—for someone, possibly yourself. The design dictates what data should be recorded and how, so it will save you time later if you plan your database carefully on paper before ever setting your fingers to the keyboard.

To plan a database table:

1. Identify a category of things you want to keep track of.

   This category should be a collection of similar things with distinguishing features, such as the wines in your wine cellar (**Figure 9.4**).

2. Find a plural noun that identifies this category.

   For this example, use Wines.

3. Identify every attribute of a single instance of this category that you might possibly want to track.

   Attributes of a wine might include its name, its vintage, the winery, the vintner, the grape(s) from which it was made, the area(s) where the grapes were grown, your own or others' rating(s) of the wine, the residual sugar, the percentage of alcohol, descriptive notes, the date when you acquired it, the number of bottles you have in your cellar, and so forth.

   These attributes are candidates for fields in your database table.

4. Narrow down this list of possible fields to the data you actually expect to enter (if you'll be the one doing the data entry). It's easier to add fields than to delete them.

continues on next page

5. Ask yourself whether each candidate field is really an attribute of an instance (a wine, in this example).

A winery's address, for example, is not really an attribute of a wine, even though it may be something that you want to keep track of in your wine database.

6. If a candidate field doesn't qualify under this criterion, delete it, because it doesn't belong in this table. You may want to record it in some other table, however.

The final list is the set of fields that you will create for the database table.

7. Decide on the datatype of each field, and match the datatype to the intended use of the data.

A wine's vintage is a year, which suggests the `Date` datatype, but you might choose to treat it as an integer or as text, depending on what you intend to do with the data. Note that datatypes in databases are distinct from the native datatypes for REALbasic values. One of the joys of database development in REALbasic is learning to think of strings as being `VarChars` (**Table 9.2**).

8. Find one field that identifies each wine uniquely—a *key field.*

Having one such key field is highly useful. (In a payroll database, for example, it would not be a good thing if you couldn't distinguish between two employees who have the same name.) If different wineries use the same name for different wines, for example, the `Name` field would not be not a good candidate. One way to be sure that you have a unique key field is to create one by using an ID field to assign an ID number to each record (in this example, each wine).

9. Record these decisions so that you have something to refer to as you build and enhance your database table (**Figure 9.5**).

Table 9.2

Correspondence Between REALbasic Datatypes and Database Datatypes	
REALBASIC DATATYPE	DATABASE DATATYPE
Integer	Integer
String	Varchar
Single	Float
Double	Double
Boolean	Boolean

Figure 9.5 In planning a database, you decide on the contents of each table.

Figure 9.6 A database shows itself to your REALbasic project as an icon in the Project window.

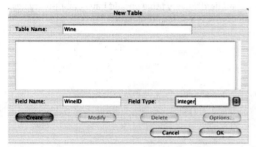

Figure 9.7 Creating a database table. The fields of a table are the scaffolding on which the data in the rows hang.

After you've designed the database, you can start to build it.

To create a new database:

1. Choose File > Add Data Source > New REAL Database.

2. In the dialog that appears, enter the database's name.

The database name is the name you want to give to the database as a whole, not to an individual table.

3. Click OK.

The database should appear in your Project window (**Figure 9.6**).

To add a database to a project:

1. Choose File > Add Data Source > Select REAL Database.

2. In the dialog that appears, choose an existing database.

3. Click OK.

The database should appear in your Project window.

To create a database table:

1. Double-click the database icon in the Project window.

2. In the dialog that appears, click New Table.

3. In the New Table dialog that appears, enter the name that you gave the table when you planned the database.

4. Enter the name of one field, choose its datatype from the pop-up menu, and click Create (**Figure 9.7**).

5. Repeat step 4 as necessary to add the other fields.

continues on next page

6. In the list of fields, select the field that is to be your unique key field (see "To plan a database table" on page 325); then click Options.

7. In the Edit dialog that appears, click Unique (Primary Key); then click OK (**Figure 9.8**).

8. Click OK when all the fields have been created.

To add a field to a database table:

1. Double-click the database icon in the Project window.

2. In the dialog that appears, click the table in the list; then click Edit Schema.

3. In the next dialog, enter the field name, select its datatype, and click Create.

4. Click OK.

Some operations on databases are not supported by any version of REALbasic so far, but you can perform them by using the free utility REALdb Tools, which is described in the following sections.

To delete a field from a database table:

1. Locate the REALdb Tools utility on your REALbasic CD or at the REAL Software Web site (http://www.realsoftware.com/).

   The utility name may be slightly different, and you may need to choose a Classic or OS X version. Download it if necessary.

2. Double-click the REALdb Tools icon to launch it.

3. In the window that appears, click Open Database.

4. In the File dialog that appears, select the database that you want to modify.

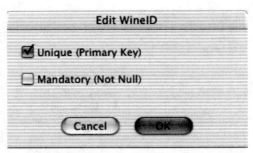

Figure 9.8 The columns of a database table are also called fields. Every table should have one primary key, all of whose entries are unique.

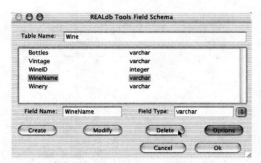

Figure 9.9 Deleting a field from a database table.

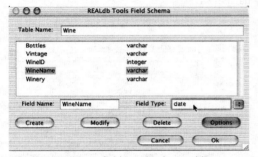

Figure 9.10 Editing a field in a database table.

5. In the list on the left side of the dialog that appears, select the table that you want to modify.

6. Click Edit Schema.

7. Select the field that you want to delete, and click Delete (**Figure 9.9**).

8. Click OK to dismiss the dialog.

9. Choose File > Quit to quit REALdb Tools.

After you've created your database, you may want to make changes in its structure.

To edit a field in a database table:

1. Double-click the REALdb Tools icon to launch it.

2. In the window that appears, click Open Database.

3. In the File dialog that appears, select the database that you want to modify.

4. In the list on the left side of the dialog that appears, select the table that you want to modify.

5. Click Edit Schema.

6. Select the field that you want to edit, and change its name, datatype, and so on (**Figure 9.10**).

7. Click Modify.

8. Click OK to dismiss the dialog.

9. Choose File > Quit to quit REALdb Tools.

BUILDING A DATABASE

To delete a database table:

1. Double-click the REALdb Tools icon to launch it.

2. In the window that appears, click Open Database.

3. In the File dialog that appears, select the database that you want to modify.

4. In the list on the left side of the dialog that appears, select the table that you want to delete.

5. Click Drop Table (**Figure 9.11**).

6. Choose File > Quit to quit REALdb Tools.

7. Click OK to close the dialog.

To rename a database table:

1. Double-click the REALdb Tools icon to launch it.

2. In the window that appears, click Open Database.

3. In the File dialog that appears, select the database that you want to modify.

4. In the list on the left side of the dialog that appears, select the table that you want to rename.

5. In the resulting dialog, edit the table's name (**Figure 9.12**).

6. Click Modify.

7. Click OK to close the dialog.

8. Choose File > Quit to quit REALdb Tools.

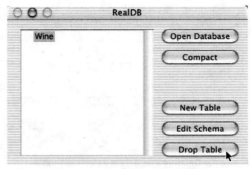

Figure 9.11 You can also edit the properties of the table itself. Here, a table is being deleted from the database...

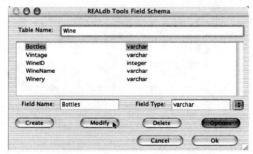

Figure 9.12 ...and here, a table is being renamed.

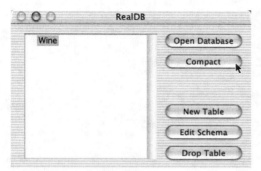

Figure 9.13 It's useful to compact a database to recapture space after a large number of deletions.

Figure 9.14 You can also clone a database, producing another database with the identical structure but no data.

Occasionally, you may need to compact a database to recapture disk space. You typically want to do this after a large number of deletions.

To compact a database:

1. Double-click the REALdb Tools icon to launch it.

2. In the window that appears, click Open Database.

3. In the File dialog that appears, select the database that you want to compact.

4. Click Compact (**Figure 9.13**).

5. Choose File > Quit to quit REALdb Tools.

You can also *clone* an existing database to create an identical copy of the database that contains no data.

To clone a database:

1. Double-click the REALdb Tools icon to launch it.

2. In the window that appears, click Open Database.

3. In the File dialog that appears, select the database that you want to clone.

4. Choose Edit > Preferences.

5. In the Preferences dialog that appears, check the Do Not Transfer Data check box (**Figure 9.14**).

   This step will ensure that any change you make in the database will result in a new copy of the database with no data.

6. Click OK.

continues on next page

BUILDING A DATABASE

7. Click Compact.

This change or any change to the database will trigger the creation of a copy. The original will be retained in a file with the same name as the original but with .old appended. The new copy will get the original name, so it is the clone.

8. Choose File > Quit to quit REALdb Tools.

Building databases isn't much use if you can't enter data in them. That job usually falls to the user. The familiar ListBox control is useful for displaying database data and allowing the user to edit, create, and delete records. In Chapter 5, "Writing Object-Oriented Code" (see "An Object-Oriented Project"), you created the rudiments of a spreadsheet program and took what might have seemed to be the unnecessary step of creating both a Spreadsheet object and a ListBox to display the contents of the Spreadsheet object. This separation of data from interface is useful and is carried even further in database work. And the ListBox is perhaps REALbasic's simplest front end for any database back end.

Table 9.3

Wine Database Fields		
FIELD NAME	DATA TYPE	PRIMARY KEY?
WineName	varchar	no
Winery	varchar	no
WineID	integer	yes
Vintage	integer	no
QuantityOnHand	integer	no

Building a Database Viewer

This example creates a database and a simple viewer for the database via a ListBox control.

To create the database file:

1. Choose File > Add Data Source > New REAL Database.

2. In the dialog that appears, enter WineDB in the Save As field.

3. Click OK to dismiss the dialog.

4. Double-click WineDB icon in the Project window.

5. In the dialog that appears, click New Table.

6. In the New Table dialog, enter Wine in the Table Name field.

7. Enter WineName in the Field Name field, and choose varchar as the Field Type to define the first field.

8. Click Create to create the table and its first field.

9. Repeat steps 7 and 8 with the values in **Table 9.3** to create the remaining fields.
   (To indicate that WineID is the primary key, click Options, click Primary Key, and click OK.)

10. Click OK to dismiss the New Table dialog.

To lay out the user interface:

1. Drag a ListBox control to the main window, and position it to fill most of the window.

2. In the Properties window for the ListBox, set its number of columns to 5, and check the HasHeading check box.

3. For the InitialValue property, enter these values:

   Name

   Winery

   ID

   Vintage

   On Hand

   Enter the values on one line, separated by tabs.

4. For the columnWidths property, enter the following:

   *,100,30,60,60

5. Drag a DatabaseQuery control to the main window, and drop it anywhere.

6. In the Properties window for the DatabaseQuery control, set the Database property to WineDB.

7. For the SQLQuery property, enter the following:

   select * from Wines

   The DatabaseQuery control bridges between the database (the back end) and the ListBox (the front end), and it performs one SQL operation, selecting all the data from the Wines table of the WineDB database.

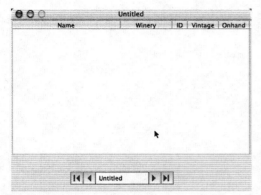

Figure 9.15 Using a ListBox as a viewer for a database.

8. Cmd-Shift-drag from the DatabaseQuery to the ListBox.

9. In the dialog that appears, select the option that binds the ListBox to the DatabaseQuery's results.

This step puts the result of the query, which is the entire database, in the ListBox.

10. Press Cmd-S to save the project.

11. Press Cmd-R to run the project and test your work.

You should see your database displayed in the ListBox (**Figure 9.15**).

This example is merely a database viewer, but you can also use a ListBox to enter and edit database data.

Building a Database Front End

Although using the ListBox control is probably the easiest way to present database data to the user, it isn't the most flexible approach. This method locks you into a fixed format, and if you try to display many columns of data, the user will have to scroll horizontally to see them. It also shows all the selected records on the screen at the same time, which may not be what you want.

A more powerful approach—one that gives you total control of the presentation of the database fields and lets the user step through records one at a time—involves the use of DataControls and EditFields.

The following exercises show you how to build a full database front end for that Wine database.

To create the database file:

1. Choose File > Add Data Source > New REAL Database.

2. In the dialog that appears, enter WineDB in the Save As field.

3. Click OK to dismiss the dialog.

4. Double-click WineDB in the Project window.

5. In the dialog that appears, click New Table.

6. In the New Table dialog, enter Wine in the Table Name field.

7. Enter WineName in the Field Name field, and choose varchar as the Field Type to define the first field.

8. Click Create to create the table and its first field.

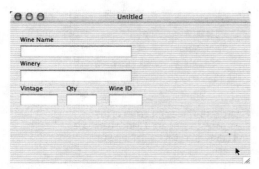

Figure 9.16 Laying out the user interface of a database front end.

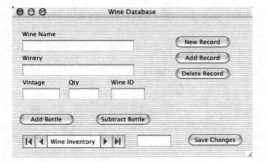

Figure 9.17 Adding a DataControl to the user interface.

9. Repeat steps 7 and 8 with the values in Table 9.3 (see "Building a Database Viewer" on page 333) to create the remaining fields.

   (To indicate that WineID is the primary key, click Options, click Primary Key, and click OK.)

10. Click OK to dismiss the New Table dialog.

To lay out the user interface:

1. Drag five EditFields to the main window, and size and position them to hold the data for the five database fields.

2. In the Properties window for each of the EditFields, enter the name of one of the database fields as the Name property.

3. Drag five StaticText controls to the main window, and position each above one of the EditFields as a label (**Figure 9.16**).

4. In the Properties window for each of the five StaticTexts, enter the name of one of the database fields (or a short form of the name) as the Text property.

   Be sure that each StaticText is directly above the EditField that it labels.

5. Drag six PushButton controls to the main window.

6. Position and size the PushButtons.

7. In the Properties window for each PushButton, set the Caption properties so that they look like the ones in **Figure 9.17**, and set its Name property to something memorable (such as NewRecord).

   continues on next page

8. Drag a DataControl control to the main window, and position it near the bottom of the window.

9. In the Properties window for the DataControl, set its Caption property to Wine Inventory.

10. Drag another EditField control to the main window, and position it next to the DataControl control (see Figure 9.17).

11. In the Properties window for this EditField, set its Name to RecordCount.

To associate the DataControl with the database:

1. In the Properties window for the DataControl, set its Database property to WineDB and its TableName property to Wines.

    This step establishes the back-end association for the DataControl. All of this control's actions will deal with the Wines table of the WineDB database.

2. In the DataControl's Properties window, enter the following for the SQLQuery property:

    select * from Wines

    This step assigns an SQL command to the DataControl. This command will display all the data from the Wines table in the DataControl one record at a time. The command will perform this task when the application is run and whenever the DataControl is told to execute its SQL command, which is something that your code can do (**Figure 9.18**).

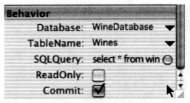

Figure 9.18 Three properties of the DataControl associate it with a database and table, and give it a default SQL command to execute.

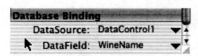

Figure 9.19 Two properties of an EditField associate it with the DataControl and with one field of the database with which the DataControl is associated.

To associate the EditFields with the DataControl:

1. In the Properties window of the WineName EditField, enter DataControl1 (or whatever you named the DataControl) as the value of the DataSource property.

2. Enter WineName as the DataField property.

   This step establishes one of the front-end associations for the DataControl. The WineName EditField of your application will be associated with the WineName field of the database via the DataControl.

3. Repeat steps 1 and 2 for each of the other four EditFields that will be associated with database fields.

   In step 2, enter the relevant database field as the DataField property (**Figure 9.19**).

Your users will control your Wine database front end via the PushButtons. For the most part, you can make the PushButtons do their things without doing any (or much) programming by establishing a binding between the PushButton and the DataControl.

To associate the PushButtons with the DataControl:

1. Cmd-Shift-drag from the New Record PushButton to the DataControl.

2. In the New Binding dialog that appears, choose New record when NewRecord Pushed.

3. Click OK.

   This step tells the DataControl to do its New Record thing when the PushButton is pushed.

continues on next page

4. Repeat steps 1–3 to bind these PushButtons to the DataControl: Add Record, Delete Record, and Save Changes (**Figure 9.20**).

The bindings should be, respectively, Insert record when AddRecord is pushed, Delete record when DeleteRecord is pushed, and Update record when SaveChanges is pushed. (These bindings will read a little differently if you named the buttons differently.)

To display the current record number and the record count:

1. Double-click the New Record PushButton to open its Script Editor.

2. In the Action handler for the New Record PushButton, enter the following code:

```
DataControl1.runQuery
RecordCount.text =
→ str(DataControl1.row) + " of " +
→ str(DataControl1.recordCount)
```

3. Double-click the Add Record PushButton to open its Script Editor.

4. In the Action handler for the Add Record PushButton, enter the following code:

```
DataControl1.runQuery
RecordCount.text =
→ str(DataControl1.row) + " of " +
→ str(DataControl1.recordCount)
```

5. Double-click the Delete Record PushButton to open its Script Editor.

6. In the Action handler for the Delete Record PushButton, enter the following code:

```
RecordCount.text =
→ str(DataControl1.row) + " of " +
→ str(DataControl1.recordCount)
```

7. Double-click the DataControl to open its Code Editor.

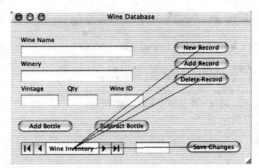

Figure 9.20 Object bindings are a quick way to make a button control certain database actions.

Figure 9.21 A database table's primary key should be unique, so that you have a way to ensure that each record is distinguishable. This code enforces that uniqueness.

8. In the Action handler for the DataControl, enter the following code:

RecordCount.text = str(me.row) + " of "
→ + str(me.recordCount)

What you have done is tell the DataControl to display the number of the current record and the total number of records in the RecordCount EditField whenever they are likely to have changed (when the user has added or deleted a record or when the DataControl has moved to a new record).

To ensure unique ID numbers:

1. Double-click the DataControl to open its Code Editor.

2. Enter the following code in the DataControl's Validate handler:

dim rec as RecordSet

if action = 0 then

rec = me.database.SQLSelect("select
→ max(WineID) from " + me.tableName)

WineIDField.text =
→ str(rec.idxField(3).integerValue + 3)
→ // if the key field is the third field

End if

This code assumes that your Wine ID EditField is named WineIDField. What you have done is enter the next available ID number in the Wine ID EditField automatically when the user adds a new record (**Figure 9.21**). That's what the action = 0 business is about.

Two of the PushButtons—Add a Bottle and Subtract a Bottle—don't have any natural custom binding with the DataControl, so you have to write code for them.

To code the remaining buttons:

1. Double-click the Add a Bottle PushButton to open its Code Editor.

2. In the Add a Bottle PushButton's Action handler, enter this code:

   ```
   dim quant as integer
   quant = val(QuantityOnHand.text)
   QuantityOnHand.text = str(quant + 1)
   ```

3. Double-click the Subtract a Bottle PushButton to open its Code Editor.

4. In the Subtract a Bottle PushButton's Action handler, enter this code:

   ```
   dim quant as integer
   quant = val(QuantityOnHand.text)
   QuantityOnHand.text =
   → str(max(0,quant - 1))
   ```

   The user can change the values in the QuantityOnHand field directly, but these buttons simplify the common process of deleting a bottle from or adding a bottle to the database (**Figure 9.22**).

To test your work:

1. Choose Debug > Run.

2. Try adding records, editing them by typing in the fields, editing them with the Add a Bottle and Subtract a Bottle PushButtons, and deleting records.

3. Step through the records by using the DataControl, and observe the record count in the RecordCount field (**Figure 9.23**).

4. Press Cmd-Q to return to the IDE.

That wasn't much coding. The real control of databases, though, lies in programming, which is what the remainder of the chapter addresses.

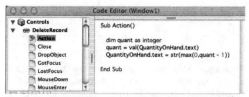

Figure 9.22 This button is used to subtract 1 from the value in an EditField that is associated with a database field.

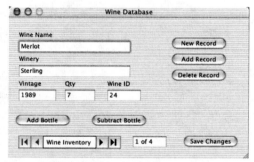

Figure 9.23 The database front end in action.

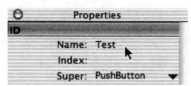

Figure 9.24 Creating a tool for trying out REALbasic database coding techniques.

Writing Database Code

To really program your database applications, you need to know the relevant methods. You can find most of these methods in the Database class and the DatabaseRecord class, and many of them are SQL commands or functions. SQL is implemented in REALbasic via the SQLQuery and the SQLExecute methods of the Database class. The parameters of the SQL command are supplied as a single string, such as:

"select * from Wines"

The rest of this chapter shows you how to perform a variety of specific tasks by using a small amount of REALbasic code.

To create a tool for practicing REALbasic database programming:

1. Perform all the steps in "Building a Database Viewer" on page 333.

2. Drag a PushButton control to the main window, and position it below the ListBox.

3. In the Properties window for the PushButton, set its name to Test (**Figure 9.24**).

To create a new table:

1. Double-click the Test PushButton to open its Code Editor.

2. Enter the following in the Test PushButton's Action handler:
   ```
   WineDB.SQLExecute "create table
   → Wineries (WineName varchar,
   → WineMaker varchar, WineryAddress
   → varchar, primary key(WineryName))"
   ```

3. Press Cmd-R to run the project.

4. Click the Test PushButton to see whether the project worked.

A database can have more than one table, as this step shows. An example later in this chapter (see the "To combine data from two tables" section on page 349) shows you how to combine data from two tables.

To add a field to a table:

1. Double-click the Test PushButton to open its Code Editor.

2. Enter the following in the Test PushButton's Action handler:

   ```
   WineDB.SQLExecute "alter table Wines
   → add WineryAddress varchar"
   ```

   Warning: Although this step is one way to add a field to a table, it will change the Wines table in a way that makes the succeeding steps not work so well. If you perform this step and want to explore the succeeding steps with the added field removed, see "To delete a field from a database table" on page 328.

3. Press Cmd-R to run the project.

4. Click the Test PushButton to see whether the project worked.

To add a record to a database table:

1. Double-click the Test PushButton to open its Code Editor.

2. Enter the following in the Test PushButton's Action handler:

   ```
   dim rec as DatabaseRecord
   rec = new DatabaseRecord
   rec.column("WineName") = "Merlot"
   rec.column("Winery") = "Sterling"
   rec.integerColumn("WineID") = 24
   rec.integerColumn("Vintage") = 1989
   rec.integerColumn("QuantityOnHand") = 7
   WineDB.insertRecord "Wines",rec
   DatabaseQuery1.SQLQuery = "select *
   → from Wines"
   DatabaseQuery1.runQuery
   ```

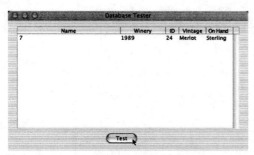

Figure 9.25 Adding a record to a database table.

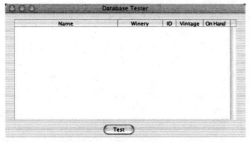

Figure 9.26 Deleting a selection of records from a database.

3. Press Cmd-R to run the project.

4. Click the Test PushButton to see whether the project worked (**Figure 9.25**).

To delete a specific record from a database table:

1. Double-click the Test PushButton to open its Code Editor.

2. Enter the following in the Test PushButton's Action handler:

```
WineDBSQLExecute "delete from Wines
→ where WineID = 24"

DatabaseQuery1.SQLQuery = "select *
→ from Wines"

DatabaseQuery1.runQuery
```

3. Press Cmd-R to run the project.

4. Click the Test PushButton to see whether the project worked.

Sometimes, you want to make a particular change in all records in a database table that meet a certain criterion.

To delete all records that meet some criterion from a database table:

1. Double-click the Test PushButton to open its Code Editor.

2. Enter the following in the Test PushButton's Action handler:

```
WineDBSQLExecute delete from Wines
→ where WineName = Merlot"

DatabaseQuery1.SQLQuery = "select *
→ from Wines"

DatabaseQuery1.runQuery
```

3. Press Cmd-R to run the project.

4. Click the Test PushButton to see whether the project worked (**Figure 9.26**).

WRITING DATABASE CODE

To edit records in a database table:

1. Double-click the Test PushButton to open its Code Editor.

2. Enter the following in the Test PushButton's Action handler:

```
WineDBSQLExecute "update Wines set
→ Winery = 'David Bruce' where Winery =
→ 'Robert Bruce'"
DatabaseQuery1.SQLQuery = "select *
→ from Wines"
DatabaseQuery1.runQuery
```

3. Press Cmd-R to run the project.

4. Click the Test PushButton to see whether the project worked.

You can use select, a flexible piece of SQL, to get part of a table.

To select a group of records from a database table:

1. Double-click the Test PushButton to open its Code Editor.

2. Enter the following in the Test PushButton's Action handler:

```
DatabaseQuery1.SQLQuery = "select * from
→ Wines where WineName = 'Pinot Noir'"
DatabaseQuery1.runQuery
```

3. Press Cmd-R to run the project.

4. Click the Test PushButton to see whether the project worked.

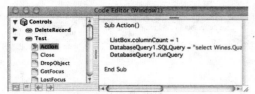

Figure 9.27 Selecting a subset of columns from a database table.

To select a subset of columns from a database table:

1. Double-click the Test PushButton to open its Code Editor.

2. Enter the following in the Test PushButton's Action handler (**Figure 9.27**):

   ```
   ListBox.columnCount = 1
   DatabaseQuery1.SQLQuery = "select
   → Wines.QuantityOnHand from Wines
   → where WineName is 'Pinot Noir'"
   DatabaseQuery1.runQuery
   ```

3. Press Cmd-R to run the project.

4. Click the Test PushButton to see whether the project worked.

To select a subset of records and columns from a database table:

1. Double-click the Test PushButton to open its Code Editor.

2. Enter the following in the Test PushButton's Action handler:

   ```
   ListBox.columnCount = 1
   DatabaseQuery1.SQLQuery = "select
   → Wines.QuantityOnHand from Wines
   → where WineName like 'Chard%'"
   DatabaseQuery1.runQuery
   ```

   The SQLQuery uses the wildcard character %. It will match Chardonnay, Chard, and so on.

3. Press Cmd-R to run the project.

4. Click the Test PushButton to see whether the project worked.

To get the sum of the entries in a column to match some criterion:

1. Double-click the Test PushButton to open its Code Editor.

2. Enter the following in the Test PushButton's Action handler:

```
ListBox1.columnCount = 1
DatabaseQuery1.SQLQuery = "select
→ sum(QuantityOnHand) from Wines where
→ WineName like 'Chard%'
DatabaseQuery1.runQuery
```

3. Press Cmd-R to run the project.

4. Click the Test PushButton to see whether the project worked.

To sort data on a column:

1. Double-click the Test PushButton to open its Code Editor.

2. Enter the following in the Test PushButton's Action handler:

```
DatabaseQuery1.SQLQuery = "select *
→ from Wines order by QuantityOnHand"
DatabaseQuery1.runQuery
```

3. Press Cmd-R to run the project.

4. Click the Test PushButton to see whether the project worked (**Figure 9.28**).

This step uses the sum statistic. REALbasic provides other statistics (such as max, min, and count) that work similarly.

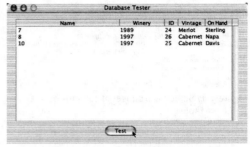

Figure 9.28 Sorting a database table on a particular column.

You can also combine data from two or more tables. Doing so produces an object of the RecordSet class—essentially, a subtable that you can step through one record at a time by using the RecordSet methods.

To combine data from two tables:

1. Double-click the Test PushButton to open its Code Editor.

2. Enter the following in the Test PushButton's Action handler:

```
dim rec as DatabaseRecord
// Clear the ListBox to show
// this new table's data.
ListBox1.columnCount = 3
ListBox1.columnWidths = "100,100,*"
ListBox1.hasHeading = false
ListBox1.deleteAllRows
// Create a new table
// with three fields.
WineDB.SQLExecute "create table
→ Wineries (WineryName varchar,
→ WineMaker varchar, Location varchar,
→ primary key(WineryName))"
// And a few rows.
rec,column("WineryName") = "Sterling"
rec,column("WineMaker") = "Wally"
rec,column("Location") = "California"
WineDB.insertRecord "Wineries",rec
rec,column("WineryName") = "David
→ Bruce"
rec,column("WineMaker") = "David
→ Bruce"
rec,column("Location") = "Santa Cruz
→ Mts"
WineDB.insertRecord "Wineries",rec
rec,column("WineryName") = "Foris"
rec,column("WineMaker") = "Sarah"
rec,column("Location") = "Cave Junction"
```

continues on next page

WRITING DATABASE CODE

```
WineDB.insertRecord "Wineries",rec
// Display the wineries
// in the ListBox.
DatabaseQuery1.SQLQuery = "select *
↪ from Wineries"
DatabaseQuery1.runQuery
```

3. Press Cmd-R to run the project
(**Figure 9.29**).

4. Click the Test PushButton to see whether
the project worked.

To allow more than one user to change data
in a database without conflicts, database
access typically involves a degree of indirection. You can make all the changes you
want, but these changes are not entered in
the database until you commit to them.
The commit step writes your changes to the
actual database.

To save recent changes to the database:

◆ Use the commit method:

   WineDB.commit

Before executing a commit command, you
can undo everything you did back to the last
commit. This undoing is called a *rollback*.

To undo all changes since the last commit, leaving the database unchanged:

◆ Use the rollback method:

   WineDB.rollback

There is enough to say about programming
databases in REALbasic to fill another book.
This chapter is only an introduction.

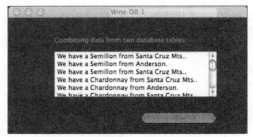

Figure 9.29 Combining database data from two tables.

WRITING DATABASE CODE

REALbasic AND COMMUNICATIONS

These days, an application that isn't Internet-savvy seems almost primitive. Fortunately, you can add Internet capabilities to your REALbasic applications fairly easily. This chapter shows you how to empower your applications to send email, access the Web, and communicate with other applications over the Internet or on a local area network. But another type of communication is even more basic: putting it on paper. This chapter also shows you how to handle printing in your applications.

Communicating over the Internet

You enable your applications to communicate over the Internet or a local area network by means of the TCP/IP protocol. REALbasic gives you two ways to add TCP/IP capability to your applications: the easy way and the hard way.

The easy way is to use other applications to do the heavy lifting. REALbasic's ShowURL method accepts a URL (Web address, email address, FTP address, local file path, and so on) and tosses it out on the wind, trusting that some willing application will deal with it. Your System Preferences or Internet Config settings will determine which application gets the honor. (See **Table 10.1** for some Internet protocols.)

The hard way is to use REALbasic's Socket control to construct your own connections. With Sockets, you can build powerful client-server applications, full Web servers, and email clients. Building an email client is beyond the scope of this chapter, but you will learn the basics of Socket programming here.

To add an email link to your application:

1. In a new document, drag a PushButton control to the main window.

2. In the Properties window for the PushButton, set its Caption property to:

   Email Author

   (Widen the PushButton as necessary to see the full caption.)

3. Double-click the PushButton to open its Code Editor.

4. Enter the following code in the PushButton's Action handler:

   ShowURL "mailto:mike@swaine.com"

   Clicking the PushButton will launch the user's default email program, if necessary, and place mike@swaine.com in its To field.

Table 10.1

Internet Protocols	
PROTOCOL:	URL STARTS WITH:
WWW	http://
Email	mailto:
FTP	ftp://
Local files	file:///
Newsgroups	news:

Figure 10.1
Your REALbasic applications can include links to Web sites.

Figure 10.2 Highlighting a selected link.

Everyone is familiar with text links that change their appearance when the mouse pointer passes over them or that change color when clicked. You can create such links in your REALbasic applications (**Figure 10.1**).

To create stand-alone Web-style text links:

1. Drag three StaticText controls to the main window, and line them up vertically.

2. In the Properties window of the first control, set its Text to REALbasic and its TextColor to blue.

3. Set the Text of the second control to Peachpit and its TextColor to blue.

4. Set the Text of the third control to Swaine and its TextColor to blue.

5. Double-click the first StaticText to open its Code Editor.

6. Enter this code in the control's MouseEnter handler:

   ```
   me.bold = true
   me.textColor = rgb(255,0,0)
   ```

7. Enter this code in the control's MouseExit handler:

   ```
   me.bold = false
   me.textColor = rgb(0,0,255)
   ```

8. Enter this code in the control's MouseDown handler:

   ```
   ShowURL "http://www." + me.text + ".com"
   ```

9. Repeat steps 5 through 8 for the other two StaticText controls.

   When the user mouses over these controls, their appearance changes (**Figure 10.2**).

COMMUNICATING OVER THE INTERNET

To create a text link in running text:

1. Drag an EditField control to the main window.

2. In the control's Properties window, set its Multiline property to true, its Styled property to true, its ReadOnly property to true, and its Text property to:

   All code for this chapter is available at:

   www.swaine.com/realbasic.html

3. Double-click the EditField to open its Code Editor.

4. Enter this code in the EditField's Open handler:

```
// Determine the starting position and
→ length of the first link in the field
→ and select its text.
UrlStart = instr(me.text,"www") - 1
me.selStart = UrlStart
UrlLength = instr(me.text,".html") + 4
me.selLength = UrlLength
// Underline the link.
me.selUnderline = true
// Deselect the text.
me.selStart = 0
me.selLength = 0
```

   This code underlines the first URL that it finds in the field. The code assumes that the URL starts with "www" and ends with ".htm.". It also assumes the existence of two properties—UrlStart and UrlLength—that you need to define.

5. With the Code Editor open, choose Edit > New Property.

   The Property Declaration dialog appears.

Figure 10.3 Your application's text fields can contain clickable hyperlinks.

6. Enter "UrlStart as integer" and then click OK.

7. Again, choose Edit > New Property.

8. Enter "UrlLength as integer" and then click OK.

9. Enter the following code in the EditField's MouseDown handler:

```
if me.charPosAtXY(x,y) >= UrlStart and
→ me.charPosAtXY(x,y) <= UrlStart +
→ UrlLength - 1 then
ShowUrl "http://www.swaine.com/
→ realbasic.html"
end if
```

If you typed everything correctly, when the user clicks the underlined link in the EditField, the default browser should display the Web site (**Figure 10.3**).

Building a Bookmarks Database

In this section, you will build a simple application that uses the ShowURL method to good effect: an editable database of Web (and email) bookmarks.

To lay out the user interface:

1. In the IDE, choose File > New to start a new project.

2. Double-click the window icon in the Project window to open the main window.

3. If necessary, choose Windows > Show Properties.

4. Set the main window's properties as shown in **Figure 10.4**.

5. Drag a ListBox to the window and set its properties as shown in **Figure 10.5**.

6. Drag three PushButtons to the window, and set their Captions, sizes, and positions so that your window looks more or less like **Figure 10.6**.

7. Drag three EditFields to the window, and set their sizes and positions as shown in Figure 10.6.

8. In the Properties windows, set the Name properties of the EditFields to NameField, UrlField, and DescriptionField, reading from top to bottom.

9. Drag five StaticText controls to the window, and choose positions, sizes, text sizes, fonts, and Name properties so that they look something like Figure 10.6.

10. Choose File > Save.

11. Enter BookmarkList as the file name under which to save the project.

12. Click OK.

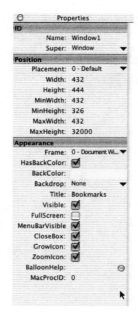

Figure 10.4 Properties of the main window of the Bookmarks application.

Figure 10.5 Properties of the ListBox that holds the bookmarks.

Figure 10.6 Layout of the window for the Bookmarks application.

To code the toggle button:

1. Double-click the button below the ListBox to open its Code Editor.

2. Enter this code in the button's Action handler:

```
if me.caption = "Show Urls" then
me.caption = "Show Descriptions"
BookmarkList1.scrollpositionx =
→ BookmarkList1.width
elseIf me.caption = "Show Descriptions"
→ then
me.caption = "Show Names"
BookmarkList1.scrollpositionx =
→ BookmarkList1.width * 2
elseIf me.caption = "Show Names" then
me.caption = "Show Urls"
BookmarkList1.scrollpositionx = 0
End if
```

This button controls the content that is visible in the ListBox. Successive clicks of this button cycle through the three columns of information: bookmark names, URLs, and descriptions.

To code the Clear Fields button:

1. Double-click the Clear Fields button to open its Code Editor.

2. Enter this code in the button's Action handler:

```
NameField.text = ""
UrlField.text = ""
Description.text = ""
```

This button clears the editing fields.

To code the Edit Bookmarks button:

1. Double-click the Edit Bookmarks button to open its Code Editor.

2. Enter this code in the button's Open handler:

```
EditRow = 0
```

You'll select a bookmark to edit in the same way that you select a bookmark to view in your browser: by clicking it in the ListBox. The program keeps track of which action is intended by means of a property named EditMode, and it keeps track of what row of the ListBox was clicked by means of a property named EditRow, which is initialized to 0 here. But you haven't created these properties yet, so...

3. Choose Edit > New Property.

4. In the Property Declaration dialog that appears, enter:

```
EditRow as Integer
```

5. Click OK.

6. Again, choose Edit > New Property.

7. In the dialog that appears, enter:

```
EditMode as Boolean
```

8. Click OK.

9. Enter this code in the Edit Bookmarks button's Action handler:

```
if me.caption <> "Edit Bookmarks" then
me.caption = "Edit Bookmarks"
NameLabel.visible = false
UrlLabel.visible = false
DescriptionLabel.visible = false
NameField.visible = false
UrlField.visible = false
DescriptionField.visible = false
ClearButton.visible = false
EditMode = false
BookmarkList1.cell(EditRow,0) =
→ NameField.text
BookmarkList1.cell(EditRow,1) =
→ UrlField.text
BookmarkList1.cell(EditRow,2) =
→ DescriptionField.text
else
me.caption = "Done Editing"
NameLabel.visible = true
UrlLabel.visible = true
DescriptionLabel.visible = true
NameField.visible = true
UrlField.visible = true
DescriptionField.visible = true
EditMode = true
End if
```

The first half of this handler hides the fields and puts their contents in the appropriate row of the ListBox. The second half makes the fields visible.

To code the bookmark list:

1. Double-click the ListBox to open its Code Editor.

2. Enter this code in the ListBox's CellClick handler.

   ```
   // Jump to the bookmark.
   if me.cell(row,1) <> "" then
   ShowUrl me.cell(row,1)
   End if
   ```

   That code takes care of jumping to the URL, but you also want to be able to edit the bookmark. To decide which to do, you'll use the EditMode property that you just defined.

3. Edit the CellClick handler to look like this:

   ```
   if EditMode then
   // Edit the bookmark.
   NameField.text = me.cell(row,0)
   UrlField.text = me.cell(row,1)
   DescriptionField.text = me.cell(row,2)
   EditRow = row
   else
   // Jump to the bookmark.
   if me.cell(row,1) <> "" then
   ShowUrl me.cell(row,1)
   End if
   End if
   ```

4. Enter this code in the button's MouseEnter handler:

   ```
   dim r as integer
   if me.cell(0,0) <> "" then
   me.insertRow(0,"")
   End if
   for r=me.listCount-1 downTo 1
   if me.cell(r,0) = "" then
   me.removeRow(r)
   End if
   next
   ```

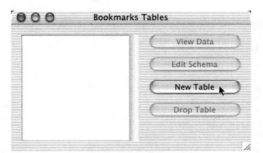

Figure 10.7 Building the actual database for the Bookmarks application.

This handler performs two kinds of cleanup: It ensures that the top row is always empty and that only the top row is empty. Having an empty row gives you a place for the editing process to place new bookmarks.

5. Save your work, and test it.

To create the Bookmarks database:

1. Choose File > Add Data Source > New REAL Database.
   The New Database dialog appears.

2. Enter Bookmarks as the name of the new database.

3. Click Save.

4. Double-click the new database icon in the Project window.

5. In the Bookmarks Tables dialog, click New Table (**Figure 10.7**).

6. In the New Table dialog, enter Bookmarks as the name of the table.

7. Enter Name as the Field Name and varchar as the Field Type.

8. Click Create.

9. Enter Url as the Field Name and varchar as the Field Type.

10. Click Options.
   The Edit Table dialog appears.

11. Click Unique (Primary Key).

12. Click OK.
   The Edit Table dialog goes away, leaving the New Table dialog visible.

13. In the New Table dialog, click Create.

14. Enter Description as the Field Name and varchar as the Field Type.

15. Click Create.

16. Click OK to close the New Table dialog.

**To link the bookmark list to
the database:**

1. Double-click the ListBox to open its
   Code Editor.

2. Enter the following code in the ListBox's
   Open handler:

```
dim recSet as recordSet
me.heading(0) = "Bookmark Names"
me.heading(1) = "Bookmark Urls"
me.heading(2) = "Bookmark Descriptions"
recSet = Bookmarks.SQLSelect("select *
→ from Bookmarks")
me.deleteAllRows
while not recSet.eof
me.addRow(recSet.field("Name").
→ stringValue)
me.cell(me.lastIndex,1) =
→ recSet.field("Url").stringValue
me.cell(me.lastIndex,2) =
→ recSet.field("Description").
→ stringValue
recSet.moveNext
wend
```

This handler loads the database data
into the ListBox.

3. Enter the following code in the ListBox's
   Close handler:

```
dim r as integer
dim rec as databaseRecord
rec = new databaseRecord
Bookmarks.SQLExecute("delete from
→ Bookmarks where Name = '%'")
Bookmarks.commit
for r=1 to me.listCount
rec.column("Name") = me.cell(r-1,0)
rec.column("Url") = me.cell(r-1,1)
rec.column("Description") =
→ me.cell(r-1,2)
```

Figure 10.8 The finished project: the Bookmarks application.

```
Bookmarks.insertRecord "Bookmarks",rec
next
Bookmarks.commit
```

This handler writes the `ListBox` data to the database.

4. Save your work, and test it (**Figure 10.8**).

5. Choose File > Build Application to save the project as a stand-alone application.

   This application is stand-alone in the sense that it doesn't need REALbasic to run, but it can't stand entirely alone. You will need to keep the database with the application.

This section completes the Bookmarks application. You should enter some bookmarks so that the application is usable. The next section discusses how to enter bookmarks and how to use the Bookmarks application in general.

Using the Bookmarks Database

The Bookmarks application lets you maintain a list of bookmarks, including Web addresses and email addresses, and lets you use these bookmarks in conjunction with your Web browser and email program. The bookmarks are saved in a REAL database automatically without any special action on your part.

To go to a bookmarked Web page:

1. Launch the Bookmarks application.

2. Click a bookmark in the list.

   If the bookmark is an HTTP link, the Bookmarks application will launch your preferred browser, if necessary, and cause it to load the Web page (**Figure 10.9**).

To send email to a bookmarked address:

1. Launch the Bookmarks application.

2. Click a bookmark in the list.

   If the bookmark is an email link, the Bookmarks application will launch your preferred email application, if necessary, and cause it to open its mail composing window with the email address filled in (**Figure 10.10**).

Figure 10.9 The Bookmarks application uses the user's default Web browser to display Web pages.

Figure 10.10 The Bookmarks application uses the user's default email client to send email messages.

Figure 10.11 Using edit mode of the Bookmarks application to create a new bookmark...

Figure 10.12 ...and to edit existing bookmarks.

To view bookmark details:

1. Click the button below the bookmark list to show URLs.

2. Click the button again to show descriptions of the bookmarks.

3. Click the button again to show the bookmark names.

To add a bookmark:

1. Click the Edit Bookmarks button.

    The bookmark editing fields and the Clear Fields button appear, and the Edit Bookmarks button changes its caption to Done Editing.

2. Click the blank line at the top of the bookmarks list.

3. Enter the name, URL, and descriptive text for the new bookmark in the appropriate fields (**Figure 10.11**).

4. Click the Done Editing button.

    The editing fields and the Clear Fields button disappear, the Done Editing button's caption changes back to Edit Bookmark, and the new bookmark data appears in the first row of the bookmarks list.

    The bookmarks list data slips down a row, leaving a new blank row at the top for data entry.

To edit a bookmark:

1. Click the Edit Bookmarks button.

2. In the bookmarks list, click the bookmark that you want to edit.

    The bookmark's name, URL, and description appear in the corresponding fields.

3. Edit the fields (**Figure 10.12**).

4. Click the Done Editing button.

To delete a bookmark:

1. Click the Edit Bookmarks button.

2. In the bookmarks list, click the bookmark that you want to delete.

The bookmark's name, URL, and description appear in the corresponding fields.

3. Click the Clear Fields button.

4. Click the Done Editing button.

The Bookmarks application uses the strong interapplication communication in the Macintosh operating system—both OS X and earlier versions. Rather than reinvent the wheel, you can program your applications to use the specialized strengths of existing applications. More examples will appear in the next chapter.

If, though, you really want to program the TCP/IP communications for yourself and not count on the presence of a browser or email program, you need to know about sockets. The next section covers the basics of socket programming.

Using Sockets

The REALbasic Socket control is a tool for managing communications that use the TCP/IP protocol—which includes most Internet communications and probably the communications on your local area network. The Socket control has methods for sending and receiving data and for opening and closing TCP/IP connections.

Using a Socket control to manage communication between computers usually requires that you know the IP address of the computer with which you intend to communicate, the port on which it will be communicating, and whether you are going to initiate the communication or wait for the other computer to initiate it. (Port numbers generally are predictable. Most Web communication happens via port 80, for example.)

You'll find the Socket control in the Tools palette, along with the user-interface controls, but Socket is not like those controls. A Socket does not appear in the application visibly, and you can create a Socket control in your code without dragging an instance from the Tools palette.

Managing a connection with a Socket follows this general pattern:

◆ Make the connection.

◆ Send or receive data.

◆ Handle errors.

◆ Eventually, break the connection.

The following steps demonstrate these processes.

To connect to another computer:

1. Drag a Socket control to the main window.

2. Drag a PushButton control to the main window.

3. Drag two EditField controls to the main window.

4. Drag two StaticText controls to the main window.

5. Position and size these user-interface elements, and set the PushButton's Caption property so that it looks like **Figure 10.13**.

6. In the Properties window for the larger EditField, set its Name to AddressField.

7. In the Properties window for the smaller EditField, set its Name to PortField.

8. Double-click the PushButton to open its Code Editor.

9. In the PushButton's Action handler, enter this code:

    Socket1.address = AddressField.text

    Socket1.port = val(PortField.text)

    Socket1.connect

    This handler sets the Socket's address and port properties to the values that the user places in AddressField and PortField, and attempts to use these values to connect to a remote computer.

10. Press Cmd-R to run the project and test it.

11. Press Cmd-Q to return to the IDE.

Figure 10.13 Using a Socket control (lower-left corner) to connect to another computer.

Figure 10.14 Receiving data with a Socket.

To receive data from another computer:

1. Follow the steps in "To connect to another computer" on the preceding page.

2. Drag two PushButtons to the main window.

3. Drag an EditField to the main window.

4. Position and name these user-interface elements as shown in **Figure 10.14**.

5. In the Properties window for this EditField, check its MultiLine and ReadOnly properties, and enter ReceiveField for its Name property.

6. Double-click the top PushButton of the two that you just added to open its Code Editor.

7. In the Action handler for this PushButton, enter this code:

```
Socket1.listen
```

8. In the Action handler for the other PushButton, enter this code:

```
ReceiveField.text = ""
```

9. In the DataAvailable handler for the Socket control, enter this code:

```
ReceiveField.text = ReceiveField.text
→ + me.readAll()
```

The PushButton scripts tells the Socket to start listening for data from the remote computer and to clear ReceiveField if it gets too full. The code runs when the Socket receives data from the remote computer; it appends the data to the contents of ReceiveField.

10. Press Cmd-R to run the project and test it.

11. Click the Listen button to listen for data.

12. If ReceiveField gets too cluttered to read, you can empty it by clicking the Clear button.

13. Press Cmd-Q to return to the IDE.

To send data to another computer:

1. Follow the steps on the preceding pages to connect to and receive data from another computer.

2. Drag one PushButton to the main window.

3. Drag one EditField to the main window.

4. Position and name these user-interface elements as the send button and blank field shown in **Figure 10.15**.

5. In the Properties window for this latest EditField, set its Name to SendField.

6. Double-click the PushButton that you just added to open its Code Editor.

7. In the Action handler for this PushButton, enter the following code:

   ```
   Socket1.write SendField.text + chr(13)
   → + chr(10)
   ```

   This handler tells the Socket to send the contents of SendField, appending the carriage -return and line-feed characters that TCP/IP likes to see at the end of a command.

8. Press Cmd-R to run the project and test it.

9. Enter data to send in SendField.

10. Click the Send button to send the data.

11. Press Cmd-Q to return to the IDE.

To handle communication errors:

1. Follow the steps on the preceding pages.

2. Drag one EditField to the main window.

3. Drag one StaticText to the main window.

4. Position these user-interface elements, and set the Name property of the StaticText control as shown in **Figure 10.16**.

5. Set the Name of the new EditField to StatusField.

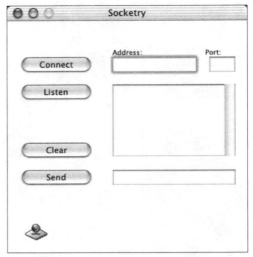

Figure 10.15 Sending data with a Socket.

Figure 10.16 Reporting transmission errors with a Socket.

Figure 10.17 Closing a connection to another computer via a Socket.

6. Double-click the Socket control to open its Code Editor.

7. In the Socket's Connected handler, enter this code:

   StatusField.text = "Connected"

8. In the Socket's Error handler, enter this code:

   StatusField.text = "Error " +
   → str(me.LastErrorCode)

   The Socket control's Connected and Error events fire when the connection is created and when any error condition occurs, respectively. The code in these handlers reports this status.

9. Press Cmd-R to run the project and test it.

10. Press Cmd-Q to return to the IDE.

To close a connection with another computer:

1. Follow the steps on the preceding pages.

2. Drag a PushButton to the main window.

3. Double-click the PushButton to open its Code Editor.

4. In its Action handler, enter this code:

   Socket1.close

5. Set this PushButton's name to Disconnect, and position it as shown in **Figure 10.17**.

6. Press Cmd-R to run the project and test it.

7. Click the Disconnect button to close the connection.

8. Press Cmd-Q to return to the IDE.

Printing

Most of what you need to know to add printing capability to your applications, you have already learned if you've read Chapter 7, "Working with Pictures." Printing in REALbasic uses graphic objects to hold the material to be printed, regardless of whether that material is graphical content or text. Your application can present a user dialog before printing—or not.

Figure 10.18 Printing the simple way: no dialog, no printer settings.

To print without a dialog:

1. Drag a PushButton to the main window.

2. Double-click the PushButton to open its Code Editor.

3. In the PushButton's Action handler, enter the following code (**Figure 10.18**):

   ```
   dim g as Graphics
   g = OpenPrinter()
   g.drawString "Hello World", 50, 50
   ```

   This example uses the OpenPrinter function to create a Graphics object associated with the default printer and then uses the DrawString method of the Graphics object to print some text.

This approach is the simplest way to print. The next example shows you how to use printer settings and a Print dialog.

To print with a dialog:

1. Press Option-Tab to open the Code Editor for the main window.

2. Choose File > New Property.

   The Property Declaration dialog appears.

3. Enter `PrinterSettings as string` and then click OK.

   These three steps create a property that you can use to keep track of the current printer settings.

4. Drag an `EditField` to the main window, and check its `MultiLine` property.

5. Drag a `PushButton` to the main window.

6. Double-click the `PushButton` to open its Code Editor.

7. In the `PushButton`'s `Action` handler, enter the following:

   ```
   dim pSet as PrinterSetup
   pSet = new PrinterSetup
   if PrinterSettings <> "" then
   pSet.setupString = PrinterSettings
   End if
   ```

   This code creates an instance of the `PrinterSetup` class and loads the value of the `PrinterSettings` property (if any value has been stored in it) into the `PrinterSetup` object's `setupString` property. REALbasic printing uses this `setupString` property to tell the printer how to behave.

   continues on next page

8. Edit the PushButton's Action handler to look like this:

```
dim page as Graphics
dim pSet as PrinterSetup
pSet = new PrinterSetup
if PrinterSettings <> "" then
EditField.text = PrinterSettings
pSet.setupString = PrinterSettings
End if
page = openPrinterDialog(pSet)
if page <> nil then
page.drawString "Hello World", 50, 50
page.nextPage
PrinterSettings = pSet.setupString
End if
```

This code invokes the OpenPrinterDialog function, which displays the standard Print dialog (**Figure 10.19**). If the user cancels the dialog, nil is returned, and the handler does nothing. Otherwise, the dialog returns a graphic object, and the handler uses it to print the text.

This chapter showed you how to make your computer talk to other computers and with a printer. The next chapter will show you how to use AppleScript and shell scripts to make your computer talk to itself.

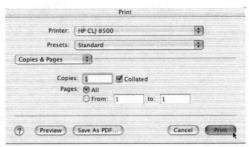

Figure 10.19 The proper way to print: present the user a standard Print dialog.

PRINTING

EXTENDING REALBASIC WITH SCRIPTING

REALbasic gives you the tools to do almost anything in your applications. But sometimes, it makes sense to go outside your application—and even outside REALbasic—to harness the power in other tools and applications, in the Macintosh Finder, or in the deeper layers of the operating system. Why build your own spreadsheet application when you already have a perfectly good professional-quality spreadsheet program in your Applications folder? Why write your own code to find files when you have a Find command?

How convenient, then, that REALbasic gives you the means to control other applications and the operating system through AppleScript, AppleEvents, and Shell scripting.

But REALbasic lets you use scripting to extend your applications in another way. With `RBScript` scripting, you can give the users of your applications the ability to write and run REALbasic code. You can make your programs programmable.

Making Programs RBScript Programmable

RBScript is a REALbasic class that you can use in your applications to execute REALbasic code in a running application. It actually implements a subset of the full REALbasic language. This subset of REALbasic is available to the user of the program while it is running, meaning that the user can do things like computing mathematical functions and performing complicated operations on string data.

An instance of an RBScript class makes a subset of REALbasic available to the user. It does have some limitations, but it includes all the math and string operations, all the basic data types (plus arrays), and all the control structures. Users of your RBScript-enabled application can create new functions, subroutines, and classes, and use them in their code.

In the following examples, you will gradually build RBScript Runner, an application that presents the user an environment for writing and testing RBScript code, complete with a library of selectable and editable example scripts. You'll start by building a minimal framework for editing and running scripts, and you'll write the traditional first program: a one-line script that displays the message "Hello World!"

Figure 11.1 Building the RBScript Runner application.

To add RBScript user scriptability to an application:

1. Choose File > New to create a new project.

2. In the Project window, double-click the Window icon to open the main window.

3. In the main window's Properties window, set its `Height` and `Width` to 384 and its `Title` to RBScript Runner.

4. Drag an `EditField` control to the main window, sizing and positioning it more or less as shown in **Figure 11.1**.

5. In its Properties window, set its `Name` to `SourceField`, its `MultiLine` property to `true`, and its `TextFont` to `Courier`.

    This field is where the user will enter the script to run. Using a monospace font, such as Courier, is traditional and useful for code.

6. Drag a `PushButton` to the main window, positioning it in the bottom-right corner of the window.

7. In the `PushButton`'s Properties window, set its `Name` to `RunButton`, its `Caption` to Run, and its `Default` property to `true`.

    The user will click this button to execute the code in `SourceField`. This code will work by invoking the `RBScript` object.

8. Double-click the Run button to open its Code Editor.

9. Enter the following code in the Run button's `Action` handler:

    ```
    RBScript1.source = SourceField.text
    RBScript1.run
    ```

    This code tells the `RBScript` object where to find the script to execute. You'd better create this `RBScript` object next.

    continues on next page

10. Drag an RBScript control to the main window.

Drop the control anywhere; it won't be visible at run time.

11. Double-click the RBScript control to open its Code Editor.

12. In the RBScript's Print handler, enter the following code:

```
OutputField.text = ""
OutputField.text = msg
```

Because this handler mentions an OutputField, you'd better create that, too.

13. Drag another EditField to the main window, and position it as shown in **Figure 11.2**.

14. In this new EditField's Properties window, set its Name to OutputField and its MultiLine property to true.

This field is where the RBScript control will place the output of the function that it executes.

15. If you like, drag three StaticText controls to the main window, positioning, sizing, and naming them as shown in **Figure 11.3**.

16. In the Properties window for SourceField, enter the following for its Text property:

```
print("Hello World!")
```

This script will be executed when the Run button is clicked.

17. Press Cmd-S to save the project, and enter RBScript Runner as its name.

18. Press Cmd-R to run the project.

The one-line script that you wrote should appear in SourceField.

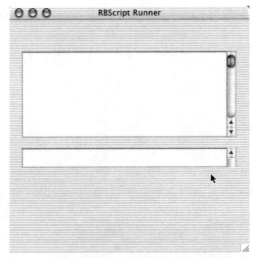

Figure 11.2 The RBScript Runner application needs fields where the user can enter the script and the script can display its output.

Figure 11.3 Adding labels to improve the user interface of the RBScript Runner application.

Figure 11.4 Running a one-line RBScript script.

19. Click Run.

The result of executing this script should appear in OutputField.

The script in SourceField is only an initial value seeded in the field. You (in your role as the user of the application) can change it, editing the text within the quotation marks, for example, and then click Run again to make the script do something different (**Figure 11.4**).

20. Press Cmd-Q to return to the IDE.

It may take a moment's consideration to realize what this simple program accomplishes. It's no trick to display a message saying "Hello World!", but it is quite a trick to write a program that lets your users write programs. And those programs don't have to be restricted, like this one, to a single line of code.

To run multiline scripts with RBScript:

1. If you haven't already done so, build the RBScript Runner application, following steps 1 through 15 of "To add RBScript user scriptability to an application" on pages 377-8.

2. In the Properties window for SourceField, enter the following for its Text property:

```
// Compute N factorial
dim i,j,N as integer
j = 1
N = 6
for i=1 to N
  j = j * i
next
print str(N) + "!= " + str(j)
```

This script will be executed when the Run button is clicked. It computes the mathematical function N factorial (written N!), with N initially set to 6.

continues on next page

3. Press Cmd-S to save your work.

4. Press Cmd-R to run the project.

   The multiline script that you wrote should appear in SourceField.

5. Click Run.

   The result of executing this script should appear in OutputField (**Figure 11.5**).

6. To compute the factorial of another number, edit the following line, substituting the other number for 6:

   N = 6

7. Click Run again to see the new result.

8. Press Cmd-Q to return to the IDE.

You can see from this example that the users of your RBScript-enabled applications can write routines very much like the routines that you write in the Code Editor when you create full REALbasic applications. But the more complicated the code is, the greater the likelihood of errors, so your users are going to need some help in the form of error messages.

Figure 11.5 Running a multiline RBScript script.

Figure 11.6 Adding error reporting to the RBScript Runner application.

To add error handling to RBScript processing:

1. If you haven't already done so, build the RBScript Runner application, following steps 1 through 15 of "To add RBScript user scriptability to an application" on pages 377-8.

2. Drag an EditField control to the main window, and size and position it like the bottom field in **Figure 11.6**.

3. In the Properties window of this new EditField, set its Name to ErrorField and its MultiLine property to true.

4. If you like, drag a StaticText control to the main window, positioning and sizing it to serve as a label for ErrorField, and setting its Name property to something appropriate (see Figure 11.6).

5. Double-click the RBScript control to open its Code Editor.

6. In the RBScript's CompilerError handler, enter this code:

   ```
   ErrorField.text = ""
   ErrorField.text = "Compiletime error "
   → str(errorNumber) + " in line " +
   → str(line) + ": " + errorMsg
   ```

7. In the RBScript's RuntimeError handler, enter this code:

   ```
   ErrorField.text = ""
   ErrorField.text = "Runtime error: " +
   → error.message
   ```

   These handlers will report on run-time and compile-time errors in the code.

continues on next page

8. In the Properties window for SourceField, enter the following for its Text property:

   // Print "Hello World!"

   dim s1,s2 as string

   s1 = "Hello"

   s2 = "World!"

   print s1 + " " + s2

   This script will be executed when the Run button is clicked. It's just a multi-line version of the familiar "Hello World!" program, but it will serve to explore error reporting.

9. Press Cmd-S to save your work.

10. Press Cmd-R to run the project.

    The script that you wrote should appear in SourceField.

11. Click Run.

    The result of executing this script should appear in OutputField (**Figure 11.7**).

12. To see what happens when an error occurs, replace one of the text strings in SourceField (including the quotation marks) with a number, and click Run again.

    You should see an error message, because your script is trying to store a number in a string variable.

13. Press Cmd-Q to return to the IDE.

Figure 11.7 Running an RBScript script with error reporting.

This example performs the basic error reporting for `RBScript` code, but its error messages aren't as informative as they could be. By studying the online documentation for the `RBScript` control, you can construct more meaningful error reporting, providing text interpretations for the errors that users are most likely to encounter when they code in your application.

Having provided your users some error reporting, you should feel free to give them the means to make even more errors. Besides allowing your users to enter code, you can allow them to enter data. You can, in fact, allow them to write code that prompts for the entry of data.

That last statement may take a minute to digest. If you want to say that your users would be writing code that prompts for data from *their* users, feel free. Personally, my head hurts just thinking about the users of the programs of the users of my programs.

✔ Tip

- `RBScript` code is compiled before running, which means that it can be relatively efficient. It also means that the code is subject to both run-time and compile-time errors.

To accept user input in RBScript routines:

1. If you haven't already done so, build the RBScript Runner application, following steps 1 through 15 of "To add **RBScript** user scriptability to an application" on pages 377-8.

2. If you want to see error diagnostics, follow steps 2 through 7 of "To add error handling to **RBScript** processing" on page 381.

3. Drag another `EditField` control to the main window, and size and position it like the bottom field in **Figure 11.8**.

4. In the Properties window of this new `EditField`, set its `Name` to `InputField` and its `MultiLine` and `ScrollbarVertical` properties to `false`.

5. If you like, drag a `StaticText` control to the main window, positioning and sizing it to serve as a label for `InputField`, and setting its `Name` property to something appropriate (see Figure 11.8).

6. Double-click the `RBScript` control to open its Code Editor.

7. Enter this code in the RBScript's `Input` handler:

```
return InputField.text
```

When the function `input` is executed during the running of the script, it triggers this handler. The handler simply returns the value in `InputField` to the script, which does with it what it will.

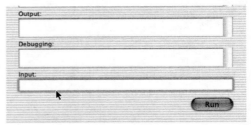

Figure 11.8 Allowing for user input in RBScript scripts.

Figure 11.9 The RBScript code reads its input value from the Input field.

8. In the Properties window for SourceField, enter the following for its Text property:

```
// Allow input to a script. User must
→ enter a number in the Input field
→ before clicking Run.
dim N as integer
N = val(input(""))
print str(1 + ((N - 1) mod 12))
```

This script will be executed when the Run button is clicked. It performs a variation on the mod function. Whereas N mod 12 returns a value in the range 0 to 11 (the remainder when N is divided by 12), this script returns a value in the range 1 to 12. It's identical to mod except that whenever mod returns 0, it returns the modulus (the number to the right of mod in N mod M). This function is useful in some contexts, such as clock arithmetic.

9. Press Cmd-S to save your work.

10. Press Cmd-R to run the project.

   The script that you wrote should appear in SourceField.

11. Put a number in InputField.

12. Click Run.

   The result of executing this script should appear in OutputField (**Figure 11.9**).

13. Press Cmd-Q to return to the IDE.

In the preceding examples, you created the beginning of a library of RBScript scripts. The next example builds an application to maintain such a library—a tool for presenting scripting possibilities to your users or for exploring RBScript scripting yourself.

MAKING PROGRAMS RBSCRIPT PROGRAMMABLE

To offer the user a library of RBScript routines:

1. If you haven't already done so, build the RBScript Runner application, following steps 1 through 15 of "To add RBScript user scriptability to an application" on pages 377-8.

2. To enable error diagnostics, follow steps 2 through 7 of "To add error handling to RBScript processing" on page 381.

3. To allow for user input to scripts, follow steps 3 through 7 of "To accept user input in RBScript routines" on page 374.

4. Drag a Popup control to the main window, and place it in the bottom-left corner of the window.

5. In the Popup's Properties window, set its Name to SampleScripts.

   This Popup will offer the user a list of sample scripts to choose among.

6. Drag a ListBox to the main window.

   You usually won't need to see its contents, so position and size the ListBox as shown in **Figure 11.10** to get it out of the way.

7. In the ListBox's Properties window, set its Name to ExampleList, its ColumnCount to 2, its HasHeading to true, its TextFont to Courier, and its ColumnWidths to 80,*.

   This ListBox will hold the scripts of your script library. Each row will hold a script name and the actual code of the script.

8. Double-click the Popup to open its Code Editor.

Figure 11.10 Adding a ListBox to hold a library of RBScript scripts.

9. Enter the following code in the Popup's Open handler:

```
dim i as integer
me.deleteAllRows
me.addRow("Example Scripts")
for i=1 to ExampleList.listCount
  me.addRow(ExampleList.cell(i-1,0))
next
me.listIndex = 0
```

This code builds the list of script names that the Popup will display. It gets the names from the ListBox.

10. Enter the following code in the Popup's Change handler:

```
ErrorField.text = ""
SourceField.text = ""
if me.listIndex > 0 then
  sourceField.text =
  → unpack(ExampleList.cell
  → (me.listIndex-1,1))
End if
```

When the user makes a choice from the Popup, this code runs. Based on the script name selected, it pulls the actual script out of the ListBox and displays it in the SourceField. In doing this, the code uses a method called Unpack, which you need to define.

11. Choose Edit > New Method.

12. In the dialog that appears, enter Unpack as the Name, s as string for Parameters, and string for Return Type.

13. Click OK.

continues on next page

MAKING PROGRAMS RBSCRIPT PROGRAMMABLE

14. Enter the following as the Unpack method's code:

```
dim s1 as string
s1 = s
while instr(s1,"•") > 0
  s1 = left(s1,instr(s1,"•")-1) +
  → chr(13) + mid(s1,instr(s1,"•")+1)
wend
return s1
```

The Unpack method converts the script from a "packed" form that lets it fit on one line in the ListBox. Scripts can have several lines, but ListBox cells can't, so you'll store your scripts packed—that is, with all return characters replaced by · (bullet) characters.

Next, you need to supply those sample scripts.

15. Using a text editor, write some RBScript scripts.

Several sample scripts have been supplied in this chapter. You can key those in or write your own.

16. Open the Properties window of the ListBox, and click the Edit button next to Initial Value to edit the initial contents of the ListBox.

17. Type the following as the first line of the ListBox's contents:

```
Example    Script
```

That's a tab between the two words. This text is the Heading for the ListBox's contents.

```
Edit Value                         OK
Example Script                     Cancel
Oneliner print("Hello World!")
Math // Compute N factorial··dim
i,j,N as integer··j=1·N=6·for i=1 to
N·  j=j*i·next··print str(N) + "!= " +
str(j)
Strings // Print 'Hello World!'··dim
s1,s2 as
string··s1="Hello"·s2="World!"··print
s1 + " " + s2
Function // Define and use a
function·//   that removes redundant
spaces··function f (s as string) as
string·  while instr(s," ")>0·
s=left(s,instr(s," ")-
1)+mid(s,instr(s," ")+1)·  wend·
return s·end function··print f("just 1
space between  words")
Sub // Define and use a subroutine·//
that prints integers or strings··sub
printAny (v as variant)·  dim s as
string·  if vartype(v)=2 or
vartype(v)=8 then·      s=v·   print s·
end if·end sub··printAny(3)
Input // Allow input to script·//
User must enter a number in the ·//
Input field before clicking Run.··dim
N as integer··N = val(input(""))·print
str(1+((N-1) mod 16))
```

Figure 11.11 In the RBScript Runner application, scripts are stored in the ListBox in this packed format.

RBScript Runner

RBScripting

```
Script:
// Compute N factorial

dim i,j,N as integer

j=1
N=6
for i=1 to N
  j=j*i
next

print str(N) + "!= " + str(j)
```

```
Output:
6!= 720
```

```
Debugging:
```

```
Input:
```

Math   Run

Figure 11.12 Using the RBScript Runner application's script library.

18. Copy each of your scripts to a separate line of the ListBox, as follows:

[name of script] [Tab] [script]

Fit each multiline script onto just one line of the ListBox by replacing all return characters in the script with · (bullet) characters. You can do this in your text editor before copying the script to the ListBox. The script will no longer be very readable, but it will pack nicely into the ListBox, and the Unpack method will clean it up. (**Figure 11.11** shows a collection of scripts in this packed form.)

19. Press Cmd-S to save your work.

20. Press Cmd-R to run the project.

21. Choose a script from the Popup.

The example script that you selected should appear in SourceField. You can edit it or leave it as is.

22. Click Run.

The result of executing this script should appear in OutputField (**Figure 11.12**).

23. Press Cmd-Q to return to the IDE.

If all went well, you have created an environment for testing RBScript scripting.

✔ Tip

■ As shown in some of these examples, you can use functions and subroutines in RBScript scripts. The trick is to define them before using them.

MAKING PROGRAMS RBSCRIPT PROGRAMMABLE

Extending REALbasic with AppleScript

AppleScript is a powerful system-level scripting language that has been around since version 7 of the Macintosh operating system. It was designed to allow applications to talk to one another and with the Finder, and to allow users to write simple stand-alone scripts to automate tasks. An art director, for example, could write one AppleScript script that invoked several applications to perform standard scaling and cropping operations on each picture in a folder of pictures; then she could rename the picture files, print a specified subset of them, and copy them all to a new folder.

AppleScript addresses a common need that application software doesn't meet: automating repetitive tasks involving data from multiple applications.

It initially took some time for AppleScript to become really useful, though. Third-party applications (as well as the Mac Finder) had to be reprogrammed to make their functionality accessible to scripting commands. In large part, that happened, and AppleScript is today a very powerful tool.

✔ Tip

- As suggested by the name, AppleScript will not work in Windows. REALbasic code intended to be used on Windows machines cannot use anything in this section.

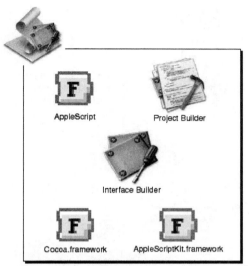

Figure 11.13 AppleScript Studio lets you build Cocoa applications with AppleScript.

Figure 11.14 Apple's Script Editor is the standard tool for creating AppleScripts.

The release of OS X set AppleScript functionality back a bit, however. Not only has Apple been slow to enable AppleScript support in the Finder, but third-party applications that support AppleScript as well as the Classic applications are still somewhat rare.

Nevertheless, Apple is clearly committed to making AppleScript as useful under OS X as it was under previous OS versions. The release of AppleScript Studio (**Figure 11.13**)—a rich environment for developing AppleScript scripts for the powerful Cocoa development platform that is part of OS X—demonstrates this commitment.

For many, though, the old familiar Script Editor application (**Figure 11.14**) will be sufficient. Whether you use AppleScript Studio or Script Editor, you will have to write some code in the AppleScript language so you can use it—unless you simply download some useful scripts written by other programmers and use those scripts. You'll find one such script at my site (www.swaine.com/realbasic.html).

If you do decide to write AppleScript scripts, you'll need a guide. Among the better recent ones is Ethan Wilde's *AppleScript for Applications: Visual QuickStart Guide* (Peachpit Press).

REALbasic's support for AppleScript is twofold:

◆ You can add compiled AppleScript scripts to a REALbasic project and invoke them just as you invoke native REALbasic commands and functions.

◆ REALbasic has several classes that support the underlying technology of AppleScript AppleEvents. Using these AppleEvent-related classes, you can build and send AppleEvents to other applications or receive AppleEvents from other applications.

To use a precompiled AppleScript in a REALbasic application:

1. Acquire a compiled AppleScript file.
   You can find some at
   www.swaine.com/realbasic.html.

2. Drag the AppleScript file to the Project window (**Figure 11.15**).

   In this example, the compiled script is called TEcount. This script, which counts words in a TextEdit document, is downloadable from www.swaine.com/realbasic.html.

3. Drag a PushButton to the main window.

4. In the PushButton's Properties window, set its Caption property to TEcount.

5. Enter the following code in the PushButton's Action handler:

   TEcount

6. Press Cmd-S to save your work.

7. Press Cmd-R to run the project and test it.

8. Open a document in TextEdit (assuming that you are running OS X; if you are not, download the STcount script from www.swaine.com and use it instead of the TEcount script).

   This document needs to be in the same folder as your REALbasic project and REALbasic itself.

9. In your REALbasic application, click the TEcount button.

   You should see an AppleScript-generated dialog that reports the number of words, characters, and lines in the frontmost TextEdit document (**Figure 11.16**).

10. Press Cmd-Q to return to the IDE.

Figure 11.15 Making a compiled AppleScript available to your application is just a matter of dropping it in the Project window.

Figure 11.16 The output of an AppleScript script invoked by a REALbasic application.

To send an AppleEvent from a REALbasic application:

1. Drag a PushButton to the main window.

2. In the Properties window of this PushButton, set its Caption property to TEopen.

3. Enter the following code in the PushButton's Action handler:

```
dim ae as AppleEvent
dim success as boolean
ae = newAppleEvent("aevt", "odoc",
→ "ttxt")
ae.folderItemParam("--") =
→ getFolderItem("p2pVogue")
success = ae.send
if not success then
  msgBox "Attempt to open TextEdit file
  → failed."
End if
```

This handler uses the AppleEvent class and the NewAppleEvent function to construct an AppleEvent and send it to the TextEdit application. The target application and the particular AppleEvent to send are specified in those cryptic codes given to the NewAppleEvent function.

4. Press Cmd-S to save your work.

5. Press Cmd-R to run the project and test it.

6. Open a document in TextEdit (or SimpleText if you are not running OS X).

continues on next page

EXTENDING REALBASIC WITH APPLESCRIPT

7. Save the document as an RTF file under the name **p2pVogue.rtf** (for compatibility with the code in this example).

Make sure that you save the file in the same folder as your REALbasic project and the same folder as REALbasic itself.

8. Close the document.

9. In your REALbasic application, click the TEopen button.

You should see the document open again (**Figure 11.17**).

10. Press Cmd-Q to return to the IDE.

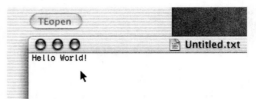

Figure 11.17 Using REALbasic to send an AppleEvent to open a document.

This section only brushes the snow off the tip of the iceberg of using AppleScript and AppleEvents within REALbasic code. A little experimentation with AppleScript itself will show you ways to extend these two examples to do other things with TextEdit files. And by studying the Wilde book or another source on AppleScript support in third-party applications, you can discover many ways to apply AppleScript to other applications from your REALbasic programs.

Although you can do a lot with AppleScript, REALbasic offers much more system-level scripting through its Shell class.

Extending REALbasic with Shell Scripting

Beneath its pretty facade, Macintosh OS X is really the Unix operating system. As a consequence, all the rich collection of Unix commands written by Unix developers over the years are available to those who know how to find them under the OS X eye candy. REALbasic gives you access to all these Unix commands via the Shell class.

If you are writing applications on a Mac to be deployed on the Windows platform, you won't have access to these Unix commands, but you will have access to the DOS command-line operating system that hides under Windows. In exactly the same way that it opens Unix under Mac OS X, the Shell class opens DOS under Windows.

The Shell class has several useful properties, events, and methods. This section covers in the Result property and the Execute method.

Result is a string property that holds the contents of the output buffer—typically, the result of the execution of some Unix or DOS command.

Execute takes a string parameter that is the literal Unix or DOS command and executes that command.

You can explore the other properties, events, and methods of the Shell class in the REALbasic Online Language Reference.

continues on next page

Using the Shell class requires not only knowledge of the class's properties, events, and methods, but also some knowledge of the Unix (or DOS) commands you want to execute. Fortunately, you don't need to be an expert in Unix or DOS to use an occasional command. For Unix in particular, just knowing the name of a command is often enough to allow you to get documentation for that command by using the Unix man (for *manual*) command.

✔ Tip

■ Unlike AppleScript scripts, Shell scripting works on both the Mac OS X and Windows platforms (but not in earlier Mac OS versions). This does *not* mean that any given Shell script will work on either platform; in general, it won't. It simply means that you can write Shell scripts for OS X, and you can also write Shell scripts—*different* Shell scripts—for Windows/DOS.

To use Shell scripting to determine your user name:

1. Drag a PushButton to the main window.

2. In the PushButton's Properties window, set its Caption property to User Name.

3. Double-click the PushButton to open its Code Editor.

4. Enter this code in the PushButton's Action handler:

```
// Geoff Perlman's script to show your
→ user name
dim myShell as Shell
dim myName as String
myShell = new Shell
myShell.execute "whoami"
// (the unix whoami command)
myName = myShell.result
msgBox myName
```

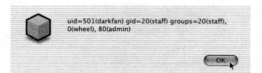

Figure 11.18 Using REALbasic's Shell class to run the Unix whoami command.

5. Press Cmd-S to save your work.

6. Press Cmd-R to run the project and test it.

7. Click the User Name PushButton.

You should see a message box showing your Mac OS X user name (**Figure 11.18**).

8. Press Cmd-Q to return to the IDE.

Several conventions in writing Unix commands are important to know. Unix commands are usually cryptic and short, and parameters of Unix commands are often single letters, supplied after a hyphen. Thus, ls -s means the ls (list directory contents) command with the s (sort by size) parameter.

You'll also need to know about Unix Shell conventions such as > and | for routing the output of a command to a file or to the input of another command for further processing. These conventions are defined by use in the following examples.

To use Shell scripting to list user directories:

1. Drag a PushButton to the main window.

2. In the PushButton's Properties window, set its Caption property to Users.

3. Double-click the PushButton to open its Code Editor.

4. Enter this code in the PushButton's Action handler:

```
// List user directory info in a file
dim myShell as Shell
myShell = new Shell
myShell.execute "ls -l users >
→ users.txt"
// (the unix ls command)
```

continues on next page

This code executes the Unix `ls` command to list the contents of a directory (the directory of users of the system) and sends the results to a file named `users.txt`.

5. Press Cmd-S to save your work.

6. Press Cmd-R to run the project and test it.

7. Click the Users `PushButton`.

After a delay that is a little hard to predict but will probably be longer than you think it should be, you should see a file named `users.txt` in the root directory of your hard drive (**Figure 11.19**).

8. Press Cmd-Q to return to the IDE.

The Unix man command is extremely useful. Give man the name of a Unix command, and it returns more than you probably wanted to know about the command, its parameters, and how to use it.

To use Shell scripting to see the documentation for Unix commands:

1. Drag a `PushButton` to the main window.

2. In the `PushButton`'s Properties window, set its `Caption` property to `Man`.

3. Double-click the `PushButton` to open its Code Editor.

4. Enter this code in the `PushButton`'s `Action` handler:

```
// Dump the documentation for the ls and
→ grep commands to two files
dim myShell as Shell
myShell = new Shell
myShell.execute "man ls > lsdox.txt"
myShell.execute "man grep > grepdox.txt"
// (the unix man command)
```

This script creates files containing documentation on the Unix `ls` and `grep` commands.

Figure 11.19 When you run the appropriate Unix `ls` command via the REALbasic `Shell` class, a new file is created.

EXTENDING REALBASIC WITH SHELL SCRIPTING

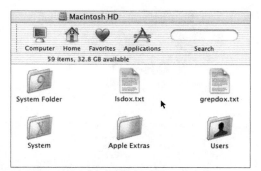

Figure 11.20 Using the REALbasic `Shell` class and the Unix `man` command to create files of documentation for Unix commands.

5. Press Cmd-S to save your work.

6. Press Cmd-R to run the project and test it.

7. Click the `Man PushButton`.

You should see two files named `lsdox.txt` and `grepdox.txt` in the root directory of your hard drive (**Figure 11.20**).

8. Press Cmd-Q to return to the IDE.

The Unix `grep` command is a powerful string search-and-replace tool.

To use the Unix grep command:

1. Drag a `PushButton` to the main window.

2. In the `PushButton`'s Properties window, set its `Caption` property to `Grep`.

3. Double-click the `PushButton` to open its Code Editor.

4. Enter this code in the `PushButton`'s `Action` handler:

```
// Use grep and piping
dim myShell as Shell
myShell = new Shell
myShell.execute "ls -l | grep mswaine >
→ mswaine.txt"
// (the unix grep command and the pipe
→ ( | ) command)
```

(In the preceding code, substitute your own user name for `mswaine`.)

continues on next page

5. Press Cmd-S to save your work.

6. Press Cmd-R to run the project and test it.

7. Click the Grep PushButton.

You should see a file in your root directory that has your user name in its name (**Figure 11.21**).

8. Press Cmd-Q to return to the IDE.

Apple should document its Unix commands, but until it gets around to doing so, any Unix or Linux manual will give you a good idea of how to use Unix commands. Documentation on DOS commands is also easy to come by if you decide that you need it.

In these first 11 chapters, you've seen how to write programs in REALbasic. In the last chapter, you'll see some things that you need to know to be a successful REALbasic programmer.

Figure 11.21 Using the Unix grep command via REALbasic.

BEING A PROGRAMMER

The preceding chapters have shown you how to use REALbasic to write programs. But there is more to being a good programmer—or a professional programmer—than just using the tools. It takes knowledge and skill in software design, debugging, documentation, and deployment.

Any advice on these topics is necessarily subjective; there is no one right way to document a REALbasic handler or to offer a choice to the user. But decades of programmer experience (and the iron heel of Apple's Human Interface Guidelines) have identified a large number of good practices that can make your programs more usable and your life easier. This chapter presents some of the most useful of these practices.

The Processes of Programming

Large applications like Adobe Photoshop or Macintosh OS X are developed by teams of programmers following more or less regimented methodologies (in Apple's case, probably less). In the approach to programming that the typical lone REALbasic programmer uses, steps in the processes of designing, debugging, and documenting an application take place whenever they seem to be appropriate. All three processes might take place during any given day in the course of a development project. This approach is the one that I use and the one that I describe in this chapter (**Figure 12.1**).

Although all three of these processes take place more or less in parallel, they require different skills, knowledge, priorities, and mindsets. So it's worthwhile to look at each in isolation to see what it involves. This chapter describes these processes and also the final process: deploying the application.

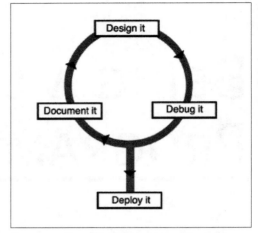

Figure 12.1 The application-development cycle.

To develop an application:

1. Design it.

   Follow the guidelines in this chapter and in the books recommended therein to come up with the initial design and to refine your application's design and the design of its user interface.

2. Debug it.

   As you write the code, continue to test it. Fix errors as you find them. Later in the development process, test the usability of your application by having users try it out.

3. Document it.

   Document your code as you write it. User documentation can wait until the features of the application begin to stabilize.

4. Repeat steps 1-3.

   Depending on your programming style, these steps might be almost simultaneous, or you might spend days on any one step before moving to the next. Listing these processes as separate steps is simply a useful way to think about the overall development process, even if it is only an approximation.

5. Deploy it.

   Later in this chapter, you will find a discussion of the things you need to do before using, posting, or shipping your application.

THE PROCESSES OF PROGRAMMING

Designing Your Applications

The word *design,* as applied to software, has at least three meanings.

One meaning is the *graphic design* of an application: the choice of typefaces and colors, the use of icons and other graphic elements, and knowledge of composition. Large commercial software projects often have a graphic designer on staff to make sure that the application meets the goals of good graphic design. This chapter doesn't have anything to do with this aspect of design, except to say that even if you can't afford a designer, you should give some thought to the aesthetics of your application. Aesthetically challenged software is often distracting and hard to use.

Usability is more properly the concern of *user-interface design,* which is the task of constructing the part of the application with which the user interacts directly. The "User-interface design" section of this chapter offers some advice on creating good user interfaces.

The third common meaning of the word *design* when used in reference to computer programs is the structure of the code that makes up the application. *Software design* addresses the goals of producing code that is easy for you or another programmer to read and maintain. Good design can make software more reusable, so that you don't have to reinvent the wheel (or the list-sorting routine) every time you create a new program. The section of this chapter titled "Software design" speaks briefly to good software design practice.

User-interface design

Good user-interface design is hard. Just look at the varied and invariably awful user interfaces that people have come up with for setting the clock in your car radio or your VCR. (For that matter, it's not clear why this has to be a user chore; why can't you just select your time zone and let the radio set its own time? The information is out there somewhere.) But a few principles can go a long way toward keeping you from making some of the most egregious user-interface design errors:

◆ Be consistent.

◆ Be clear.

◆ Keep it simple.

✔ Tips

■ Know your environment and follow the user-interface guidelines for the platform on which you intend to deploy your application. (See the sidebar "User-Interface Design Resources" on page 410.)

■ Know your user. If you are the target user of your application, this is easy. Otherwise, you need to identify the target users, determine their needs and strengths and limitations, do user testing, and *listen*.

DESIGNING YOUR APPLICATIONS

Good user-interface design starts with the big picture: the layout of the screen or window.

To design an effective screen layout:

◆ Place elements where the user expects them to be (**Figure 12.2**).

The user's mental model of each aspect of your application is conditioned by the way other applications work and by the other aspects of your application. Be consistent with established conventions, with Apple's Human Interface Guidelines, and with your own application.

◆ Eliminate screen clutter.

Examine every element on your screen, and ask yourself what function it is serving. For most applications, *looking cool* is not a valid function. Eliminate any element that doesn't have a clear function.

◆ Put the user in charge.

The screen belongs to the user. Your job in laying out the screen is to provide the user the means to get something done (**Figure 12.3**).

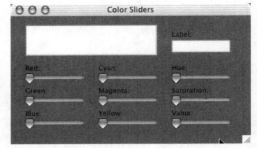

Figure 12.2 Place user-interface elements where users are used to seeing them.

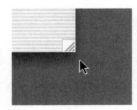

Figure 12.3 Even as simple a thing as making a window resizable can give the user a greater sense of control and make your application more accommodating.

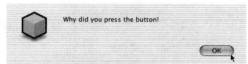

Figure 12.4 It's a lesson that some of the largest software companies haven't learned: Don't insult, confuse, or annoy your users.

User-interface design is not static. One of the experts in the field, Alan Cooper, argues that application developers should think in terms of *interaction design* rather than interface design. Certainly, an important goal of design is to produce a good interaction with the user, and dialogs are a key part of this goal.

To create effective user dialogs:

◆ Use dialogs when you need to collect some information from the user before proceeding or to offer warnings or advice.

◆ Use a confirming dialog if the action that the user is about to take could have undesirable consequences and is irreversible: "Are you sure you want to erase your hard disk? This action is irreversible."

◆ Be courteous. Your program is a guest on the user's computer. Many dialogs in commercial applications insult, confuse, or annoy users. Avoid this mistake (**Figure 12.4**).

◆ Respect the user's time. Keep dialog text to the absolute minimum required to get the idea across clearly.

◆ Ask yourself whether each dialog is necessary. Design is the art of making choices. Sometimes, it's appropriate to offer the choice to the user, but often, choices left to the user are really choices abdicated by the designer.

◆ Follow user-interface guidelines scrupulously in the use and placement of buttons and text.

◆ Be forgiving. Users make mistakes. Whenever possible, let them undo actions. When this isn't possible, warn users clearly in advance.

✔ Tip

■ Icons can be effective tools for communicating in a user interface, but only if they are self-explanatory.

The user interface of your REALbasic application will be made up of controls. Using the right control for each job will make your user interface more transparent and usable.

To use user-interface controls effectively:

- Use check boxes and radio buttons to let the user set options (**Figure 12.5**).
- Use check boxes when the options are independent of one another.
- Use radio buttons when only one of the options must be chosen.
- Use push buttons to initiate actions.
- Use pop-up menus to allow the user to choose items from a list. Unlike the options in check boxes, the options in a pop-up menu are not constantly visible.
- Use dialogs to request further information immediately.
- Use edit fields for information that the user can enter at any time.
- Always consider whether a menu item would be the best way to implement a controlling feature. The most-used applications typically give nearly all their main windows to the user's document and place most of the control of the application in menus.

✔ Tip

- Label radio buttons with adjectives, not nouns or verbs. This practice is almost always clearer (**Figure 12.6**).

Figure 12.5 Use check boxes and radio buttons to let users set options.

Figure 12.6 Label radio buttons with adjectives, not verbs. A radio button indicates a state, not an action.

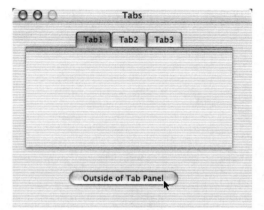

Figure 12.7 Place all elements at the right level. A button belongs inside a TabPanel only if it applies to only one Tab.

Figure 12.8 Don't depend on color to convey information.

To use tab panels effectively:

◆ Group contents logically. For every user-interface element, ask yourself, "On which panel does this belong?"

◆ Place any user-interface element that applies to the entire window outside the TabPanel (**Figure 12.7**).

◆ Title the tabs meaningfully and briefly.

◆ Don't get carried away. Some commercial applications use multiple rows of tabs, which you can accomplish in REALbasic by placing TabPanels within TabPanels. This arrangement is invariably ugly and usually confusing. Avoid the temptation.

To use color effectively:

◆ Design in black and white, and add color afterward.

◆ Never rely on color as the only way to convey information. Unless you are the only user of your application, you don't know whether your users can discriminate colors (**Figure 12.8**).

◆ Test your color choices by setting your monitor to grayscale. If you can't distinguish two colors in grayscale, adjust the value of one and retest.

◆ Use color to distinguish, not to identify. Color can show that two things are not the same, but users will not remember what you have decided that magenta stands for.

Getting out of the way

As users, we make the most productive use of software when we are the least conscious of what we are doing. You can't type rapidly if you have to consciously decide about each keypress. If you think about every step you take, you'll walk funny. The same goes for performing tasks on computers.

As programmers, we generally should strive to make our software as transparent as possible, so that users start to use its capabilities quickly and without thinking about what they are doing (**Figure 12.9**).

This rule does have exceptions. At times, the user needs to be very conscious of what is happening, such as when the program is warning about a potentially damaging action. But in general, software should present the user the best tools for getting the job done and get out of the way.

Many books on user-interface design available, and Apple's Human Interface Guidelines are available online.

Figure 12.9 Strive to make your software as invisible as possible.

DESIGNING YOUR APPLICATIONS

User-Interface Design Resources

◆ *User Interface Design for Programmers*, by Joel Spolksy (Apress, 2001). Windows-oriented but entertaining and original. A good book for beginning programmers or experts.

◆ *About Face: The Essentials of User Interface Design*, by Alan Cooper (IDG Books, 1995). Even more Windows-oriented than the Spolksy book, but recommended if you intend to deploy applications on the Windows platform. Cooper has been called the father of (Microsoft's) Visual Basic but is highly irreverent about Microsoft's user-interface designs.

◆ *Tog on Interface*, by Bruce Tognazzini (Addison Wesley, 1992). A dated but still-important book by Apple's long-time Human Interface evangelist.

◆ *The Humane Interface: New Directions for Designing Interactive Systems*, by Jef Raskin (Addison Wesley, 2000). Innovative ideas in user-interface design from the creator of the Macintosh project at Apple. Jef will tell you to break the rules, so know what they are first.

◆ You can find Apple's Human Interface Guidelines here:

`http://developer.apple.com/techpubs/mac/HIGuidelines/HIGuidelines-2.html`

These are the rules. The site has both Classic and OS X Aqua guidelines. Apple doesn't want to encourage anyone to write pre-OS X software, though, so the Classic guidelines could disappear.

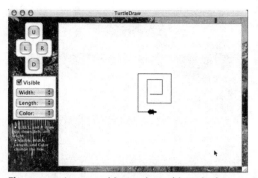

Figure 12.10 Let your objects mirror objects in the task domain.

Software design

REALbasic is a hybrid language, based on an early programming language but extending it with the software design philosophy of a later era. The key to designing REALbasic applications that are easy to understand, easy to maintain, portable, reusable, and easy to extend is using the added-on object-oriented features of the language.

Object-oriented programming really means programming with classes. By creating a class, you *encapsulate* in one unit properties and behavior that you can reuse elsewhere in the same application or export for use in other applications.

It takes practice to get comfortable with object-oriented programming, but the benefits repay the effort. Learn to think in terms of classes, and you will write better code.

When you get comfortable with the idea of object-oriented programming, think very hard about the objects that you are creating (really, classes, but objects are instances of classes). They should correspond to objects in the task domain. If you are writing a spreadsheet program, your objects likely would include cells, and possibly rows, columns, and sheets. If you are writing a drawing program, your objects probably would include drawing objects, such as pens, crayons, and erasers (and possibly turtles), as well as a drawing-surface object. And a drawing-surface object should have the kinds of properties that we associate with a drawing surface, such as dimensions, texture, and reflectivity. Drawing objects should be able to draw, so a pen object should have a draw method, which would likely have things in common with a crayon's draw method but not be identical to it.

The more your objects mirror the objects in the task domain, the easier your code will be to write, the less likely you are to take a wrong turn in design, and the more intuitive your program is likely to be for its users (**Figure 12.10**).

Debugging Your Applications

When I was an arrogant young computer-science student, one of my professors looked over a monstrously long, monstrously messed-up program that I had written and was in the process of debugging, and told me, "To have so much code written and so little of it actually running shows poor programming practice."

I took his advice to heart and ever since have debugged my code as I programmed, getting each component running before adding the next frill. I advise the same to anyone who wants to avoid tearing hair out or incurring the scorn of Professor Mitchell Wand.

There are two kinds of errors, and you *will* encounter both of them daily in your programming. These errors are compile-time errors and run-time errors.

Compile-time errors are those errors that REALbasic can tell, without even running the code, are just wrong. Typically, they are errors in your use of the REALbasic syntax. REALbasic will refuse to run the program and display an error message that, unfortunately, probably won't help you much (**Figure 12.11**).

Run-time errors don't get found until the program runs, or tries to run. On finding a run-time error, REALbasic will terminate the program and drop you out to the operating system or the IDE, depending on whether you're running an application or running a project from the IDE. In this case, REALbasic will display a different kind of error message, which probably will be even less helpful (**Figure 12.12**).

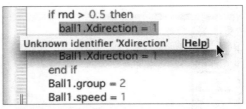

```
    if rnd > 0.5 then
        ball1.Xdirection = 1
Unknown identifier 'Xdirection'    [Help]
        Ball1.Xdirection = 1
    end if
    Ball1.group = 2
    Ball1.speed = 1
```

Figure 12.11 A compile-time error message.

```
Function Validate(action as integer) As Boolean
    Dim rec as RecordSet
    if action = 0 then
        rec = me.database.SQLSelect("select max(MovieID) from " +
        MovieId.text = str(rec.idxfield(2).integerValue + 2)
Unhandled NilObjectException raised    [Help]
        End Function
```

Figure 12.12 A run-time error message.

DEBUGGING YOUR APPLICATIONS

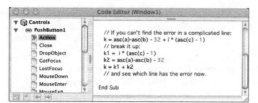

Figure 12.13 Sometimes, you need to break complicated calculations into several lines to find the errors in them.

To be fair, sometimes REALbasic will nail the error precisely, such as when you have failed to mention a variable in a `dim` statement before using it. But determining what went wrong is usually a dark art, requiring subtle detective work on your part.

✔ Tips

- When your code perpetrates a compile-time error, REALbasic highlights the line on which the error occurred. If you don't see anything wrong with the line, try breaking it into smaller components (**Figure 12.13**).

- The most common compile-time error, at least for us fumble-fingered programmers, is that you didn't type what you meant to type. The skill required here is proofreading skill: the ability to look at a line of text and see what it really says, not what you think it ought to say. This skill is acquirable.

Things to check when you get a compile-time error:

◆ Does the line have the same number of right and left parentheses? It helps if they're all where they belong, too.

◆ Is every period really a period and every comma really a comma? The alien wisdom of keyboard user-interface design placed these similar-looking keys next to each another, making mistakes easy (**Figure 12.14**).

◆ Is every space in place? Missing or extra spaces are the hardest errors to spot, but REALbasic cares.

◆ Watch out for missing assignment statements. The following line will give you an error:

new Date

And it should. You haven't put this new Date anywhere. You need to assign it to a variable:

dim d as Date
d = new Date

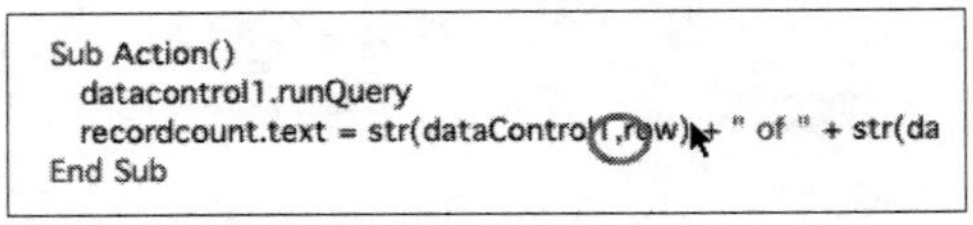

✔ Tips

■ One of the most common and hard-to-find errors is the fencepost error: getting the value of the counter on a loop wrong by 1. The error gets its name from this problem: How many fenceposts do you need to build a fence 100 feet long with the fenceposts 10 feet apart? If you divided 100 by 10 and got 10, you had the right idea, but you committed a fencepost error.

■ If your program seems to be locked up, it may be in an infinite loop. Get out of the situation as best you can, and examine the loops in your program, especially while loops. Look for a loop with a termination condition that could, under some circumstance, fail ever to evaluate to true.

```
Sub Action()
    datacontrol1.runQuery
    recordcount.text = str(dataControl1,row)+ " of " + str(da
End Sub
```

Figure 12.14 Debugging your code starts with proofreading it. Is that comma really a period?

Bug-tracking tools

REALbasic gives you several tools for tracking down the bugs in your code, including commenting out lines of code, the MsgBox function, and the Debugger.

To comment out lines of code:

1. In the Code Editor for a handler, select a line or several consecutive lines that seem to be problematic.

(See "To comment several lines of code" on page 421 for more information on using this commenting capability.)

2. Press Cmd-'.

The selected lines will appear commented with a single quote mark in front of them.

3. Press Cmd-R to run the program.

The selected lines will not be executed when the program runs. (Commented lines are never executed.) If the problem goes away, you have narrowed down your search for the error to this section of code. If the problem persists, you need to look elsewhere.

DEBUGGING YOUR APPLICATIONS

To use the MsgBox function to debug your code:

1. Locate a spot in your code where you'd like to know what it's doing (because it apparently isn't doing what you thought you told it to do).

2. Insert a line of code like this:

   `msgBox "Now entering Print method."`

   or

   `msgBox "The value of i is " + str(i) + "."`

   This code will display the indicated text when the program gets to this point in its execution. Some suggestions: It's often useful to report the value of a variable or some branching of the code, such as entering a method or taking a branch of an `if` statement. It's often merely annoying to put the `msgBox` line at a place in the code where it will get executed several times every second (**Figure 12.15**).

3. Think what you expect to happen when you run the program.

   It's useful actually to articulate what you expect:

   The `msgBox` should display "Now entering the Print method" twice shortly before the program terminates.

   Then if you *don't* see the expected outcome, you'll know you're onto something.

4. Run the program, and see what happens.

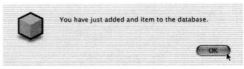

Figure 12.15 The `MsgBox` function is a handy debugging tool.

```
Function Validate(action
  ● Dim rec as RecordSet
    if action = 0 then
```

Figure 12.16 A breakpoint has been set in the Debugger.

```
    Dim rec as RecordSet
  ◆ if action = 0 then
        rec = me.database.SQLSelect("select
        Movield.text = str(rec.idxfield(2).inte⌐
    end if
```

Figure 12.17 When the program gets to the breakpoint, it stops execution and points to the line.

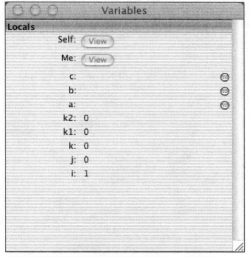

Figure 12.18 The Variables window is a debugging tool that shows you the values of the variables in your code.

The MsgBox function is handy for getting the answer to a specific question about what your code is doing, but the Debugger, a component of the IDE, gives you a lot more information and a lot more control. The Debugger lets you step through the execution of a section of your program, observing its activity one line at a time.

To use the Debugger to debug your code:

1. Select the line of code where you want to start watching your program execute.

2. Choose Debug > Set Breakpoint.

   A red diamond appears next to the selected line in your code (**Figure 12.16**).

3. Press Cmd-R to run the program.

   When the program gets to the selected line, it stops and drops you back into the IDE, but more specifically into the Debugger. A green arrow appears beside the line that will be executed next (**Figure 12.17**).

4. Next, do one of the following:

   ▲ Choose Debug > Step Over to move forward one step in this routine.

   ▲ Choose Debug > Step Into to move into the first line of the subroutine if the preceding line was a call to a subroutine.

   ▲ Choose Debug > Step Out if you have stepped into a subroutine and want to move back out to the calling routine.

   ▲ Choose Debug > Run to leave the Debugger and let the program run normally.

5. To see what is happening to the local variables in your program as you step through it, look at the Variables window (**Figure 12.18**).

   You may need to select Windows > Variables Window to show it.

Your code can run perfectly but still not run well. You can use many techniques for optimizing code to make it run faster or to use less disk space or memory. Following are a few speed tips.

Optimizing your code

Usually, you have to consider the speed of only certain sections of your code—those that do complicated things or that are repeated many times. So before you spend time trying to speed your code, it is useful to investigate just how slow particular sections of the code are. Adding a couple of lines (temporarily) that report how long a section of code takes is a good way to find this out.

To time a section of code:

1. Insert this code before the first line of the section of code that you want to time:

   ```
   startTime = ticks
   ```

2. Add this line of code to the beginning of the code's handler:

   ```
   dim startTime as integer
   ```

3. Insert this code *after* the last line of the section of code that you want to time:

   ```
   msgBox "That operation took " +
   → str((ticks - startTime)/60) +
   → " seconds."
   ```

4. Press Cmd-R to run the program.

   The program will display the number of seconds that the section of code took to execute (**Figure 12.19**).

You can modify this technique to display ticks (sixtieths of a second) or hours.

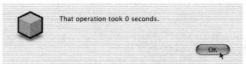

Figure 12.19 Timing your code can help you find ways to improve its performance.

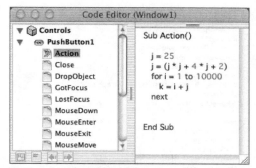

Figure 12.20 Moving calculations outside a loop can often speed code.

Most of the time, you'll find that the code in loops is using most of the program's computation time. Several tricks can speed loop code significantly.

To optimize loop code:

◆ Move those calculations that do not depend on the loop index outside the loop:

```
j = 25
for i = 1 to 10000
   k = i + (j * j + 4 * j + 2)
next
```

becomes (**Figure 12.20**):

```
j = 25
j = (j * j + 4 * j + 2)
for i = 1 to 10000
   k = i + j
next
```

◆ Combine loops if they have the same counter:

```
for i = 1 to 100
   dogButton.caption = "dog " + str(i)
next
for i = 1 to 100
   catButton.caption = "cat " + str(i)
next
```

becomes:

```
for i = 1 to 100
   dogButton.caption = "dog " + str(i)
   catButton.caption = "cat " + str(i)
next
```

Although programming has evolved in varied ways over the decades, certain bugs seem to persist unchanged from era to era like cockroaches. The loop-optimizing techniques in this section are adapted from a 1972 book on Fortran programming but are very relevant to 21st-century programming in REALbasic.

Documenting Your Applications

You need to consider at least three issues in documenting your code: comments, naming, and user documentation.

The code of a computer program is a one-way act of communication from a person to a computer. But this does not mean that only the computer needs to be able to read the code. Because you will revisit your code to find bugs, make enhancements, and re-use classes and code snippets, you need to be able to read the code yourself. And a few weeks after you have finished a program, it will become remarkably opaque to you unless you comment it effectively.

It is unlikely that you will add too many comments to your code. Because comments are ignored in the execution of a program, they have no effect on program speed. You should use them wherever they can clarify your code.

If a line of REALbasic code starts with a comment mark, the rest of that line is a comment. If the comment mark appears within the line, everything to the right of it on the line is a comment (**Figure 12.21**).

```
//Opens Movie in MoviePlayer
f = GetOpenFolderItem("video/quicktime")
if f <> nil then
  m = f.OpenAsMovie
  movieTrailer.movie = m
  movieTrailer.stop
end if
// Writes the file path to MovieLink edit field
s = f.name
if f.directory then
  s = s + ":"
end
while f.parent <> nil
  f = f.parent
  s = f.name + " : " + s
wend
MovieLink.text = s
```

Figure 12.21 Comments explain your code.

```
//Opens Movie in MoviePlayer
//The MoviePlayer is labeled as MovieTrailer
f = GetOpenFolderItem("video/quicktime")
if f <> nil then
    m = f.OpenAsMovie
```

Figure 12.22 Commenting a block of lines.

REALbasic supports three kinds of comment marks:

◆ The single quote ('). This is consistent with the comment mark in Visual Basic:

' This is a comment.

◆ The double slash (//). This is consistent with the comment mark in some other languages:

// This is a comment.

◆ The remark mark (REM). This is consistent with original Basic:

REM This is a remark (comment).

✔ Tips

■ There is no obvious reason to use REM to indicate comments, and there is some reason not to use //. (The Code Editor supports the ' mark more fully.) But you can use any comment mark that works for you. Whatever you use, however, be consistent.

■ If you regularly use the technique of commenting out sections of code for debugging purposes, you might want to be able to distinguish these temporarily commented lines from real comments. In this case, you might want to use the double slash (//) mark for real comments.

To comment several lines of code:

1. In the Code Editor for a handler, select the lines that you want to comment.

   The lines must all be executable—that is, none of the lines can already be commented.

2. Press Cmd-'.

   The selected lines will appear commented (**Figure 12.22**).

DOCUMENTING YOUR APPLICATIONS

To uncomment several commented lines of code:

1. In the Code Editor for a handler, select the lines that you want to uncomment.

2. Press Cmd-'.

   The selected lines will have their comment marks removed. This technique works only if the comment mark used was the single quote (').

To comment a handler:

1. Comment the handler as a whole.

   At the very top of the handler, explain what the entire handler does:

   ```
   // Displays a one-month calendar
   // for the month supplied.
   ```

2. Comment any coherent blocks of code.
   A for loop is a good example of a coherent block of code.

   ```
   // Draw the grid:
   for c = 0 to 7
     g.drawLine c*gridWidth+gridLeft,
     → gridTop, c*gridWidth+gridLeft,
     → gridBottom
   next
   for r = 0 to nRows
     g.drawLine gridLeft,
     → r*gridHeight+gridTop, gridRight,
     → r*gridHeight+gridTop
   next
   ```

3. Comment any tricky lines.
   This is one occasion when you might want to place the comment on the same line as the executable code:

   ```
   gridWidth = me.width \ 7
   → // Note integer division.
   ```

✔ Tips

- Give your variables and objects meaningful names. One strategy is to include the kind of object and its use in its name, such as `UserNameListBox` or `Write_File_Menu`. Because a name needs to be a single word, many programmers pack multiword phrases into names by using intercap (`UserNameListBox`) or underscore (`Write_File_Menu`) style. Variable names might include an indication of the variable's type, such as `intAmount` to hint that this amount is an integer variable. Whatever you choose, be consistent.

  User documentation is any help that you give your users in understanding your program. Documentation can be electronic or printed; it can be text, diagrams, or video.

- Get help with creating user documentation. Even if it's only free feedback from a user, get another pair of eyes on your docs. After spending long hours immersed in your program, you'll find it almost impossible to see the program as a user will see it.

To write effective user documentation:

◆ Use proper English.

(Or proper French, or proper Swahili.) Bad grammar, usage, or spelling in the documentation will brand your work as amateurish and reduce its ease of use.

◆ Don't be afraid to use technical terms.

Define your jargon and then use it freely and without embarrassment. But use only as much jargon as you need, and use it consistently.

◆ Write plainly.

User documentation is not a branch of the entertainment industry, and nobody is going to be impressed by your erudition. 'Tis a gift to be simple.

◆ Don't trust spelling checkers and grammar checkers.

Use them, but don't rely on them. If you can't spell, find some person who can to read your documentation.

◆ Outline.

Don't worry about following any particular style of outlining; just get the skeleton of your documentation built before you begin fleshing it out.

◆ Write a reference, not a tutorial.

This guideline is not always the right advice, but if it is *possible* to write your documentation as a reference, you probably should. Users want to be in control (**Figure 12.23**).

◆ Be brief, but be comprehensive.

Users want to be able to find the answers to their questions in the documentation. What they *don't* want is to spend any more time with the documentation than is absolutely necessary. The documentation is something between them and the program. Make that something a door, not a wall.

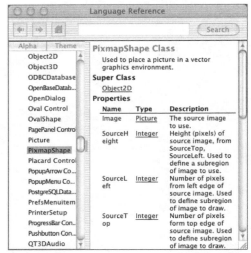

Figure 12.23 Consider making your user documentation a reference rather than a tutorial. References have longer useful lives.

Deploying Your Applications

You've written a fine application—intelligently designed, clearly documented, flawlessly coded. Now how do you deliver it to its intended audience? How do you deploy your application?

Your deployment choices depend on what that intended audience is. If you have written the application for yourself, deployment may be as simple as choosing File > Build Application and starting to use the application. If your intended audience is a few other people in your company, the process might be much the same.

But if your application is a mission-critical tool for your company or some other company, or if you intend to release it to the general public for free or for money, the deployment process may need to be a little more involved. Among the things that you may want to concern yourself with are detailed version numbers (to help you manage your development cycle), a custom application icon (to give your application a professional look), and a Macintosh creator code (so that the Mac operating system can launch your application when files of the appropriate types are clicked).

To assign a custom icon to your application:

1. Create several sizes of the icon that you want to use in your application, using: the resource-editing program ResEdit; an icon-editing program; or a graphics program.

   You need several sizes of icons for a Macintosh application. To see just how many and what sizes, see steps 3-4.

2. Copy one of the icon images to the Clipboard.

   Some icon-editing programs may let you copy all the icon images at the same time.

3. Choose File > Build Settings.

   The Build Settings dialog appears.

4. Click the Icons button.

   The Application Icon dialog appears (**Figure 12.24**).

5. Paste the icon image into the corresponding-size box.

   If you are using an icon-editing program, you may be able to paste all the images at the same time. Otherwise, repeat steps 2 and 5 for each image.

6. Click OK to dismiss the Application Icon dialog.

7. Click OK to dismiss the Build Settings dialog.

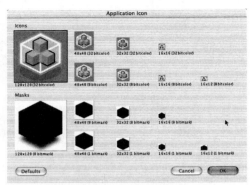

Figure 12.24 The Application Icon dialog.

Figure 12.25 Entering a creator code.

To register a creator ID for your application:

1. Select a four-character code that the Mac operating system can use to recognize your application.

   Creator codes need to be unique. You can check to see whether your code is available by visiting the Apple Web site:

   `http:developer.apple.com/dev/cftype/`
   `→ faq.html`

2. Choose File > Build Settings.

   The Build Settings dialog appears.

3. Choose Macintosh Settings from the pop-up menu.

4. Enter your creator code (**Figure 12.25**).

5. Use your Web browser to go to
   `http://developer.apple.com/dev/`
   `→ cftype/`.

   This URL is the Creator Code Registration page.

6. Click the registration-form link to go to the page containing the form.

7. Fill in the form, and click Submit.

8. Click OK to dismiss the Build Settings dialog.

To set the version information for your application:

1. Choose File > Build Settings.

    The Build Settings dialog appears.

2. Choose Version Information from the pop-up menu at the top of the dialog.

3. Enter the three-decimal version number in the Version text boxes.

    The convention for version numbers is that the first digit refers to a major release and subsequent digits refer to respectively less-significant updates.

4. Enter the Short Version, the Long Version, and the Package Info in the appropriate fields (**Figure 12.26**).

    The Short Version is your application's version number as it will appear in the Finder's list view. The Long Version and Package Info text will appear in the Get Info window for your application. The Long Version is a good place for your copyright notice.

5. Click OK to dismiss the Build Settings dialog.

I'll leave you with one final caution on application development. In building computer applications, as in any complicated project, always remember Hofstadter's Law:

"It always takes longer than you expect, even when you take into account Hofstadter's Law."

It certainly does.

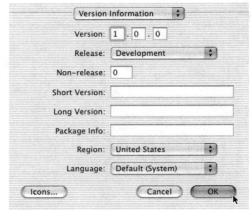

Figure 12.26 Entering version information.

DEPLOYING YOUR APPLICATIONS

INDEX

&<;/&>; syntax, 46
< > characters, 46, 90, 127
= (equals sign), 127, 128, 160
' (single quote), 421
~ (tilde), 169
3D animation, 296–299
3D graphics, 275
3D modeling, 297
4D Server, 322, 323
216-color palette, 234

A

About Face: The Essentials of User Interface Design, 410
AbsolutePath property, 190, 200, 201
AcceptPictureDrop method, 224, 244
Action handler, 94
actions, time-dependent, 293–295
Add Data Source command, 327, 333
Add File Type dialog, 186, 189
additive primaries, 231
AmbientLight property, 299
ampersand-and-semicolon syntax, 46
and operator, 126
animation files, sources of, 296
animations, 275–299. *See also* movies
    changing bit depth of, 282
    changing speed of, 282
    creating specific types
        sprite, 276–292, 307–319
        time-aware, 293–295
    displaying 3D, 293–295
    freezing, 279
    making responsive to key presses, 284–285
    stepping through, 279
    testing, 279, 280
App class, 167, 207, 208
App function, 167

Apple
    application-development process, 402
    documentation, for Unix commands, 400
    Human Interface Guidelines, 401, 410
AppleEvents, 391, 393–394
AppleScript, 6, 390–394
AppleScript for Applications: Visual QuickStart Guide, 391
AppleScript Studio, 391
Application class, 167, 208
application-development process, 22, 402–403
Application Icon dialog, 426
applications. *See also* projects
    adding Internet capabilities to, 351, 352–355
    adding printing capabilities to, 372–374
    adding user scriptability to, 375, 377–379
    allowing user to launch, 206–208
    assigning custom icons to, 426
    building, 5, 6–8, 22
        bookmarks, 356–366
        database front end, 336–342
        database viewer, 333–335
        Deus Web Wizard, 23–29
        guestbook, 80–100
        HTML editor, 31–72
        ping-pong game, 307–319
        RBScript Runner, 376–389
        spreadsheet, 178–183
        turtle graphics, 261–274
    contrasted with projects, 32
    converting projects to stand-alone, 71, 100
    crashing of, 22
    debugging, 22, 29, 412–419
    deconstructing, 23
    deploying, 402, 403, 425–428
    designing, 402, 404–411
    documenting, 402, 403, 420–424
    extending capabilities of, 375
    naming, 71

applications *(continued)*
  prototyping, 5
  registering Creator code for, 427
  selecting/manipulating files with, 185, 202, 217
    (*See also* files)
  setting version information for, 428
  testing, 29, 35
  time-aware, 293–295
arrays
  of controls, 155–156
  creating, 117, 155–156
  defined, 117
Ask A Question text property, 26
assignment statement, 76, 116–125
Atari, 307
autocompletion feature, 109

B

Back button, 112
back end, database, 322
BackColor property, 241, 245
Backdrop property
  for Canvas control, 241, 246, 247, 250, 270
  for SpriteSurface control, 276
  for Window control, 245
background color, 241, 245
background picture, 245, 270
Ball class, 309–310
Barry, Andrew, 2, 7
BASIC programming language, 3, 101, 151
behaviors, 102–103
BevelButton control, 25, 245
binary files, 220–222
BinaryStream class, 220–222
binding, object, 102–103, 340
bit depth, 282
Blue property, 230
BMP files, 239
Bold property, 242
Bond, Taylor, 23
Bookmarks application, 356–366
  adding/deleting bookmarks in, 365, 366
  building database for, 356–366
  editing bookmarks in, 365
  launching, 364
  purpose of, 364
  viewing bookmarks with, 365
Bookmarks database
  creating, 361
  laying out user interface for, 356
  linking bookmark list to, 362–363
Boolean values
  in branching code, 130–133
  combining with parentheses, 127
  comparing numbers/strings using, 127

  defined, 77
  negating, 126
  performing logical and/or on, 126–127
BorderWidth property, 264
branching code, 130–133
browser pane, Code Editor, 104, 105
browsers, language read by Web, 32
bug-tracking tools, 415–417. *See also* debugging
Build Application command/dialog, 71, 100, 274
Build Settings command/dialog, 274, 427–428
Bushnell, Nolan, 307
buttons
  adding to dialogs/toolbars, 25, 66–67, 88
  coding, 94–95, 97, 265, 267–268
  creating, 245, 262–263, 267, 313–314
  framing, 272
  labeling, 408
  resizing, 25
  setting Default property for, 25

C

C++, 101
calculations, 125, 254, 348
Camera object, 298
Canvas control, 246–253
  adding images to projects with, 86
  controlling, 251–253
  displaying images with, 247
  drawing grid lines with, 248
  making images transparent with, 241
  and Mouse events, 247, 253
  performance considerations, 254
  power/flexibility of, 246
  properties of, 246
  rotating text with, 249–250
case, changing, 122
case-sensitivity, xi, 18, 128
Caution icon, 68–69, 243
CellAction handler, 179
child class, 153
Child method, 194
Circle control, 229
classes
  adding properties to, 163
  creating constructors for, 166
  creating instances of, 154–156, 177
  creating new, 162–165, 174–176
  customizing event handlers for, 164
  encrypting/decrypting, 171
  hierarchy of, 152
  importing/exporting, 170
  and inheritance, 152–153
  and object-oriented programming, 151, 411
  removing, 168–169
Clear command, 11, 12

Clipboard, 110, 117, 244
cloning, database, 331–332
CMY color model, 231, 232, 252, 273–274
CMY function, 230, 234
CMYK color model, 273
Cocoa applications, 391
code
    branching, 130–133
    commenting out lines of, 415, 420, 421–422
    compiled *vs.* interpreted, 4, 383
    controlling sequence of instructions in, 129
    copying from Online Language Reference, 115
    debugging, 22, 29, 412–419
    deciding where to put, 172
    documenting, 440–424
    editing, 18, 110
    encrypting/decrypting, 171
    finding and replacing, 111–112
    gray arrows in, xi
    learning to write, xi
    looping, 134–136, 145, 254, 414
    object-oriented, 3, 73, 151, 172, 411 (*See also* objects)
    optimizing, 418–419
    placing in modules, 173
    printing, 112
    repeating, 134–136
    reusing, 152
    setting focus in, 91
    timing sections of, 418
    use of case in, xi, 18
    using objects in, 157–159
    writing, 39, 101, 104, 343–350 (*See also* Code Editor)
Code Editor, 104–112
    creating methods in, 138
    customizing, 107–108
    editing code in, 18, 110
    finding/replacing code in, 111–112
    opening, 104–105
    parts of, 104
    purpose of, 17, 104
    resizing panes in, 18, 108
    setting properties via, 76
code snippets, 115
coding. *See* code; scripting
Collision event, 291, 292, 313
Color data type, 230
color models
    converting between, 232
    descriptions of, 230–231
    viewing relationships among, 260
Color Picker, 233, 234, 273
color properties, 230
Color Sliders tool, 231, 255–260

colors
    allowing user to choose, 234
    populating Colors window with, 232, 233
    representing information in, 230–231
    setting values for, 230, 252, 255
    tips for effective use of, 409
    transforming, in pictures, 251–252
    Web-safe, 234, 235–236
Colors window, 232, 233
columns, 324, 347, 348. *See also* fields
comments, code, 415, 420, 421–422
commit method, 350
communication errors, 370
communications, tool for managing. *See* Socket control
Compact command, 331
companion Web site, xi
comparison operators, 127, 160–161
comparison statements, 126–128
compile-time errors, 381, 412, 413, 414
compiled languages, 4, 383
computers, managing communication between, 352, 367–371
concatenation, 119
conditional statements, 130–133
constructors, 166
control arrays, 155–156
Control class, 224, 246
controls. *See also* specific controls
    creating array of, 155–156
    creating instances of, 154–155
    creating new class based on, 165
    managing behavior of, 156
    purpose of, 13
    referring to, 156
    viewing documentation for, 114
Cooper, Alan, 407, 410
Copies property, 242
"copy and append" operation, 110
CopyFileTo method, 191, 197
Count property, 194, 199
CountFields property, 213
crashes, application, 22
CreateAsFolder method, 198
CreateBinaryFile method, 221
CreateTextFile method, 198
CreationDate property, 200
Creator code, 186, 188, 190, 427
cropping pictures, 242
cross-fades, 300
"cut and append" operation, 110
Cyan property, 230

D

data. *See also* databases
   manipulating, 116
   sending/receiving, 369–370
   writing to file, 98–99
data source, 322
data types, 77, 163
database applications, 8, 322, 323
Database class, 322, 343
Database Design for Mere Mortals, 321
database design models, 324
database tables. *See also* databases
   adding/deleting fields in, 328–329, 344
   adding/deleting records in, 344–345
   combining data from two, 349–350
   components of, 324
   creating, 327–328, 343, 361
   deleting, 330
   editing fields/records in, 329, 346
   examples of, 324
   getting sum of column entries in, 348
   planning, 325–326
   renaming, 330
   selecting records in, 346–347
   sorting data in, 348
DatabaseQuery control, 334–335
DatabaseRecord class, 343
databases
   adding to projects, 327
   allowing user to change data in, 350
   basic information about, 322–324
   building front end for, 336–342
   building viewer for, 333–335
   cloning, 331–332
   compacting, 331
   creating, 327, 333, 336–337
   defined, 324
   displaying data in, 323, 332
   entering data into, 332
   planning, 325–326
   purpose of, 321
   recommended book on, 321
   saving, 350
   undoing changes to, 350
   version of REALbasic required for, 321
DataControl object, 323, 336–341
Debugger, 417
debugging, 22, 29, 412–419
Decrypt command, 171
Delete method, 191, 197
delimiter property, 215
deployment, application, 402, 403, 425–428
design
   application, 402, 404–411
   database, 324

   interaction, 407
   software, 411
   user-interface, 404, 405–410
destructors, 169
Deus Web Wizard, 23–29
   creating tabs for, 27–28
   creating windows for, 27
   creators of, 23
   purpose of, 23
   replicating toolbar for, 24–26
   testing, 29
dialogs, creating effective user, 407
digital clock, 294–295
Dim statement, 77, 116–125
Directory property, 198
documentation, 402, 403, 420–424
Do...Loop structure, 136, 212
DOS commands, 395, 396, 400
dot notation, 77, 157, 158
Double data type, 77
double slash (//), 421
Draw methods, 242, 248, 254
DrawCautionIcon method, 243
drawing
   graphics, 261
   grid lines, 248
   text, 248
drawing area, TurtleDraw
   creating, 262–263
   properties of, 263
   setting color of, 273–274
   tracking boundaries of, 264, 269
DrawLine method, 242
DrawPicture method, 242, 254
DrawPolygon method, 242
DrawString method, 242, 248
drop shadows, 226
DropObject event, 224, 244
DWW. *See* Deus Web Wizard

E

Edit File Type dialog, 189
Edit Schema command, 329
Edit Tab window, 28
EditableMovie class, 300, 304
EditField control
   and database front end, 336, 337–338, 339
   and focus, 91, 165
   placing text in, 248
   properties of, 26
   purpose of, 33–34
editor pane, Code Editor, 104, 105
effects, visual, 300, 304
electronic guestbook. *See* guestbook application
Else keyword, 130, 131, 132

ElseIf keyword, 130, 131
email links, 352, 364
Enabled property, 89
EnableMenuItems event, 38–39
encapsulation, 411
Encrypt command, 171
EndIf keyword, 130, 131, 132
EndSelect keyword, 133
EOF (end of file) property, 210, 220
equality operator, 127, 128, 160
Erase option, TurtleDraw, 273–274
error-handling, 370, 381–383, 412–414
Eval method, 183
event-driven programming, 4, 60
event handlers
    commenting, 422
    customizing, 164
    defined, 17
    editing, 18
    purpose of, 60
Execute method, 395
Exit keyword, 135
Export Class command, 170
ExportPicture function, 239

F

Facts and Fallacies of Software Engineering, xi
fencepost error, 414
FieldOfView property, 299
fields
    adding/deleting, 328–329, 344
    defined, 324
    editing, 329, 346
    input (*See* user-input fields)
    key, 326
    planning, 325–326
file:/// protocol, 352
file dialogs, 202–208
    for launching applications, 206–208
    for saving files, 205–206
    for selecting/opening files, 202–203
    for selecting/opening folders, 204
File menu, adding items to, 51, 56
file path. *See* path
file types, 186–189
    creating new, 188–189
    declaring, 187
    enabling applications to work with, 187–188
    modifying, 189
    predefined, 186
    purpose of, 186
    removing, 189
File Types dialog, 54, 187–189
files, 185–222
    adding to projects, 11
    allowing user to choose where to save, 205–206

allowing user to select/open, 202–204
copying, 197
creating, 198
deleting, 197, 201
distinguishing from folders, 198
getting information about
    creation date, 200
    file size, 200
    modification date, 200
    pathname, 200
hiding/revealing, 199
implicit opening of, 206–208
key concepts in working with, 186
    file types, 186–189
    FolderItem class, 190–195
launching, 198
locking/unlocking, 199
moving, 197
naming/renaming, 197, 201
reading, 209–213, 216, 217, 218, 219, 220–221
referring to, 186, 190
saving pictures to, 217–218
sequential (*See* sequential files)
testing for existence of, 196
testing for locked, 199
types of (*See* file types)
writing to, 98–99, 214, 216, 221–222
FillColor property, 233
FillPolygon method, 242
Find and Replace operations, 111–112
Finder, Macintosh, 375, 390
FirstPage property, 242
FloodLight property, 299
focus, 91, 93, 165
FolderItem class, 190–195
    creating instances of, 191–195
    documentation for, 190
    properties/methods of, 190–191
    purpose of, 186
folders
    allowing user to select/open, 204
    creating, 198
    deleting, 201
    determining number of items in, 199
    distinguishing from files, 198
    renaming files in, 201
For...Next structure, 134–135, 254
Forward button, 112
fractals, 261
FrameRate property, 276
FrameSpeed property, 282
front end, database
    building, 336–342
    purpose of, 322
FTP, 352
functions, 139, 192

G

games
  classic video, 307
  creating ping-pong, 307–319
  and SpriteSurface control, 284, 310–313
GetFolderItem method, 191–195
GetOpenFolderItem function, 202
GetSaveFolderItem function, 205
GetTrueFolderItem method, 191, 192
Glass, Robert L., xi
Goal class, 310
Golden Rectangles, 229
GotFocus handlers, 93
graphical controls, 224–229, 244, 246
graphics. *See also* images; pictures
  3D, 275, 296–299
  and Canvas control, 244, 246
  masking parts of, 226–227
  performance considerations, 254
  tools for creating, 224–229
Graphics class, 242–243
Graphics property, 240, 241, 242, 246
gray arrow, in lines of code, xi
greater-than operator, 127
Green property, 230
grep command, 399–400
grid lines, drawing, 248
Group property, 291, 292
GrowIcon property, 33, 262
guestbook application, 80–100
  adding elements to
    buttons, 88
    images, 86–87
    text, 87
  coding buttons for, 94–95, 97
  converting to stand-alone application, 100
  creating elements for
    main window, 82–83
    time-controlled text message, 95–97
    user-input fields, 83–85
  enhancing, 100
  managing user input for, 89–92
  product concept, 80
  product specification, 80–81
  prompting users for input to, 93
  roughing out, 82–88
  saving data to file, 98–99
  testing, 88, 92, 100

H

handlers
  commenting, 422
  customizing, 164
  defined, 17

  editing, 18
  purpose of, 60
hardware requirements, x
HasBackColor property, 245
Height property, 34, 224, 240
"Hello World!" script, 376–379
Hernandez, Michael J., 321
hierarchy, class, 152
Hofstadter's Law, 428
<HR/> tag, 49–50
HSV color model, 231, 232, 252
HSV function, 230, 234
HTML
  editors, 32
  files, 32
  improving readability of, 140
  tags (*See* tags)
HTML Editor application, 31–72
  converting to stand-alone application, 71
  creating elements for
    HTML editing field, 33–34
    Indent menu item, 141
    New menu item, 51–53
    Open menu item, 63–64
    Save Changes dialog box, 65–70
    Save menu items, 55–62
    Symbols menu, 46–50
    Tags menu, 36–45
  improving readability of HTML produced by, 140
  purpose of, 31, 32
  specifying file types for, 54
  testing, 35, 70
http:// protocol, 352
Hue property, 230
Human Interface Guidelines, Apple, 401, 410
Humane Interface: New Directions for Designing Interactive Systems, The, 410
HyperCard, ix, x, 5, 8
hyperlinks. *See* links
HyperText Markup Language, 32. *See also* HTML

I

icons, 407, 426
IDE, 2, 9, 22
If structure, 130–132, 213
images. *See also* graphics; pictures
  animating, 275 (*See also* animations)
  displaying with Canvas control, 247
  importing, 86–87, 237
  layering, 250
  responding to clicks within, 253
  rotating, 249–250
ImageWell control, 224, 225, 228, 244
Import Class command, 170

importing
    classes, 170
    images/pictures, 86–87, 237
Indent method, 140–150
    creating, 142
    creating menu item for, 141
    purpose of, 140
    writing code, 143–149
        to control indent size, 150
        to handle indent levels, 147–149
        to insert indents, 145–146
        to remove existing indents, 143–144
Index property, 155, 156, 263
IndexCount property, 240
IndexedImage property, 240
inequality operator, 127
infinite loops, 414
inheritance, 152–153
input fields. See user-input fields
instances
    creating, 154–156, 177
    deleting, 169
instantiation, 154
instr method, 144
Integer data type, 77, 264
integrated development environment. See IDE
interaction design, 407
interface design, 404, 405–410
Interface Guidelines, Apple Human, 401, 410
interface objects, 13
Internet applications, 8
Internet Config settings, 352
Internet protocols, 352
interpreted languages, 4
IP addresses, 367
IsA operator, 161
Italic property, 242
Item method, 194

J

Java, 101
JPEG files, 217, 239

K

Kemeney, John, 3
key field, 326
key presses, making animations responsive to,
    284–285
Kurtz, Thomas, 3

L

label properties, 315
Language Reference window, 78, 113, 159

LastPage property, 242
Launch method, 191, 198
launching application
    creating document upon, 208
    by double-clicking document, 208
    by dropping file on it, 206–207
Left property, 224
Length property, 200
less-than operator, 127
library, script, 386–389
LimitText property, 89
Line control, 224, 225, 263–264
LineColor property, 264
links
    email, 352
    text, 353–355
Linux, 400
ListBox control
    creating picture picker with, 244–245
    creating script library with, 386–389
    displaying spreadsheet data with, 178–183
    entering/editing database data with, 335
    and focus, 165
    reading tab-delimited data into, 211–213
    viewing databases with, 323, 332, 334–335
Lock properties, 34, 224, 262
Locked property, 199
logical operators, 126–127
Logo programming language, 261
Looping property, 303
loops, 134–136, 145, 254, 414, 419
LostFocus handlers, 90, 91
ls command, 397

M

Mac OS 9, 6
Mac OS System 7.6.1, x
Mac OS X
    and AppleScript, 391
    building applications for, 6
    creating files for, 186
    and Shell scripting, 395–396
    and system requirements, x
    and Unix, 395–396
MacCreator property, 190
Macintosh
    building applications for, 6
    creating files for, 186
    Finder, 375, 390
    programming environment for, ix
    scripting language, 390–394
    and Shell scripting, 395–396
    sound files, 218
    system requirements, x
MacType property, 190

"Made with REALbasic" program, 5
Magenta property, 230
mailto: link, 352
man command, 398–399
Mask property, 240
mathematical operators, 125
me function, 78, 159
menu editor, 19
Menu handlers, 106
Menu icon, 19
menu items, 19–21
menus, 19–21, 36
Method Declaration dialog, 235
methods
    adding to classes, 164
    adding to modules, 173
    creating, 98–99, 138, 142, 175–176
    deleting, 139
    parts of, 137
    passing values to, 138
    referring to, 157–158
    returning values from, 139
Microseconds function, 293
Microsoft Office, 6
Microsoft Windows. See Windows systems
MIDI files, 218
Mode property, 96, 294, 295
ModificationDate property, 200
modules, 173
Morph method, 252
Mouse events, 224, 247, 253
MouseX property, 224
MouseY property, 224
MoveFileTo method, 197
Movie class, 300
movie files, 219. See also movies
MoviePlayer control, 219, 275, 300–304
movies, 300–304. See also animations
    controlling start/stop time for, 303
    editing, 304
    hiding controls for, 303
    letting user choose, 302
    loading, 301–302
    looping, 303
    setting up, 301
    tools for working with, 300
MP3 files, 218
MPEG files, 218
MsgBox function, 415, 416
MultiLine property, 34

N

Name property, 33, 34, 190, 197
naming
    applications, 71

files, 197, 201
menus, 19, 36
objects, 423
tables, 330
variables, 423
navigation buttons, 262–263, 265, 272
New Class command, 162, 163, 165, 208
New menu item
    creating, 51
    enabling, 52–53
    purpose of, 51
    testing, 51, 53
New Method command/dialog, 138, 175, 235
New Module command, 173
New Property command/dialog, 57, 79, 163, 175
New Table dialog, 327
New Window command, 10, 12, 162
NewAppleEvent function, 393
NewBall method, 316
NewDocument event handler, 208
NewDragItem method, 224
NewGoals method, 318–319
NewPaddles method, 317
NewPicture function, 240, 241
news: protocol, 352
newsgroups, 352
NewWalls method, 318
NextBall method, 319
NextFrame event, 276, 278
nil object, 161, 169
not operator, 126
NotePlayer control, 305, 306
NthField property, 213
numbers
    comparing, 127
    converting to/from strings, 123–124
    reading/writing, 222

O

object binding, 102–103, 340
object-oriented programming
    benefits of, 151
    deciding where to put code, 172
    defined, 3, 73, 411
    development of, 3
object properties. See properties
Object3D class, 296, 298
objects
    changing properties of, 16, 75
    characteristics of, 74
    comparing, 160–161
    creating, 74, 411
    defined, 151
    deleting, 169
    naming, 423

INDEX

referring to, 77–78, 157–159
rotating, 299
testing class of, 161
using in code, 157–159
Online Language Reference, 113–115
OOP, 15. *See also* object-oriented programming
Open File dialog, 202–203
Open Folder dialog, 204
Open handler, 166
Open menu item, 63–64
OpenAsBinaryFile method, 220
OpenAsMovie method, 219
OpenAsPicture method, 217, 237, 239
OpenAsSound method, 218
OpenAsTextFile method, 191
OpenDialog class, 203
OpenDocument event handler, 208
OpenGL, 296
OpenStyleEditField method, 216
operators
    comparison, 127
    logical, 126–127
    mathematical, 125
or operator, 127
Oracle, 323
Oval control, 224, 225, 226–227

P

Paddle class, 308–309
padlock icon, 171
Page properties, 264, 269
Paint class, 246
Paint handler, 243, 248
Palindrome property, 303
parameters, method, 137
parent class, 153
Parent property, 193
parentheses, grouping elements with, 127
path
    returning to FolderItem class, 200–201
    testing validity of, 196
Period property, 96, 294, 295
Photoshop files, 239
PICT files, 217, 239
Picture class, 240–241, 246
picture picker, 244–245
picture properties, 240
pictures. *See also* graphics; images
    allowing user to choose folder/file type for
        saving, 239
    allowing user to select/open, 238
    animating, 304
    converting to different formats, 239
    creating, 241
    cropping, 242

importing into projects, 237
making transparent, 241
manipulating, 240
reading from files, 217, 237
rotating, 249–250
saving, 217–218, 238–239
scaling, 243
transforming colors of, 251–252
ping-pong game, 307–319
    creating elements for
        Ball class, 309–310
        EditFields for names/scores, 314
        game window, 307
        Paddle class, 308–309
        Run button, 313–314
        Speed pop-up menu, 315
        Wall class, 310
    creating properties/methods for, 316–319
    inspiration for, 307
    setting up SpriteSurface for, 310–313
Pitch method, 299
Pixel property, 242, 254
PNG files, 239
Pong, 307
PopupMenu control, 315
port numbers, 367
Position property, 299
posterization, 251
Potter, Andrew, 23
PowerPC, x, 6
primary colors, additive *vs.* subtractive, 231
printing
    with dialog, 372
    properties for controlling, 242
    without dialog, 373–374
Priority property, 291, 292
procedures, 139
product specification, 80–81
Professional version, REALbasic, 9, 321, 323
programming
    creating behaviors without, 102–103
    database, 343–350
    environment, ix, x
    event-driven, 60
    by imitation, 24–29
    languages, 3, 101, 151, 261
    object-oriented, 3, 73, 151, 172, 411
    process of, 402–403
Project Window, 10, 11
projects. *See also* applications
    adding databases to, 327
    adding files to, 11
    adding windows to, 10
    contrasted with applications, 32
    converting to stand-alone applications, 71, 100
    creating objects in, 74

projects *(continued)*
  defined, 10
  developing spec for, 80–81
  importing pictures into, 237
  opening, 10
  removing classes/objects from, 168–169
  roughing out, 82–88
  saving, 11
  starting new, 10, 33
properties. *See also* specific properties
  adding to classes, 163
  changing, 16, 75
  creating, 56–57, 79, 175
  defined, 75
  getting information about, 78–79
  referring to, 77–78, 157–159
  setting values for, 76
  viewing names/values for, 15
prototyping tool, using REALbasic as, x, 5
PushButton control, 25, 88, 262

Q

Quesa, 296
QuickDraw 3D, 296
QuickTime movies, 300–306
  allowing user to choose, 302
  controlling start/stop time for, 303
  dragging into applications, 219
  editing, 304
  hiding controls for, 303
  loading, 301–302
  looping, 303
  playing sound from, 305–306
  reading, 219
  setting up, 301
  supported file types, 239
  tools for working with, 300
Quit command, 29, 35
quote ('), 421

R

RadioButton control, 156
Raskin, Jef, 410
RB3DSpace control, 275, 296, 298, 299
RBScript, 4, 375–389
RBScript class, 376
RBScript Runner application, 376–389
  accepting user input in, 384–385
  adding error handling to, 381–383
  building, 377–379
  offering library of scripts in, 386–389
  purpose of, 376
ReadAll method, 210
ReadDouble method, 222

ReadLong method, 222
ReadShort method, 222
ReadSingle method, 222
REAL Software, xi, 5
REALbasic
  code syntax, 101, 113
  creator of, 2
  IDE, 2, 9, 22
  installing, 9
  launching, 9
  programming language, 3–4, 73, 101, 151
  purpose of, x, 1
  scripting system, 4, 375–389
  Standard *vs.* Professional version, 9, 321, 323
  system requirements, x
  ways of using, 5–8
  Windows version, x, 7
  writing code in, 101, 104 (*See also* Code Editor)
REALdb Tools utility, 328–332
records
  adding/deleting, 344–345
  defined, 324
  editing, 329, 346
  selecting, 346–347
RecordSet class, 349
RecordSet method, 349
Rectangle control, 224, 225, 226, 244, 272
RectControl class, 224, 246
Red property, 230
Refresh method, 243
RefreshRect method, 243
relational databases, 324
REM statement, 421
replace method, 144
ResourceForkLength property, 200
Result property, 395
return value, method, 137, 138
RGB color model, 231, 232
RGB function, 230, 234
RGBSurface property, 240, 254
Roll method, 299
rollback method, 350
rotating objects, 249–250, 299
RoundRectangle control, 224, 225, 272
rows, 324. *See also* records
Run button, 313–314
Run command, 29, 35
run-time errors, 381, 412

S

Saturation property, 230
Save As dialog, 205
Save As menu item, 61–62
Save Changes dialog, 65–70
  adding buttons to, 66–67

adding Caution icon to, 68–69
creating, 65
displaying, 69
testing, 70
Save command, 35
Save menu item, 55–62
    code for saving files, 58–59
    creating, 56
    enabling, 58
    handling, 61
    testing, 62
SaveAsDialog class, 206
SaveAsPicture method, 217, 238, 239
SaveStyledEditField method, 216
scalar values, 155, 157, 160
scaling pictures, 243
Script Editor, 391
script library, 386–389
scripting, 375–400
    with AppleScript, 6, 390–394
    with RBScript, 4, 375–389
    with Shell class, 395–400
scrolling, 283–284
Select Case structure, 130, 133, 156
SelectColor function, 234
SelectFolder function, 204
SelectFolderDialog class, 204
self function, 159
Separator tool, 25
sequential files, 209–216
    changing delimiter character in, 215
    inserting line into middle of, 215
    reading, 209–213, 216
    writing to, 214, 216
Set Breakpoint command, 417
SetCMY method, 258
SetHSV method, 259
SetRGB method, 258
SGL files, 239
shareware, 23
Shell class, 395
Shell scripting, 395–400
    determining user name with, 396–397
    displaying Unix documentation with, 398–399
    listing user directories with, 397–398
    platform considerations, 395–396
    searching and replacing with, 399–400
Show Colors command, 233
Show Properties command, 15, 26
Show Tools command, 12, 13, 14
ShowModal method, 203, 204, 206
ShowURL method, 352
Single data type, 77
slashes (//), 421
Socket control, 352, 367–371
software design, 411

Sound class, 305
sound files, 218, 305–306
spec, product, 80–81
speed, animation, 282
Spolksy, Joel, 410
spreadsheet application, 174, 178–183
Spreadsheet class, 174–183
    creating, 174
    creating instance of, 177
    creating properties/methods for, 175–176
    using for spreadsheet application, 178–183
spreadsheet files, 209
Spreadsheet object, 332
sprite animation, 276–292
    animating walking figure in, 281–282
    changing bit depth of, 282
    changing speed of, 282
    changing Sprite images in, 280
    characteristics of, 276
    creating, 277–278
    creating new Sprites for, 286–291
    making responsive to key presses, 284–285
    managing Sprite interaction in, 291–292
    scrolling SpriteSurface in, 282–284
    single-stepping, 279
    testing, 279, 280
Sprite class
    animating, 289–291
    creating, 277, 286–291
    defined, 276
    managing interactions of, 291–292
    properties of, 276
SpriteSurface control, 276–292, 310–313
SQL, 322, 323
stand-alone applications, converting projects to, 71, 100
Standard version, REALbasic, 9, 323
StaticText control, 26, 87, 248
strComp function, 128
strings, 118–124
    assigning, 118
    changing case of, 122
    comparing, 128
    concatenating, 119
    converting to/from numbers, 123–124
    defined, 77
    determining ASCII value of, 123
    determining length of, 119
    extracting part of, 120
    removing spaces from, 122
    replacing part of, 121
StringWidth method, 242
Strout, Joseph, 296
Structured Query Language. See SQL
Styled property, 216
styled text, reading/writing, 216

subclasses, 153, 163, 167
submenus, 42–43
subtractive primaries, 231
super class, 152–153
Super property, 52
Symbols menu, 46–50
    adding items to, 46–47
    creating, 46
    enabling items in, 47
    testing, 47, 48, 50
system requirements, x

T

tab-delimited files, 209, 211–213, 215
Tab Panel Editor, 27
tables. *See* database tables
TabPanel control, 27, 409
tabs
    attaching text boxes to, 28
    creating, 27–28
    tips for effective use of, 409
tabular data, reading, 211–213
tags
    avoiding manual entry of, 32, 140
    examples of, 32
    indenting, 140, 145–149
    nesting, 140, 145
    symbols for marking, 46
    unmatched, 49
Tags menu, 36–45
    adding items to, 37
    adding submenu to, 42–43
    creating, 36
    enabling items in, 38–39, 43–44
    purpose of, 36
    testing, 38, 41, 45
TCP/IP protocol, 352, 367
test mode, 35, 71
testing applications, 29, 35
text
    drawing, 248
    rotating, 249–250
    viewing 3D objects as, 297
text editors, 32
text files, 54, 198, 209, 216
text links, 353–355
text streams, 209–215
TextFont property, 242
TextHasChanged property, 60
TextInputStream class, 209–215
TextOutputStream class, 209, 214–215
TGA files, 239
Then keyword, 130, 131, 132
Ticks function, 293, 418
TIFF files, 239

tilde (~), 169
time-aware applications, 293–295
time-controlled text message, 95–97
Timer control, 95–96, 294–295, 305–306
Title property, 33
Tog on Interface, 410
Tognazzini, Bruce, 410
toolbars
    adding separators to, 25
    creating, 24
    creating text box for, 26
    putting buttons on, 25
tools. *See also* controls
    adding/removing, 14
    displaying name of, 14
    resizing, 14
    types of, 13
Tools palette, 13–14, 224
Top property, 34, 224
Transparency property, 240
transparent, making pictures, 241
turtle graphics, 261
TurtleDraw application, 261–274
    building, 274
    creating/coding elements for
        About control, 270–271
        background picture, 270
        Color button, 268
        customization buttons, 267, 272
        drawing area, 262–263, 269, 273–274
        Erase option, 273–274
        Line control objects, 263
        navigation buttons, 262–263, 265, 272
        user instructions, 270–271
        Visible button, 268
        Width/Length buttons, 267
    creating TurtleDraw method for, 266
    defining properties needed by, 264
    initializing, 269
    purpose of, 261
    setting properties for, 261
.txt extension, 54
Type code, 186, 188, 190

U

Underline property, 242
Undo command, 168
Unix commands, 395–400
URLs, 352
UseFocusRing property, 92
user directories, using Shell scripting to list, 397–398
user documentation, 420, 423, 424
user-input fields
    controlling order of entry in, 90–92

creating, 83–85
limiting entry in, 89–91
preventing entry in, 89
prompting users for input in, 93
testing, 92
writing data to file, 98–99
user-interface design, 404, 405–410
User Interface Design for Programmers, 410
user name, using Shell scripting to determine,
   396–397

V

Value property, 230
values
   assigning to variables, 76, 118, 125
   comparing, 127–128
   negating, 126–127
   passing to methods, 138
   returning from methods, 139
variables
   assigning values to, 76, 118, 125
   creating, 116–117
   doing math with, 125
   naming, 423
   purpose of, 76
vector-graphics classes, 254
Version Information menu, 428
video games. *See* games
video tools, 300
Visible property, 199, 264
Visual Basic, x, 5, 7, 8
visual effects, 300, 304
Visual QuickStart Guides, xi, 391
Volume function, 193

W

walking-figure animation, 281–282
Wall class, 310
Web browsers, language read by, 32
Web-safe colors, 234, 235–236
Web sites
   book's companion, xi
   loading movies from, 302
   REAL Software, xi
Web Wizard. *See* Deus Web Wizard
WebColor method, 234, 235
While structure, 136, 144
Width property, 34, 224, 240
Wilde, Ethan, 391
window editor, 12
windows
   adding/removing items in, 12
   creating, 10, 27
   redrawing, 243

referring to, 159
resizing, 12
setting background color for, 245
Windows systems
   building applications for, x, 7
   creating files for, 186
   running REALbasic on, x, 7
   and Shell scripting, 395–396
   sound files, 218
Wine database, 325–332
wipes, 300
WireFrame property, 299
Write method, 214
WriteDouble method, 222
WriteLine method, 214, 215
WriteLong method, 222
WriteShort method, 222
WriteSingle method, 222
WWW protocol, 352
WYSIWYG, 12

X

Xerox Palo Alto Research Center, 3

Y

Yaw method, 299
Yellow property, 230
yin-yang symbol, 227, 254

Z

ZoomIcon property, 33, 262